RELIGIONS / GLOBALIZATIONS

RELIGIONS / GLOBALIZATIONS

THEORIES AND CASES

Edited by Dwight N. Hopkins, Lois Ann Lorentzen,

Eduardo Mendieta, & David Batstone

Duke University Press / Durham and London 2001

© 2001 Duke University Press

Printed in the United States of America on acid-free paper ⊛

Typeset in Trump Medieval by Tseng Information Systems

Library of Congress Cataloging-in-Publication Data

appear on the last printed page of this book.

CONTENTS

ACKNOWLEDGMENTS

D wight N. Hopkins wishes to acknowledge the support of his secretary Nathelda McGhee for her diligent administrative efforts, his research assistant Kurt Buhring for timely help, Will Coleman for reading and giving valuable suggestions for Hopkins's essay in this volume, and Linda E. Thomas for her continual, stimulating intellectual critiques. And he appreciates the ongoing support of the former dean (W. Clark Gilpin) and current dean (Richard A. Rosengarten) of the Divinity School of the University of Chicago.

Lois Ann Lorentzen spent part of her sabbatical in Chiapas, Mexico. She is grateful to Michael Stanfield for his suggestion that she visit the highlands of Chiapas; as always his friendship and insights are appreciated. Sabbatical time and funding were provided by the University of San Francisco (USF). She is grateful to the Faculty Development Fund Committee and the Dean's Office of the College of Arts and Sciences at USF for consistently supporting her work. Lois is also appreciative of the opportunity provided by Javier Riojas Rodriguez to teach short courses on environmental ethics in Mexico. The insights, friendships, and connections provided by Javier and by graduate students at the Universidades Iberoamericana in Mexico City, Puebla, and Leon were invaluable. Dwight N. Hopkins, Eduardo Mendieta, and David Batstone again proved to be invigorating, challenging, and provocative intellectual compatriots! Thanks to Gerardo Marin for his unfailingly patient support and wonderful meals. And finally she thanks her father, Dr. Ernest Stanley Lorentzen, for giving her both religion and the world!

David Batstone offers his acknowledgments for Wendy, Jade, Zak, Jesse, Caelin, and Bill Smith.

All four co-editors thank Reynolds Smith for his perseverance on this project.

For the majority of cultures around the world, religion thoroughly permeates and decisively affects the everyday rituals of survival and hope. Reflected in diverse spiritual customs, sacred symbols, and indigenous worship styles, global religions are permanent constituents of human life. In fact, for most of the world's peoples, religion helps to construct the public realm. The norm, therefore, is not a false divide between secularity and spirituality but the coexistence and interweaving of the so-called holy and profane.

Moreover, as the contributors to this volume substantiate, religions embodied in disparate human cultures have served as the foundation for national differences, racial conflicts, class exploitation, and gender discrimination, on the one hand, as well as for the resolution of hostility and the achievement of full humanity for those at the bottom of all societies, on the other. Religious spirituality remains both endemic to controversy and empowering for social transformation.

Worldwide religious dynamics have accompanied contemporary economic and political events. With the breakup of the Communist governments of Eastern Europe and the Soviet Union, formerly smoldering religious embers have erupted into prairie fires interconnected with national, racial, ethnic, territorial, and linguistic wars. Peoples from an earlier Marxist-Leninist era strive for ultimate meaning in their lives, and consequently religion rushes in to fill the void left by a transforming state apparatus.

Similarly, the destabilizing of the geopolitical configuration caused by the collapse of the Berlin Wall and the effects of having a single world superpower have produced regional disputes often clothed in religious language. A manifestation of globalization—the breakdown of familiar boundaries and power balances—allows religion to be deployed to help refabricate new communities.

In the "Third World" or "Two-Thirds World" and in many U.S. minority communities, we find some of the clearest representations of a spirituality of resistance and positive social amelioration. The growing pressures of the global economy—energized by further squeezing by the World Bank, the International Monetary Fund, U.S. monopoly corporations, and local elites—have fostered a persistent resurgence of indigenous grassroots communities, often bolstered by liberation theologies and a politicized spirituality of survival and freedom.

Furthermore, in the global arena, trends such as growing crime, fear, economic hardships for citizens at the bottom of society, and periodic right-wing religious groups, in addition to decentralized activism to fight them, have encouraged us to take a deeper look at religion's role in life-and-death issues in people's everyday lives.

Religion matters. In the contemporary period, we find not fewer but more religious movements. The essays in this volume use theoretical and material approaches to explore religion in the context of globalization. Indeed, these essays interrogate the religions of globalization.

GLOBALIZATION

"Globalization" is a word that can make some people apoplectic with ire, and others giddy with excitement. The speed with which globalization has taken over scholarly debates, as well as public discussions in the popular media, is remarkable. It has become a favorite word of all kinds of state philosophers, pundits, essayists, awry prophets of doom, and shameless unapologetic visionaries of the nouveaux riches of techno-capitalism. It is hard not to take sides, just as it is equally difficult not to be perplexed by the intractability of possibilities that are both closed off and opened up by the processes that go under the name of globalization. All of this should raise some flags and thus should command some healthy skepticism.

The authors in this volume enter the globalization debate wary of its faddishness, yet convinced that globalization does signify *something*. To many, globalization is merely the new lingua franca of finance capital, as well as the continuation of Western neocolonialism, now carried out by other means. Many others even speculate that globalization is just modernity accelerated and raised to a higher power. Others still see it as a radical qualitative change in the nature, extent, and depth of the transformations brought on by all the different processes that in one way or another are gathered underneath a verb that has taken on the mantle of an epochal noun. "Globalization," like its predecessors, "modernity," "colonialism," and "post-modernity," is a term that describes, evaluates, and points to a series of social processes whose outcomes remain speculative. Globalization is also a way for society to name itself, and thus to determine itself vis-à-vis those who have yet to be globalized, or are in the processes of globalization. To this extent, "globalization" is a term charged with ideological and geopolitical baggage and implications.

Some contributors to this volume criticize the deleterious and disastrous effects brought about by globalization, effects that span from the economic, to the cultural, to the ecological. Deforestation, depletion of fisheries, propagation of infectious diseases, destabilization of national economies, homogenization of cultures, destruction of national film industries, extinction of local languages, sexual tourism, and exile and migration are all pointed to as negative effects of globalization. Others underscore the positive and benign aspects of globalization, which can promote democracy, human rights, the rights of women and gays, the protection of biodiversity, and the development of supranational movements (NGO). Globalization is both McDonaldization and MTVization—the reign of infotainment, as Benjamin Barber calls it—but also the use of the Internet for counterinsurgency tactics; it is Michael Jordan, but also Subcommandante Marcos; it is Danielle Steel and Stephen King, but also Gabriel García Márquez, Salman Rushdie, and Buchi Emecheta.

Should a theorist's primary unit of analysis indeed be the "global"? Is globalization the macrodeterminant that trumps the regional, national, tribal, and local? Does globalization reflect domination or liberation for local cultures? Does globalization create, as Walter Mignolo suggests, the conditions for "barbarian theorizing," or for new forms of spirituality, as some contributors to this volume assert? Are transnational phenomena such as panindigenous movements of dual citizenships reflective primarily of the global or the local? Does globalization bring about more conformity or more heterogeneity? Can an overemphasis on globalization as a determinant miss seeing local agency? The contributors to this volume provide a variety of responses to the preceding questions, manifesting the contradictions and tensions endemic to the concept of globalization. These essays reflect ongoing struggles in both theory and practice to come to terms with the religions of globalization.

RELIGION AND GLOBALIZATION

This book seeks to explore ways in which religion and globalization are intertwined. If religion is one of the most fundamental means of organizing human life, then the seeds of globalization may lie within religion itself. We cannot talk about globalization without talking about religion, and we cannot talk about religion without considering how it might have laid the foundations for globalization's inception and launching. Does religion prepare the ground, both culturally and socially, for globalization? Some contributors will claim that the "hyper-globalization" of certain religions, such as the Iberian Catholic Church, promoted the idea of the world as one place. Others ask whether globalization transforms the conditions for the existence, maintenance, and furtherance of religion. Insofar as globalization challenges the nation-state, might it not also resist the ways in which religion has been pillaged and mobilized for nationalist causes? Might a dialectical tension exist between religion and globalization, a codependence and codetermination, manifesting in different modes of religious revitalization? Religion, in various contexts, may serve as an agent of homogenization or an agent of heterogenization. Under both guises, religion both furthers and resists globalization. The essays in this volume explore some of the formative and fundamental tensions and intertwinements between religions and globalization.

PART ONE / THEORETICAL FRAMEWORKS

DWIGHT N. HOPKINS

The Religion of Globalization

The many different interactions between globalization and religion can be approached from a variety of theological perspectives and ethical practices.[1] The World Council of Churches (wcc) marks one such engagement. The wcc constitutes the largest transnational institutional manifestation of diverse communities of Christian faith. It encompasses the denominations of Protestantism (e.g., Episcopal, Presbyterian, Methodist, Congregational, Baptist, etc.), structural dialogue with the Roman Catholic Church, a strong presence of and leadership by Eastern Orthodox Churches, and an assortment of new syncretized or indigenized forms of Christian religions located throughout Africa, Asia, and Latin America. The wcc takes seriously the Christian imperative to make all peoples followers of Jesus Christ the light of the world. In this regard, Christianity perceives its domain as a form of discipleship on a global stage where, by way of the preached word, theological instruction, sacramental ritualization, iconographic representation, and a persistent witness of love, justice, and reconciliation, the message of Jesus the Christ will truly become the embodied vision of a new and ultimate future that is to come for all peoples.

The Council for a Parliament of the World's Religions, in contrast, pursues the multilateral engagement of diverse communities of faith—from African indigenous religions, the great religions of Asia, Islam, Judaism, Protestantism, and Catholicism, to any forms of faith expressions, on the global scale, that agree to civil conversation through mutual encounter. Whereas the wcc might have an evangelistic prescriptive dimension, the Parliament pursues across national borders conversations guided by enlightened dialogue shared by each religion offering its unique gifts to the universal human community regardless of any particular doctrinal demands and tradition's commands. Moreover, again contrasting the wcc, the Parliament refrains from any explicit involvement in political problematics. Its primary "ought" manifests in its broadening of the tent of interlocutors so that changes in the human condition follow logically from more and more people getting to know one another. The metaphor and reality of a parliament mean respectful interchange and exchange of the broadest possible distribution and differentiation of faith communities throughout the world. The wider the contact and knowledge of the other, the increased possibilities of living together in harmony.

A third paradigm of religion and globalization contact appears in the Pluralism Project.[2] Here the revelation of globalization is implosion. Instead of seeking a variety of ways of unifying religious communities outside the United States, the project examines the multiplying reality of a rapid heterogeneity of religions within the United States. This study of the increased religious diversity in the United States focuses especially on the growing multidimensional nature of religions brought by immigrant groups. In a word, the analysis does not follow lines of investigation from the powerful colonial center to its intertwinement with religions in the colonies or geographic peripheries of the world. Quite the opposite, instead of ascertaining the dominant religions' missionary explosion outward all over the earth (especially Christian world evangelization from North America to the Third World), the Pluralism Project study reverses the angle of vision. It observes implosion: how is it that non-Christian religions from the rest of the world (particularly from the Third World) are undergoing a process of potential long-term saturation in the American domestic Christian landscape? It seeks to discern how Americans of all faiths are crafting a positive pluralism.

This essay pursues an alternative claim. The argument is that globalization of monopoly finance capitalist culture is itself a religion. Such a religion feeds on the most vulnerable peoples in the world theater. Consequently, a theology of liberation is one necessary response to the rapacious appetite of globalization qua religion. The Ecumenical Association of Third World Theologians (EATWOT) signifies this response.[3] The majority of this article defines the contours of globalization as a religion. At the end, I examine the schematic theological position of EATWOT.

Religion is a system of beliefs and practices comprising a god (which is the object of one's faith), a faith (which is a belief in a desired power greater than oneself), a religious leadership (which determines the path of belief), religious institutions (which facilitate the ongoing organization of the religion), a theological anthropology (which defines what it means to be human), values (which set the standards to which the religion subscribes), a theology (which is the theoretical justification of the faith), and revelation (which is the diverse ways that the god manifests itself in and to the world).[4]

God, more specifically, is the ultimate concern of a community of believers. This god is the final desire and aim that surpasses and circumscribes all other penultimate realities, dreams, wants, and actions. It controls all things and motivates its believers to gear their entire life in pursuit of, and in obedience to, this god. It subordinates the believers and all of creation to the power of itself. It possesses the believers and compels them to pursue it because it has the ability to never be totally fulfilled, and it possesses the power to never be finally contained and controlled by its followers. This ultimate concern, moreover, is the ground of being for its believers. The foundation of their ontology rests on this god. Their very being in the world is determined by god. In a word, this god is the highest life-and-death concern.

The god of the religion of globalization is the concentration of monopoly, finance capitalist wealth. The god of globalization, in this sense, is not merely a belief in the accumulation of capital for private possession by owners operating inside one country, a signification of the lower stage in the development of capitalism. On the contrary, the god of globalization embodies the ultimate concern or ground of being where there is a fierce belief in the intense concentration, in a few hands, of monopoly, finance capitalist wealth on the world stage. It is an extreme form of the private ownership and control of capital in various forms of wealth spurred on by the rapid movement of finance and capital on a global scale. Monopoly, finance capitalist wealth, as god in the religion of globalization, is a power in its own right that makes its adherents bow down to it and pursue any means necessary to obtain it. All who believe in it are possessed by it; it is the final goal above all else.

Furthermore, it is transcendent; it has no allegiances to individuals, institutions, and boundaries. "Far more wealth than ever before is stateless, circulating wherever in the world the owner can find the highest return. Thus spending by investors in industrialized countries on overseas stocks increased 197-fold between 1970 and 1997, and each nation's capital market is beginning to merge into a global capital market."[5] This god of monopoly, finance capitalist wealth is not confined or defined by anything except its own internal drive for increased concentration of more wealth. Like the traits of a supernatural phenomenon, it does manifest in the tangible (hence its immanence). At the same time, the tangible does not exhaust its power (hence its transcendence). Ultimately, the telos (a religious term denoting the final providence of a god) is to reproduce itself by making the entire world of humanity and the ecology constituted by the intense concentration of monopoly, finance capital. Instead of characterizing itself as love, liberation, justice, or reconciliation, this god is Mammon.

The sectors of the world, located mainly in the United States, that represent those with the most faith in this object of concern (i.e., Mammon) are the small groups of families who comprise the religious leadership in the religion of globalization. They are a select group set aside like priests who maintain knowledge of the laws of this god and the demands it requires of its followers. Their knowledge signifies a certain type of gnosis—insider information, networking among each other, direct access to the power and benefits of their god, the larger parameters and long-term vision, setting the pace in the pursuit of this god, defining what it means to be a true believer, confidence to determine the lives of their followers, influencing public opinion, and the decision-making power over who and who will not enter the priesthood. For instance, the United Nations Development Programme's "Human Development Report of 1992" defined this priesthood by way of income distribution. "The richest 20% of the world's population receives 82.7% of the total world income, while the poorest 20% receives only 1.4%. The gap between the rich and the poor is continuing to grow."[6] The richest 225 individuals in the world constitute a combined wealth of more than $1 trillion. This is equal to the annual income of the poorest 47 percent of the world's population. And the three richest people on earth own assets surpassing the combined gross domestic product of the forty-eight

least-developed countries.[7] The priests are the minute group of families who privately own, control, and distribute wealth and the means
of production.

The religious-like institutions that facilitate the transcendent
flow of monopoly-finance capitalist wealth or the god in globalization are numerous. However, three in particular comprise what can
be termed a Trinity. They are the World Trade Organization (WTO),
international banks (including the International Monetary Fund and
the World Bank), and monopoly capitalist corporations. The WTO
exists to monitor and enhance international trade. Its name con-
notes, prima facie, that it is an objective world body adjudicating and
massaging global trade for the world's peoples, perhaps by pursuing
a scientific neutral line of interaction. Yet, de facto, it functions in
the interest of the god of monopoly, finance capitalist wealth. Determined to a great extent by U.S. interests, among others, the WTO
is the part of the Trinity maintaining an asymmetrical balance of
trade mainly by advocating and practicing free trade so that the god
in the religion of globalization can have unimpeded free access to the
developed world and the Third World (Africa, Asia, Latin America,
and the Pacific Islands). It pushes for an increased consumer market for finance capitalist investment. Moreover, it is influenced by,
and weighted toward, the small group of priests of globalization's
religion.

The second person of the Trinity (international banks along with
the IMF and the World Bank) serves to set conditions of loans, particularly to the Third World, so that underdeveloped countries become
converted to global religion. Third World countries receive financial loan packages that demand that these countries reshift resource
focus away from domestic priorities in order to repay international
loans. Indeed, the deeper the debt, the more loans are required to
continue the repayment process on earlier acquired loans. Once the
initial initiation rite of loan procurement is accomplished, Third
World countries become full members (that is, dependent members)
of this global religion. In this sense, international banks are akin
to missionaries who travel the world seeking new converts into the
system. And similar to the history of Christianity, the indigenous
resources or ways of being in the world or faith of a people are replaced, wiped out, or syncretized with the arrival of this foreign religion.[8] Monopoly capitalist corporations (e.g., MNC), the third per-

son of the Trinity, are the direct institutional instruments of the priests of this religion. The MNC signifies an interlocking ownership and control of wealth and finances. It can interlock wealth across industries and within industries, and it can have headquarters in one country with subsidiary "missionary" outposts in other nations. For instance, U.S. soft drink companies can also have part ownership in concentrated fruit products, newspapers, the media, airlines, television stations, Hollywood studios, clothing manufacturing, fast-food lines, and automobile companies. Such a concentration of wealth, or the god of globalization, enables MNC to shift wealth and investments throughout the globe to undercut, underprice, and buy off an entire range of companies in the Third World, thereby "proselytizing" more members and areas of the earth into the religion.

Like all religions, the religion of globalization advances a theological anthropology. Theological anthropology defines and regulates what it means to be a human being in the system of a religion. What does a god require of human beings in order to be human? For the priests of the religion of globalization, the god of globalization calls on them to act out an ontology (the very being of who they are) in the quest for the epitome of the ideal person. Such a human being is one who has the most concentrated financial wealth accumulation on a global scale. Ideally, since religions have a proclivity for utopia, a small group would control the world's capital. Here capital includes both the majority of the human population (real people) and the ecology (the earth's natural and human-made resources). Theological anthropology is, moreover, a realized eschatology where the final eschaton (the end time) finds "a new heaven and a new earth" signifying the absolute social relations among human beings as defined by the god of concentrated wealth. In other words, to be a human being in the eschatological utopia is to have the extreme asymmetrical social relations with the smallest group possible endowed with the highest concentration of monopolized financial wealth.

In contrast, theological anthropology for the majority of the world (poor and working peoples, and those with lesser wealth and income) suggests another reality of what it means to be human in the religion of globalization. Before globalization, especially in Third World indigenous communities, human beings were valued for who they were as members of the human race created by some divine power.[9] Now globalization rebaptizes them into a new man and woman. The measure of worth becomes what one consumes. Globalization's religion forges new tastes and sensibilities throughout the world while it attempts to manufacture one transcendent culture — the culture of market consumption. A true human being becomes one who actually possesses commodities or one whose orientation in life is to possess commodities. Though the vast majority of Third World peoples are poor, the religion of globalization attempts to transform them into adherents of the faith by inducing a desire to perceive themselves as owning products from the United States and the developed capitalist world. This touches the core issue. The new religion not only wants people to purchase products. It also desires for people to reconceive of themselves as people. To change into something new, people must, in addition to redirecting their purchasing habits, refeel who they are in the present and reenvision their possibilities differently in the future. People are baptized into a lifestyle to fulfill the desire for commodities and to follow further the commodification of desires.

Globalization relentlessly pursues this refashioning of the new man and woman throughout the globe. It seeks a homogenized monoculture of the market to transform people being valued in themselves to people being determined by their dependency on commodities. A world culture producing one definition of humanity is predicated on serving the market. The market of monopoly, finance capitalism benefits the small group of priests in the religion of globalization. In contrast, most of the world's people are left out. "The pragmatic [and positive] analysis of economists and financiers is based on the principle of exclusion. Growing poverty and exclusion have [be]come a dominant social and political development of our era. Inequality and exclusion are not distortions of the system. They are a systematic requisite for growth and permanence."[10] Restated, the majority of the world that operates within the religion of globalization experiences a theological anthropology of exclusion from the earth's resources, victimization at the hands of extreme social polarization, and a truncated humanity.

The spreading of different values is closely linked to theological anthropology. As one redefines oneself, by accepting the new religion's reconfiguring of the human person, one internalizes values appropriate to the new man or woman. At least, the point of the religion of globalization is to craft new values to accompany the new person. First is the value of individualism. If monopoly, finance capital is to succeed as the new god throughout the earth, it has to decouple the idea, particularly in Third World indigenous cultures, that the individual is linked to, defined by, accountable to, and responsible for his or her family and extended family. A sense of communalism and sacrifice of individual gain for the sake of a larger community stands in stark contradiction to the new religion of globalization. Once an individual converts to the new religion and reorients his or her self-worth and feeling of worthiness to a mode of individual gain, regardless of the well-being of those around him or her, this person has successfully undergone the rite of confirmation into the new religion and an acceptance of faith in the new god as a personal lord and savior. The value of individualism (individual gain by any means necessary) centers the god of monopoly, finance capitalism.

Individualism opens up the additional value of accumulation of things for the individual's primary benefit. In other words, gaining and amassing personal possessions as a means of acquiring more personal possessions flows from a focus on the self for the self. Accenting such a worth in life manifests in diverse manners. It downplays sharing. It weakens the art of negotiation and compromise. It blinds a vision of mutuality. And it fosters a utilitarian way of being in the world where people, places, and things become tools for, and stepping stones toward, increased personal profit. On the political level, such a value breeds a type of "monopoly capitalist democracy" constituted by subordination of the many for the few. This form of democracy employs the many to attain more resources for the few. As a political value, such a democracy equates the common good and the larger civic welfare with pragmatic results for the elite. In the economic sphere, it is a feeling internal to the individual that prompts the pursuance of profit to facilitate more personal profit. It privileges the importance of commodities. A commodity, in this sense, means valuing economic wealth as one of the highest virtues in defining the new human being. Akin to an addiction (when left to mature), it motivates, gnaws at, and compels the new converted person toward the determination of life-and-death issues based on whether or not one has enough wealth. The ownership of wealth commodities and the hunger for this ownership control the perception of life's and death's worth.

A positive worldview of individualism and the thirst for commodities lead more easily to valuing the United States and other developed finance capitalist countries. These centers epitomize a culture and perfection of individualism and commodification. Therefore when one's values accept and imitate the attributes of globalization, they have an inclination to gravitate toward the geographic and imaginative locations where those values have advanced more fully. The "West" becomes a place, like a utopia, of meaning to fulfill one's theological anthropology. For the sectors of Third World countries that are able to migrate toward these valued centers, the worth of being human is brought closer to a realized individualism and commodification. For the elite who remain in developing countries, energies and resources are deployed, metaphorically or literally, to purchase or imitate the latest thought forms, things, and lifestyles from New York, Paris, and London. For the overwhelming majority (agricultural laborers and farmers in the rural areas and the employed, underemployed, and unemployed in urban communities), the values of globalization breed the conditions for the possibility of desiring those things from the West. The religion of the new human being moves one's senses through space, time, and imagination to the "altars" of the monopoly finance capitalist god of concentrated wealth. Lacking god's material gifts, one values and feeds on the desire for materiality.

This god has a theology.[11] Theology denotes a rational understanding, justification, and meaning making of a god. Theology derives from two root words—*theos* and *logos*. *Theos* means god, and *logos* means interpreting, questioning, understanding, explaining, or reasoning about something or someone. Thus theos plus logos renders a rational understanding or reasoning about god. In religious discourse, moreover, theology takes on an added sense of justification of one's faith to the public. What rationale does one give to account for one's faith in the public domain of competing and conflictual faith claims? What system of views, theoretical arguments, and coherent conclusions does one advance in the common conversation? Theology makes sense of faith in god. If the god is concentrated monopoly, finance capitalist wealth, then how does one imagine and explain faith in this god? In a word, theology clarifies the attributes and ethics of a god. A primary elaboration and justification of concentrated monopoly, finance capitalist wealth is the theology of neoliberalism.[12]

Neoliberalism, as the theological justification for the god of the religion of globalization, has three prominent dogmatics or doctrines. First is the emphasis on free markets—a movement to open up global markets, especially in the Third World.[13] Actually, the market is not free for all countries because as transnational corporations enter or deepen their hold in developing countries' domestic economy, corporations are free to repatriate their profit from loans and investment at the expense of the welfare of the poor and the market share of local businesses. The criterion on entry is to adhere to and pursue concentrated monopoly, finance capitalist wealth. However, some form of freedom does occur for developing countries. They enjoy the freedom to restructure domestic growth based on linkages to export industries. Yet these exports are intertwined with serving the needs of the developed finance capitalist countries; a process that disrupts the economic planning for domestic well-being. Export orientation, furthermore, is driven by the quest for diverse forms of foreign currency. Thus free markets provide favorable terms for transnational monopoly corporations to enter developing countries, and they provide unfavorable terms for developing countries' efforts at exporting. Free markets translate into unrestricted entry of the god of globalization.

Privatization, the second theological justification, is a condition imposed on Third World countries by transnational corporations. If a developing country opens its market borders, it has to agree to refocus domestic resources of the state government away from providing health, education, welfare, jobs, and other safety nets for its citizens. Instead, accumulated resources of the state go into repayment of debt on loans invested by monopoly-finance capitalists and create whatever conditions these corporations require to enhance their other types of investment in the developing country. Consequently, neoliberalism theology promotes, as one condition for various investments, the practice of privatization of social services for the vast majority of the people; for the Third World, this means the poor. Not only do domestic private businesses seek to substitute for the previous role of the government, but transnational corporations also enter the arena of profiting from private services provided to the public, at least to those who can afford the costs. However, exceptions to the transformed function of Third World states do occur. Local governments, as additional conditions for foreign investments, undergird the environment of monopoly-finance corporate presence by way of tax breaks, transfer payments, an increased military, and a burgeoning prison network, the latter being geared to the unemployed, opposition forces, and criminal sectors.

The third theological justification is deregulation. The religion of globalization offers a "common-sense" explanation for this final justification. It seems to "make sense" that a government enmeshed in regulations implies a heavy state bureaucracy consuming scarce resources, time, and personnel that could be deployed more efficiently elsewhere in the domestic economy. Thus if Third World countries are to enjoy the benefits ("grace") of the god of monopolized capitalist wealth, the theology of neoliberalism calls for stripping governments of their historic role of regulating the harmful effects of business practices imposed on people and the ecology. If transnational corporations invest, they require unimpeded access to natural resources despite inherent deleterious impacts on the earth. Similarly, statutes prohibiting the pollution of nature's waters are weakened, if not abolished, in some instances. Upsetting the natural cycles and regenerating processes of nature kills the environment. Because the ecosystem is interconnected, human beings' physical relation to, and aesthetic appreciation of, the plant, animal, water, and air dimension of creation are impaired. In a word, the destruction of nature leads to increased morbidity and mortality of the human population.

Deregulation, in addition, fosters an environment of a free market, which directly impacts workers' jobs, income, and family security, all for the interest of monopolized businesses. One of the reasons U.S. monopolies transfer operations to Third World countries is to enjoy a situation of weak trade union organization. In certain cases, trade unions do not function or are impractical. Without a viable opposition from the workers who produce the profits, profits are relatively guaranteed to flow directly to the owners of transnational monopolies. Furthermore, without bargaining power or protection for the profits they make, rural and urban workers suffer the threat of job loss, real declining income, and instability in their families. Lack of adequate income connects with health deregulation. Specifically, the Third World government relaxes food quality restrictions, control on the standards of medicines, monitoring of toxicity levels in drinking water, and any mandatory physical examinations for the populace, particularly pertaining to infants and children. Without sufficient income, working people are incapable of satisfying health needs, which are now catered to by the business sector owing to privatization.

Moreover, deregulation undercuts the function of the state. A transnational monopoly business from the United States enters a developing country and provides inequitable conditions for investment. Investment will come if the state will loosen tax codes. These codes were originally established to do at least three things. One was to protect local businesses from being totally undercut by foreign investors. If these investors payed taxes, then that would, to a degree, cut away from some resources that could be used by foreign businesses to underprice local goods. Two, taxes were initially put into place to prevent monopoly capitalists from repatriating 100 percent of their investments, thus leaving the local citizens with no real benefits from the profits that the local government had permitted the foreign company to extract. And three, lack of tax income severs the local political machinery from a role of providing welfare benefits for the indigenous population. Actually, this function of the state became moot with neoliberalism's doctrine of privatization. In sum, deregulation in neoliberalism theology promotes a theological justification that supports the abolition of diverse forms of government regulation of the market and capital ownership and distribution.

Third World leaders who oppose the theology of neoliberalism's three-prong approach of free market, privatization, and deregulation pinpoint the particular harm experienced by developing countries. Most of the geography and people's residences are in the rural areas, and therefore agriculture proves key to any hope and vision of achieving sustainable development. Yet here is where profound undermining of Third World potential growth takes place. For instance, in Asia, forests and agricultural lands are being depleted and destroyed. "Steel bars and iron poles for factories are replacing trees; golf courses and plush residential areas are taking the place of rice fields, and other forms of technologies employed in newly-built industries prove to be destructive to all forms of life."[14] Even if developing countries reach for the promise of finance capital, they would have to rely heavily on the agricultural sphere. But in this sector is where the gospel of globalization realizes the underdevelopment of agricultural possibilities.

The doctrine of neoliberalism is the explanatory arm of the god of concentrated monopoly finance wealth. It says that one partakes of the grace of this god by offering unhindered access to further wealth concentration. Then Third World peoples will experience a "trickle-down" effect from the good works of transnational monopolies.

THE REVELATION OF GOD IN GLOBALIZATION

All religions posit some god, a force greater than any one human being. God surpasses the ability of one person, place, or thing to contain it. The potency of god compels its disciples to have faith that god will be with them and that god will help them to enjoy the benefits that god's grace offers. Even after devotees of the religion die, god continues to live. In this sense, god is absolute transcendence. At the same time, god reveals itself through concrete manifestations to its believers and followers. Revelation enables the adherents to know that this god is real, has power, and yields results. The priests in globalization (the small group of families with disproportionate private ownership and distribution power of the world's wealth) and those who accept the leadership of this "clergy" act as if concentrated monopoly, finance capitalist wealth is a god. And its revelation appears in definite economic, political, and cultural unveilings that disclose and award further opportunities for a concentration of monopolized-finance wealth. The transcendent god reveals itself in immanent processes.

Globalization is a religious system of capitalist wealth concentration on a global scale, rapidly pursuing its object of faith—an indefinite increased concentration. The religion of globalization is constituted by a god, a faith, religious leadership, a trinity of religious institutions, a theological anthropology, values, and a theology. As a system, it makes no distinction between a sacred or secular sphere; it is all-pervasive.

Regarding its economic revelation, globalization pursues the integration of all markets throughout the world.[15] One of its chief ethical practices is to lock developing countries into a dependent state by advancing loans and making these countries go into debt. Once linked into this system, countries undergo an endless spiral of more debt and capital drain. To repay the interest on original debt (not including the principal), developing countries take out more loans from mainly U.S. corporations. Likewise, they take out additional loans and thereby undergo deeper loan and debt consumption to meet the repayment schedule of the interest on the second loan, which was acquired to meet the dept repayment schedule of the first loan. As mentioned previously, loan advancements from transnational monopoly businesses come with specific strings attached. The primary requirement is a free market—the ability of finance capital to penetrate the domestic economy of the debtor nation. This quick influx of investment can (after accumulating profit) just as easily exit a country and thus disrupt the local financial arrangements and currency values. As a result, gross unemployment and mega-downsizing occur.

Debt repayment imbalances and the volatility of investments structurally adjust domestic Third World economies in an adverse manner. "The growth of agriculture is relatively delinked from local people's requirements and oriented toward export markets. . . . Savings and investments are tuned to the global requirement of transnational capital. National economic activities in general (production, consumption, and markets) are subordinated to international economic forces."[16] Developing countries gear their domestic resources toward the export needs of the United States. These countries shift from production for domestic consumption to cash crops for export. Thus the majority of the populace (especially in the rural areas) suffer undernutrition, malnutrition, and, in extreme cases, starvation. Moreover, an unequal exchange exists in the export industries. Another requirement of loan advancement is that not only are local resources geared to the international market, but these export products cannot receive any subsidies from local governments. Goods therefore enter the global market and have to compete with similar products produced by multinational monopolies capable of realizing underpricing strategies. Contrasting the free market conditions set by global monopoly business for developing countries, the United States and other developed capitalist governments establish exclusive markets—a wall of protection against select Third World products. Protective legislation includes tariffs, quotas, and most-favored-nation status. A globalized free market means a carte blanche for the flow of monopoly finance capital into Third World arenas and restricted freedom of export to these financial centers.

An additional feature of globalization is the "new pattern of global division of labor with different countries specializing in the production of components of a single product like the motor car. This resulted in the increased movement of goods from one country to another, but within units of the same" monopoly capitalist institution.[17] This slows down or makes impossible effective trade union organizing for the rights of local workers. Workers do not see the assembled finished product produced by their labor, thus adding to worker disinterest in their jobs and in the process of production. Lack of interest can impact the desire to resist economic injustices. And because parts of a car, for example, are manufactured throughout different locations of the Third World, it is pretty much impossible to call for a worldwide strike against a globalized automobile industry. Using various countries as part of the international production division of labor unbalances employees' attempts at raising wages, thus leading to increased economic hardship.

Moreover, globalization brings on the ritual sequence of forced devaluation of local currencies which gives rise to the printing of more monies to pay for debt interests and other needs of foreign investors. The printing of money induces hyper inflation. Hyperinflation exacerbates workers' and other citizens' purchasing power and leads to increased dependency on jobs provided by foreign industries. In austere situations, purchasing power is further compromised when international lending institutions demand a cap on wages as another precondition for financial and capital investment. From both the pricing and income sides, the ritual of the religion of globalization positions workers in a defensive economic posture.

The intensification of worldwide finance capital mobility creates an unprecedented movement of people across geographic boundaries. The phenomenon of worker migration has become a permanent feature of the earth. The relocation of transnational firms in rural areas tends to displace peasants, rural labor, and small farmers, who, in turn, travel to cities and quasi-urban areas. The intense pressures of a tight and unfavorable job market in cities push urban workers to cross national borders into neighboring and distant Third World countries. Those who can secure the means or are fortunate enough to be contracted by international monopolies travel to the United States and other job sites in the developed capitalist centers. The system of globalization offers a push-and-pull dynamic that feeds the poor's and working poor's economic hardships as well as dreams of a better life for heads of households and their children.

Finally, the economic revelation of the religion of globalization is enhanced greatly by the notion of distanciation or time-space compression brought about by computer technological and telecommunications advances. Distanciation or time-space compression allows instantaneous international activity of concentrated monopoly finance capitalist wealth. This god travels the world (and thus is transcendent) with a literal press of a computer button. It never sleeps as the priests and their representatives of the religion trade and invest twenty-four hours a day (again, another mark of transcendence). The reality of time-space (distanciation) means that the time normally prescribed by the distance between geographies no longer holds. In prior times, capital and business transactions took place within a small town or village. People walked, rode horses, and later drove their cars to a bank or an investment center. Human beings actually met face-to-face, especially in terms of physically examining investment possibilities before decision making.

Now with the advent of cyberspace and computer technology, monopoly finance capitalist wealth moves at the "speed of light" and compresses the former travel distance required by separate geographies. The god of the religion of globalization defies all parameters. Commodity exchange, investment activities, and profit mobility occur instantaneously everywhere and anywhere. Within an instant via computer, E-mail, the Web, or cell phone, the priests of globalization can conduct business in Cape Town, Tenerife, Rio, Sri Lanka, and Honolulu. If "people in Tokyo can experience the same thing at the same time as others in Helsinki, say a business transaction or a media event, then they in effect live in the same place, space has been annihilated by time compression."[18] The annihilation of space indicates the further supernatural strength of the god of the religion of globalization because it cannot be restrained by various confines of the natural, material reality.

Politics, a second revelation in the religion of globalization, concerns how the god of increased monopoly finance capitalist wealth weakens the sovereignty and decision-making powers of local states, particularly in Third World nations. Globalization redefines the state. As indicated previously, as part of the initiation into the global dynamic, developing countries' governments make policy not for the benefit of labor, the environment, the domestic economy, or the marginalized sectors of society but in the interest of what will facilitate intensified wealth concentration.

Globalization propelled by MNCs is no respecter of national boundaries. The free mobility claimed by this process is possible only for a few. You have to pay a price to be part of this exclusive system. The policies of liberalization and withdrawal of subsidies, which are the conditions imposed by the IMF and the World Bank, have resulted in curtailing the power of the State. The global institutions tend to destroy the idea of the nation-state and the state is forced to abdicate its social responsibilities. While the state is rendered powerless, it has become a mere tool of the rich and the powerful. Its sole function is to suppress any organized resistance by ordinary people to the unjust system.[19]

The state does not become obsolete. It reconfigures its past functions (which were geared to the well-being of its own citizens) into a quasi-standing committee or outpost rendering services for transnational corporations. The state abdicates its former obligations to the common public good in areas such as health, welfare, and education. Privatization, including multinational businesses, becomes the deliverer of social services for a price.

In addition, the state, deploying its political clout, works as a leverage for corporate accumulation of wealth. It can allow transnationals the privilege of paying no or small real estate taxes. It permits these businesses freedom from sales taxes and income taxes for a set period of time. Municipal authorities, in various instances, provide free water and sewer lines and then give discounts on utility bills. Similarly, they gratuitously offer free landscaping of buildings and factories. The state, moreover, grants businesses the "right" to not pay taxes on investment income. Therefore the state functions as a welfare agency for corporate wealth accumulation.[20]

Thus, as a result of the religion of globalization, new goals and content emerge for the state. The concept of an independent, freestanding nation-state, negotiating the considerations of contained national interests of its citizenry, becomes moot. The state apparatus is pulled by and into the exigencies of globalization. In this sense, it lacks power. On the other hand, it still commands the reins of discipline and punishment for any recalcitrant citizens daring to cause an unstable environment for transnational investments. The state accepts the task of making, monitoring, and managing its own people as outlaws.

Not only do the political implications of globalization reveal themselves in the transformed politics of the state, but politics likewise impinge on place, location, and geography within Third World countries, in addition to other regions and nations. More exactly, the power dynamics and administrative resources begin to play out differently in the physicality of major cities that house concentrated business transactions. Just as nation-states are no longer what they used to be, so the major metropolises of the earth have become global cities.

> National and global markets as well as globally integrated operations require central places where the work of globalization gets done. Further, information industries require a vast physical infrastructure containing strategic nodes with hyperconcentrations of facilities. Finally, even the most advanced information industries have a work process—that is, a complex of workers, machines, and buildings that are more placebound than the imagery of an information economy suggests. . . . Global cities are centers for the servicing and financing of international trade, investment, and headquarter operations.[21]

Finally, the politics of democracy on a world stage are made in the image of the god of globalization. Everything that this god touches has the potential of becoming its disciple for the furtherance of intensified monopoly finance capitalist wealth. To date, globalization is the highest form of capitalist democracy, a top-down democracy imposed against the profit of the majority. Democracy, in the discourse of the U.S. civil society, suggests the right of all citizens to make decisions by exercising the franchise. And in the common sense of American civic responsibility, because the United States has the highest form of democracy, such a political system of social relations among citizens needs to be exported over the entire earth. Yet the politics of real American democracy, as evidenced in its imposition throughout the world, include a power differential. Governments "elected" by their own people receive the benefits of being the friend of the free market as long as they serve the religion of globalization. In this scenario, leaders of the state appear to be elected by the majority vote of its populace, but in effect powerful "votes" of global finance capital sway domestic policy-making priorities, for governments exist at the decision and pleasure of transnational deliberations. "In other words, decisions came to be made on a transnational basis—a transfer of political power from the 'debtor' nation states to international agencies."[22] This new form of democracy inverts true democracy; people's power is replaced by elite finance capitalist power. And this latter unveiling of power does not even trickle down to the people. In fact, the structure of power has been transformed by capitalist liberal democracy and the freedom of the market.[23]

In addition to offering an economical and political disclosure of itself, the god of concentrated monopoly finance capitalist wealth reveals itself by creating a recognizable culture in the world arena. It attempts to forge a popular cultural consensus and a popular lifestyle. Television serves as a major pioneer in developing a common way of being and worldview. It is not unusual, for instance, to discover destitute black South Africans in local townships addicted to daily showings of semipornographic daytime soap operas from the United States. Crowded into one small room, the many viewers could be more conversant in the politics, economics, families, personalities, and dreams of these fictional characters than they are of the complexities of their own real country. Such visual pop art for mass international consumption not only creates an illusion about what American societies are actually like but moreover stimulates the imagination of the Third World voyeur into what he or she or the ideal should be. The vision of the real and the ideal, hopes and failures, can often be more powerful in molding a popular opinion than massaging aspirations to become something a viewer knows he or she will never be. A rural, semirural, or urban slum dweller in the Third World might be stimulated to desire a trip to the United States or to imitate all that is seen on the television screen. Yet one's real circumstances testify to the unlikelihood of becoming an American. However, television soap operas spark ways of imitating and incorporating the visual lessons from fictional people into the cultural trappings of the viewers. They might use their own native dress but wear it like their favorite daytime TV star, for example. One does not have to live in America to be American; one can indigenize America and become a hybrid international "citizen" at home.

Global cultural beachheads also manifest in the great television trio of MTV, CNN, and ESPN. If one is an American who travels throughout the world from hotel to hotel and from one home to another home (in both the Third World and the Second [European] World), one can literally feel a sense of knowing and experience a degree of familiarity by hearing MTV videos, observing the up-to-the-minute news of CNN, and catching the latest American sports tournaments within twenty-four hours on ESPN. These three channels convey a desired reality on several levels. Music entertainment markets aesthetics to diverse age groups within a country. It differentiates lifestyles for focused groups. However, the impact of MTV does not cease once the viewer leaves the television area of one's home or hotel. On the contrary, MTV operates as a public relations link in a chain of the entertainment market. What is seen on MTV can be purchased for listening pleasure from the local record shop. Similarly, MTV megastars are constantly on global concert tours. Via their private airplanes, they descend from the heavens already equipped with prefabricated road shows that do not have to be dovetailed to local environments. And T-shirts, cups, balloons, written literature, and related paraphernalia blanket the global concert venue like natural precipitation.

CNN presents the norms for worldwide crime, government, health, business, beauty, and other forms of human titillation and arousal. Whether broadcast from Atlanta or New York, CNN gives watchers in developing countries the notions of what is worthy and humanly normal material to be reported on. The monopoly capitalist owners of CNN allow and portray only certain types of crimes and human interest news items. What the globe perceives might not be what the globe approves of. But because everyone is seeing the same types of news items, then those items become normal. And more and more newspersons adopt the visage of movie stars when anchorpeople look more and more like male and female models. Furthermore, they no longer present news in a straightforward manner (à la the Walter Cronkite era). Now interpersonal banter ensues in between hard news reportage. Similarly, some news reporters become superstars themselves. Viewers follow them regularly as they cover the volatile hot spots all over the globe. Usually backgrounded by streaming heat-seeking missiles in the nighttime air or lodged amid a sea of bone-thin, hungry children, the elite globe-trotters and mega-stars of CNN function like human interest stories within the news foci that they are covering.

ESPN offers the ultimate sports entertainment panorama. It exoticizes places with faraway fishing junkets. It has the potential to instigate, aggravate, and manipulate relations between Third World countries, especially with nuanced portrayal of soccer matches. It legendizes America by the triumphant hoopla of U.S. basketball heroes. Similar to the role MTV plays for the world tours of entertainers, ESPN helps to market merchandise. During the heyday of the Michael Jordan Chicago Bulls era, team insignia could be found in the remote areas of Tibet.

Further intricate unfoldings of the cultural revelation of the religion of globalization appear with the McDonaldization of the world, closely pursued by KFC and Burger King. What these fast-food monopoly capitalist corporations have in common with Pepsi and Coca-Cola is the refined art of creating and altering the food tastes of the indigenous populations in developing countries. They effect a smooth strategy: U.S. soft drink monopolies undercut the prices of locally brewed soda pop, purchase a monopoly on the coin soda dispensing machines in a country, and flood the market with massive advertising linking their product with youth, sex, sports, and happy faces. With cigarettes, for example, transnationals often give away free samples for a certain period of time. Once a significant segment of the people become drug addicts on nicotine, acts of gratuity revert to the normal acts of sales and purchase.

Globalization has become the vehicle of cultural invasion. Technology is power. It becomes the carrier to those systems and ideologies (values and cultures) within which it has been nurtured. The tendency is to create a mono-culture. By mono-culture we mean the undermining of economic, cultural and ecological diversity, the nearly universal acceptance of a technological culture as developed in the West and the adoption of its inherent values. The indigenous culture and its potential for human development are vastly ignored. The tendency is to accept efficiency with productivity without any concern for compassion or justice.[24]

Culture is an industry inventing and spreading aesthetic sensibilities, fantasy and imagination, the pursuit of pleasure, and the creation of compassion on a global scale. In addition to the financial institutions of culture cited so far, Nike, Hard Rock Cafe, Planet Hollywood, Pizza Hut, pornography, Kentucky straight bourbon, and Hollywood film industry monopolies aid the god of the religion of globalization to remake the world in its own image. In the cultural industry, mergers and recombinations of satellite, television, cable, software, and broadcasting companies serve to circulate this god throughout every possible nook and cranny of the world theater.[25]

CONCLUSION

This essay began with paradigmatic contrasts of religion and globalization. The wcc, it was stated, signifies, within the Christian community, an ecumenical move to proclaim the gospel of Jesus Christ to all the lands of the earth. The Council for a Parliament of the World's Religions offers a different approach. It desires interfaith and interreligious unity by having all belief expressions around the world come together and share gifts of communication, peace, and intrahuman harmony. The third model, the Pluralism Project, exemplifies the implosion of religious realities within the United States and hopes that knowledge of this new phenomenon might service civil interactions among new neighbors.

The essay then turned to the major claims of the argument. Not only is there religion and globalization, or a globalized religion, or religion in globalization, or global religions coming inward to the center; in fact, globalization itself is a form of religion. There is a religion of globalization that embodies the accoutrements of many other religions. God in this religion is the concentration of monopoly finance wealth, which functions both transcendently and immanently. It gives faith to its believers that it is the one and only supreme god—a notion made even more plausible with the fall of the Berlin Wall and the adoption of aspects of the market economy by some sectors of the former Soviet Union and by certain economists in the People's Republic of China. God has religious leadership constituted by the extremely small group of global billionaire families.

To foster the aims of this god, the trinity of the World Trade Organization, international banks (including the IMF and World Bank), and monopoly capitalist corporations acts as messengers or "angels" delivering this new gospel throughout the land. Theological anthropology functions as a didactic for how people should relate to and be in relation to god, and it teaches the human values from god. Theology, the justification and explanation of this religion, trumpets the tripartite grace of neoliberalism: free markets, privatization, and deregulation. Finally, the argument concluded with the ongoing complexities germane to all gods and religion: how does a divine or supernatural reality make itself known? This raises the question of revelation. And globalization, among other possibilities, unveils itself as affirming and transforming potentialities through the media of economics, politics, and culture.

Another essay is required to unpack a fifth paradigmatic expression of the interplay between religion and globalization. Liberation theologians in the international organization EATWOT begin with the broad vista of liberation of the least in society, as particularized among oppressed and marginalized peoples and the ecology in African, Asian, Latin American, and Pacific Islander regions of the world. EATWOT also includes Third World communities that are discriminated against in the United States (e.g., African Americans, Asian Americans, Hispanic-Latinos, and Native Americans–American Indians). EATWOT's understanding of religion and globalization accents agency and the coconstitution of a new human self with the God of freedom for the oppressed. EATWOT offers a new spirituality of resistance to domination and a sustained struggle for freedom and justice, anchored in the plight of the poor but yielding a full humanity for all.[26]

NOTES
1. For relevant reading on "globalization," see Samir Amin, *Re-reading the Postwar Period: An Intellectual Itinerary* (New York: Monthly Review Press, 1994); Arjun Appadurai, *Modernity at Large: Cultural Dimensions of Globalization* (Minneapolis: University of Minnesota Press, 1996); Israel Batista, ed., *Social Movements, Globalization, Exclusion: Social Movements, Challenges and Perspectives* (Geneva: World Council of Churches, 1997); Zygmunt Bauman, *Globalization: The Human Consequences* (New York: Columbia University Press, 1998); Peter Beyer, *Religion and Globalization* (Thousand Oaks:

Sage, 1994); Wade Roof Clark, ed., *World Order and Religion* (Albany: State University of New York Press, 1991); U. Duchrow, *Alternatives to Global Capitalism: Drawn from Biblical History, Designed for Political Action* (Utrecht: International Books, 1995); Mike Featherstone et al., eds., *Global Modernities* (Thousand Oaks: Sage, 1995); Irving Hexhma and Karla Poewe, *Making the Human Sacred: New Religions as Global Cultures* (Boulder: Westview Press, 1997); Susanne Rudolph Hoeber and James Piscatori, eds., *Transnational Religion and Fading States* (Boulder: Westview Press, 1997); Roland Robertson, *Globalization: Social Theory and Global Culture* (Thousand Oaks: Sage, 1992); Saskia Sassen, *Globalization and Its Discontents: Essays on the New Mobility of People and Money* (New York: New Press, 1998); Robert J. Schreiter, *The New Catholicity: Theology between the Global and the Local* (Maryknoll: Orbis Books, 1997); William H. Swatos, ed., *Religious Politics in Global Perspective* (New York: Greenwood Press, 1989); Malcolm Waters, *Globalization* (New York: Routledge, 1995); and John Witte Jr. and Johan D. van der Vyver, eds., *Religious Human Rights in Global Perspective: Religious Perspectives* (Boston: Martinus Nijhoff Publishers, 1996).

The Ecumenical Association of Third World Theologians publishes the journal *Voices from the Third World*, which contains continuous theoretical, theological, and practical discussions on globalization and religion. Some pertinent editions are June 1993, December 1995, December 1996, June 1997, December 1997, June 1998, December 1998, and June 1999. Also review David R. Loy, "The Religion of the Market," *Journal of the American Academy of Religion* 65, no. 2 (summer 1997).

2. The Pluralism Project is located at Harvard University. The Web site is www.fas.harvard.edu/pluralism.

3. I am a member of the board of trustees of the Council for a Parliament of the World's Religions and chair of the international theological commission of EATWOT, and I was a delegate to the eighth assembly of the WCC, held in Harare, Zimbabwe, in December 1998. Documentation on the WCC and the Parliament can be obtained from the World Council of Churches, 150 Route de Ferney, P.O. Box 2100, 1211 Geneva 2, Switzerland, and the Council for a Parliament of the World's Religions, P.O. Box 1630, Chicago, IL 60690 (Web site: www.cpwr.org). For a detailed sociological and theological genealogy of EATWOT, see my *Introducing Black Theology of Liberation* (Maryknoll: Orbis Books, 1999); James H. Cone, *For My People: Black Theology and the Black Church, Where Have We Been and Where Are We Going?* (Maryknoll: Orbis Books, 1984); and Theo Witvliet, *A Place in the Sun: An Introduction to Liberation Theology in the Third World* (Maryknoll: Orbis Books, 1985).

4. Mary John Mananzan, a Filipina member of EATWOT, writes the following about globalization: "EATWOT theologians see Globalization as a new religion that has its dogma (profit), its ethical principles (laws of the market), its prophets and high priests (International Monetary Fund–World Bank, Trans National

Corporations), its temples (Megamalls), its rituals (stock market biddings), its altar (market), its victims for sacrifice (greater majority of excluded peoples)." See her "Five Hundred Years of Colonial History: A Theological Reflection on the Philippine Experience," *Voices from the Third World* 21, no. 1 (June 1998): 242. For definitions of religion, see Peter Beyer, *Religion and Globalization* (Thousand Oaks: Sage, 1994), 5; and Paul Tillich, *Systematic Theology*, vol. 1 (Chicago: University of Chicago Press, 1951).

5. Nicholas D. Kristof and Edward Wyatt, "Who Sank, or Swam, in Choppy Currents of a World Cash Ocean," *New York Times*, 15 February 1999.

6. J. B. Banawiratma, "Religions in Indonesian Pluralistic Society in the Era of Globalization: A Christian Perspective," *Voices from the Third World* 22, no. 1 (June 1999): 38.

7. See *Forbes*, 12 October 1998, 4; and *As the South Goes* 6, no. 1 (spring 1999), a publication of the Institute for the Elimination of Poverty and Genocide, 9 Gammon Ave. S.W., Atlanta, GA 30315.

8. For the process of Christianity's relation to indigenous religions, see Tink Tinker, *Missionary Conquest: The Gospel of Native American Cultural Genocide* (Minneapolis: Fortress Press, 1993); and Charles H. Long, *Significations: Signs, Symbols, and Images in the Interpretation of Religion* (Minneapolis: Fortress Press, 1986).

9. Regarding theological anthropology, see John Mbiti, *African Religions and Philosophy* (Garden City: Anchor Books, 1970); Mbiti, *Introduction to African Religion* (Portsmouth: Heinemann, 1975); Tsenay Serequeberhan, ed., *African Philosophy: The Essential Writings* (New York: Paragon House, 1991); Laurenti Magesa, *African Religion: The Moral Traditions of Abundant Life* (Maryknoll: Orbis Books, 1997); Thomas D. Blakely et al., eds., *Religion in Africa* (Portsmouth: Heinemann, 1994); and Thomas Lawson, *Religions of Africa* (San Francisco: Harper and Row, 1985).

10. Israel Batista, "Social Movements: A Personal Testimony," in *Social Movements, Globalization, Exclusion: Social Movements, Challenges and Perspectives*, ed. Israel Batista (Geneva: World Council of Churches, 1967), 3.

11. For references on theology, see Bradley C. Hanson, *Introduction to Christian Theology* (Minneapolis: Fortress Press, 1997); Peter C. Hodgson and Robert H. King, eds., *Christian Theology: An Introduction to Its Traditions and Tasks* (Minneapolis: Fortress Press, 1985); and Alister E. McGrath, *Christian Theology: An Introduction* (Cambridge: Blackwell, 1994).

12. Readings on the historical backdrop and current contours of neoliberalism and its attendant characteristics of free markets, privatization, and deregulation can be found in Samir Amin, *Re-reading the Postwar Period: An Intellectual Itinerary*; Robert Gilpin, *The Political Economy of International Relations* (Princeton: Princeton University Press, 1987); Ana Ezcurra, "Globalization, Neoliberalism, and Civil Society," in *Social Movements, Globalization, Exclusion: Social Movements, Challenges and Perspectives*, ed. Israel Batista

(Geneva: World Council of Churches, 1997); Vandana Shiva, "Democracy in the Age of Globalization," *Essay: The Social Movements;* Peter McIsaac, "Structural Adjustment Programmes: Capitalist Myth in Africa," *Voices from the Third World* 21, no. 1 (June 1998); and Mathew Kurian, "Evolution of the Market and Its Social Implications," *Voices from the Third World* 21, no. 1 (June 1998).

13. Neoliberalism pursues its project just as aggressively in Europe, the former Eastern bloc, and the remaining socialist countries. I underscore the Third World primarily because it includes the largest human and ecological resources in the world.

14. Carmelita Usog, "Doing Theology: Contextualized Theology (God-Talk, Women Speak)," *Voices from the Third World* 21, no. 1 (June 1998): 197.

15. See the "Report of the Ecumenical Association of Third World Theologians Evaluation Commission," *Voices from the Third World* 19, no. 2 (December 1996): 222–23.

16. Dalip Swamy, "An Alternative to Globalisation," *Voices from the Third World* 20, no. 1 (June 1997): 130–31.

17. C. T. Kurien, "Globalization—What Is It About?" *Voices from the Third World* 20, no. 2 (December 1997): 20.

18. See Zygmunt Bauman, introduction to *Globalization: The Human Consequences* (New York: Columbia University Press, 1998); and Malcolm Waters, *Globalization* (New York: Routledge, 1995), chap. 3.

19. K. C. Abraham, "Together in Mission and Unity: Beholding the Glory of God's Kingdom," *Voices from the Third World* 22, no. 1 (June 1999): 144–45.

20. *Time,* 9 November 1998, 36.

21. Sassen, *Globalization and Its Discontents,* xxii–xxiii.

22. Ezcurra, "Globalization, Neoliberalism, and Civil Society," 82.

23. For a concise summation of what I call the politics of the god of the religion of globalization, see Bauman, 65–69.

24. Abraham, "Together in Mission and Unity," 144.

25. For another perspective on culture and globalization, see Arjun Appadurai, *Modernity at Large: Cultural Dimensions of Globalization* (Minneapolis: University of Minnesota Press, 1996), chap. 2. Appadurai proposes a theoretical framework with five foci highly marked by their disjuncture. His categories of ethnoscapes, mediascapes, technoscapes, financescapes, and ideoscapes are helpful. Aspects of this five-pronged schematic are taken into consideration in my perspective. However, I would argue that from the experiences of the world's poor (and not those of the elites and experts of different fields), there is less disjuncture among the five than Appadurai asserts.

26. For details on EATWOT, see note 3. For a comprehensive outline of this new spirituality, see Mary John Mananzan, "Five Hundred Years of Colonial History," 231–32.

ENRIQUE DUSSEL

The Sociohistorical Meaning

of Liberation Theology (Reflections

about Its Origin and World Context)

In previous works I have dealt with the origin and development of liberation theology from the viewpoint of the history of the church or from a theological perspective.[1] Now, however, I will reflect on the sociohistorical world "context" that gave birth to its emergence. My goal is to prove that this is a "phenomenon" with global significance.

THE "MODERNITIES" AND THE WORLD
RELIGIONS IN THE NORTH-SOUTH DIALECTIC

From the emergence of the Christian era up to 1492, neither Europe nor the Latin Roman Empire had ever been considered the "center" of the cultural, political, or economic world. The Latin-Germanic Europe had always been considered a peripheral and subordinate sector of a system with a "center" placed elsewhere. This "center" had first been positioned between Egypt and Mesopotamia (from 3000 B.C.E.) and later in the Seleucid and Ptolemaic region, having also the area between Baghdad and Samarkanda as a hinge to connect with China and the Mediterranean (from 750 to 1350 C.E.).[2]

On the other hand, Europe had not given any sign of its scientific, philosophical, theological, economic, or even technological superiority over the Chinese, Hindu, or Muslim cultures of the time (the latter covering from the Atlantic Morocco to the Philippines).[3] The fortuitous act of taking the Atlantic Ocean toward the system's "center," then located in India, produced the invasion of America and the conquest of its indigenous cultures. Annexing large territories[4] to Europe created such a comparative world unbalance that historians, philosophers, theologians, and others granted the Atlantic a status of privilege, producing the interpretative mirage of always locating Europe at the "center" of the First World system.[5] "Scientific" histories of the eighteenth century, particularly those of German romanticism, ideologically incorporated Greece into Western Europe,[6] in a doting process of recovering the past of the modern "centrality" of Europe.

The invasion of America—wrongly called "discovery"—placed Europe for the first time in history (only now and for the first time in the context of world history) in the "center." The management of this "centrality" constitutes the phenomenon of modernity. By establishing the "centrality" of the Atlantic,[7] Europe-America set Nordic Europe free from having to go through the Mediterranean— and therefore, through Rome—to connect with the Euro-Asiatic system.[8] The two farthest points from the "center" became thus Japan on the East and the Europe of the North and Baltic Sea in the West.[9] The event of the invasion of America allowed Nordic-Germanic Europe[10] to avoid going through the Mediterranean Rome. In other words, in a very short period of time (1492–1517), the major event of the Protestant separation of the Nordic German people of the Roman-Mediterranean Christianity, initiated by Luther at Erfurt, took place. Occurring toward the south of Europe after the emergence of Protestantism, the "Catholic Reformation" was the reaction of Roman-Mediterranean Christianity, thereby initiating the appearance of "Catholicism."

Hispanic modernity (modernity I), centered in Seville, established the First World system by bringing together Europe and Latin America and by producing, through its conquest of Mexico and Peru,[11] the first "modernization" via the inspiration of what later became the expressed Catholicism of the Council of Trent. Modernity I was characteristically mercantilist and monetary (of early capitalism) and was driven by an imperialist project that failed with Charles V in 1557, when he abdicated owing to his financial downfall. In spite of this incident, modernity I brought about the first missionary expansion of Mediterranean Christianity, now modern and anti-Protestant, in the first marginalized and colonial world of Europe.

Dutch modernity (modernity II), centered in Amsterdam (1630–1680),[12] was also mercantilist but religiously Reformed and, properly speaking, bourgeois. It organized its expansion simply by founding two commercial companies (West and East Indies), initiating the "modern" capitalist process with a new scientific, philosophical, and theological paradigm (following Descartes or Spinoza). In the eighteenth century, England and Scotland, with the Calvinist or Presbyterian Edinburgh as center, took the lead of the world system and established the first Protestant missionary expansion in the marginalized and colonial world.

Islam, which since the second century had expanded from the Arab peninsula to the Córdoba's Caliphate and Morocco's kingdoms west of Maghreb,[13] had joined the Turks in taking Constantinople and would later threaten the borders of Vienna. Its expansion continued toward the south of the Sahara from the ninth century to the present. The military and economic crisis of the Muslim world[14] drove it from the "center" of the Euro-Asiatic system to the periphery of the world system dominated by Europe until 1945.

This was the way in which the world religions—Confucianism, Taoism, Hinduism, Buddhism, and others—received not only the political and economic impact of Europe's world system organization but also the presence of Christianity, both Catholic and Protestant. That is, Christianity became present for the first time in the "peripheral and colonial" world.[15] The implantation of Christianity in this diverse peripheral and colonial world helps illuminate the specific perspective in which liberation theology emerges.

From this point on, liberation theology becomes a "reinterpretative and critical reflection" arising at the end of modernity (in the ancient colonial world of the Hispanic and preindustrial modernity I), within the only southern and peripheral Christianity of the poor. This fact produces, inside of a culturally "dominant" Christianity,[16] the awakening of a "prophetic and political" responsibility, in radical contrast to Islamic "fundamentalisms" that claim direct power from the Right. It also yields a Christianity that transforms from within: the definite "popular imagination" that emerged from the impact of the Catholic modernity I.[17] This is a "critical" Christianity from the perspective of the impoverished masses of the South, which could not develop within the Christianities of the rich North of Europe and the United States. It is also a transmodern and postecumenical reflection, for its point of departure (rather than the divided churches—both Protestant and Catholic—of modernity) is its reference to the oppressed and excluded masses.

THE CONDITION OF THE SOUTH FROM THE DOWNFALL OF "POPULISM" TO THE "REAL SOCIALISM," 1945-1989

At the end of the so-called Second World War[18] in 1945, the United States defeated Germany and Japan and established its supremacy over the United Kingdom.[19] It took almost ten years (1945-1954) for the new power to consolidate its sovereignty as a world "center."[20] Once this new stage of reorganization of the center of the world's system was completed, the United States confronted, at the periphery, a perpetually sovereign China, a politically independent Latin America (since the beginning of the nineteenth century), and the new liberated European colonies.[21]

In Latin America, from the economic crisis of 1929 to the coup d'état against Arbenz in Guatemala of 1954 (organized by the CIA),[22] the emerging nationalistic bourgeoisie managed a certain industrial development. This effort led to a belief in the possibility of an economic development based in the nationalistic decisions of a populist state,[23] guided by a charismatic popular leader.[24] This was the promising beginning of the most stable capitalism developed in Latin America.

The "globalization" of the market began with North American "penetration" into Latin America by way of the "doctrine of development" upheld by UNESCO's Economic Commission for Latin America. This initiative was coupled with financial investments and developing technological dependence for the substitution of imports, thus beginning the expansion of transnational companies. Military support was added to bring down populist governments in the territory.[25] Subsequently the Alliance for Progress opened the so-called Decade of Progress (1954-1964). The acclaimed "development" never took place. Instead, countries in the area suffered extraordinary extraction of their national wealth, inflationary instability, mobilization of their popular sectors, and increasing impoverishment. In 1954 the present process of "globalization" under the global supremacy of the United States over Latin America was initiated.

The history of this process encompasses establishing a structure of increasing dependency by stages. There was resistance, both successful and not so successful revolutionary movements against this tendency. Only by taking into account the horizon of this historical context can we understand the origin and development of the theology of liberation.

According to national oligarchies and the intelligence services of the United States, the only way to stop the situation from worsening and to create stability was to move to another form of state rule: military dictatorships of national security states.[26] The economic paradigm based on "globalization" deepened the dependency already started with the Decade of Development.[27] Recent military dictatorships, from the one in Brazil in 1964, to the one defeated in Haiti in 1994, tried to develop a viable capitalism of increasing dependence.[28] A number of consecutive failures (such as the shortcomings of the "Brazilian Miracle," the Malvinas' war led by the Argentinean military, the North American productivity crisis,[29] and the effects of starting the payment of the interest on the public debt)[30] led to reestablishing civil governments by "democratic" elections.[31]

The last stage in the recent development of formal democratic countries in Latin America was characterized by a political stability of the people's elected representative regimes. This stage was also limited by an increasing impoverishment, caused by the not so "orthodox" generalized use (until 1989) of a neoliberal "globalization" economic policy.

Parallel to the military dictatorships, for more than thirty years,[32] there was a revolutionary process aimed at various noncapitalist alternatives, successful only in Cuba, Nicaragua, and Chile. This movement caused great popular hope, drawing the participation of many young people, social organizations, and Christian political parties.[33]

In summary, the coming together of poverty and the increasing oppression of massive believing communities, the emergence of alternative revolutionary movements to capitalism, and the refined analysis by the "Theory of Dependence" of the causes of the economic deterioration after the downfall of populist governments (in a Latin American context, where the church had been structurally restored by the impact of the Second Vatican Council)—all created the conditions, specifically in 1968, for the emergence of a theological perspective that, from this time on, came to be known as liberation theology.

LIBERATION THEOLOGY AS RUPTURE OF THE RELIGION-DOMINATION IDENTITY IN THE PROCESS OF GLOBALIZATION-EXCLUSION

After a short or long period of development that took centuries, religions of the world identified themselves with cultures that contributed to their origin. This identity with culture, that is, with the dominant classes, was called Confucianism in China and Brahmanism in India. In Islam, it became the official interpretation and management of the Koran by the power of the Caliphate. And in the history of the Christian Church, it was known as Christendom.[34]

While the coexistence of these regional communities (e.g., from China, India, and even to the world of Islam and Europe) led to interpenetrating mutual destruction or domination, the identity between world religion and culture was not significantly challenged, because this latter opposition emerged internally. Contrary to this trend, the expansion of European Christendoms[35] from the sixteenth to the eighteenth century produced different significant crises in the world religions of the South. In Latin America, this expansion brought the penetration of a world religion previously nonexistent in the region.[36] But the secularization process led by the European Enlightenment (Aufklärung) of the eighteenth century produced, since the nineteenth century, the most decisive factor in questioning the relationship between political power and religious and cultural identity.

For the most part, traditional world religions played the role of resisting the foreign "modernization" process brought about by conquest. This included resistance against Europe's cultural influence and its secularizing impact. The encroachment of these three elements (conquest, culture, and secularization) prompted the world religions of the South to defend their popular traditions from the impoverishing and dominating conquest, the imposition of a foreign culture, and the atheism or unbelief proper to the Enlightenment. Paradoxically, southern world religions' identification with ancestral political and economic powers led them to strive for a "return to the authenticity of the past," similar to the thrust of "fundamentalist" religions. Therefore, movements of religious revivalism in Africa or Asia frequently had in the past, and continue to have in the present, the ambiguous impulse toward both defending their own identity and simultaneously affirming a premodern past that can hardly move beyond modernity.

While the theology of liberation emerged from the intellectual university and working-class elites beginning in 1968, it was not driven by an ideal of a return to a past identity. Its critical difference from the cultural, political, economic, and religious groups (e.g., inheritors of Christendom) placed it in conflict with them, as well as with the oligarchies and the bourgeoisie. Liberation theology's stance derived from its break with, or critical position regarding, such cultural, economic, political, and religious dominant realms and its commitment to the classes, groups, and popular movements oppressed by the dependent capitalism or excluded from the process of modernizing globalization. The source of this commitment was twofold. First, it originated from a rereading of the Gospels. Second, it arose from a reinterpretation of the life and preaching of the historical Jesus, which allowed Christians in Latin America to discover a new meaning of the social and even revolutionary changes taking place in South America at the end of the sixties.

The commitment for social and even revolutionary change of many young Christians who discovered such responsibility[37] led them to a "crisis of faith," or even to its very loss. What happened was that a certain traditional "interpretation" proved inadequate for the needs of a political praxis at a time of deep crisis. Thus liberation theology emerged as a way of rethinking or reformulating Christian interpretation[38] to make possible a new vision of events—both social and even revolutionary ones—by which the commitment to the poor and participation in their struggles meant building God's reign as taught by the founder of Christianity.

This was a worldwide historical event. Certain militant groups of a world religion, by being located in the "South,"[39] brought about a rereading of its foundational text,[40] the reestablishment of a direct connection with its founder,[41] and thus an advancing of the struggle of the oppressed and excluded of society.[42] Such struggles were now based in the Gospels[43] and relied on the resources of popular imagination (i.e., its traditions, myths, and rites). This stance sharply contrasted many of the leftist revolutionary movements of the time.

The latter, given their atheistic foundation, fought against this popular religious experience as the foundation of the people's struggle against repressive systems. Liberation theology hermeneutically reinterpreted the religious assumptions of the historical popular conscience to facilitate the liberation of the poor and the transformation of political, economic, social, and religious institutions. In so doing, this theological perspective remembered and was inspired by ancient and fundamental moments of the Christian faith. Among the most important of these events were the liberation of the slaves from Egypt, the profoundly antiritualistic and justice-oriented proclamation of the prophets for the oppressed, as well as the whole proclamation of the founder of Christianity contained in the Gospels. Along with these principles, liberation theology included new insights brought about by such liberating events as the ones produced by Bartolomé de Las Casas for the well-being of the Native Americans during the sixteenth century, or those contributed by Miguel Hidalgo, founder of Mexico, during the nineteenth century.

Liberation theology is a creative and complex synthesis[44] of apparently contradictory tensions. Without falling into traditionalism, it claims to participate in the most ancient prophetic traditions and to learn from the very founder of Christianity. It professes the struggle for greater justice in the life of the numerous human sectors of society excluded from the modernizing globalization process but avoids falling into technological anachronisms or destructive ecological positions. It affirms the ancestral religion of the people with a profound liberating and transformative hermeneutic against tragic historical resignation. It shows the importance of the political realm but rejects the direct use of power by theologians as in the case of Islamic "fundamentalism." It is critical of capitalism, not from the perspective of a feudalistic past or a premodern conservatism, but from a yearning for the realization of a future alternative of greater justice for the majority sectors of society. Those who claim this theological perspective are willing to risk a commitment to positions that draw on democratic socialism and, at the same time, learn from its present failures. Its commitment to the world of the poor and the experience of Ecclesial Basic Communities moves those who hold this theological perspective to learn to live with respect and tolerance and promote democratic participation.

Paradoxically, even if liberation theologians are subjected to persecution both inside[45] and outside[46] the church, their presence has become increasingly widespread inside the Christian community[47] and has a deeper impact in the secular realm. The latter is evidenced by the Mayan rebellion of January 1994 at Chiapas, the Lavalás popular movement led by Father Aristide in Haiti, or the public declarations of Frei Betto on the crisis of land occupation in Brazil.[48] These are events attributed to liberation theologians by public opinion and the media. Surely the reference is not merely to the actions of some theologians or to an internal Catholic or Protestant academic and theological reflection of the type of modernity I and II. The reference is rather to *a rereading of Christianity that has taken root in the massive and numerous oppressed peoples of the continent,* who have been intentionally excluded from the process of globalization. This perspective manifests in the "popular imagination," its myths, rites, and the historical remembrance of its liberators, among whom we find people such as Moses, Isaiah, Jesus Christ, Francis of Assisi, Bartolomé de Las Casas, Hidalgo, Rutilio Grande, Romero, Ellacuría, and many others. The most dynamic militant representatives of this theological perspective speak of liberation from a domination that began during the conquest with the invasion of the American continent five hundred years ago, and from which it is difficult to find an immediate resolution. For this reason, in spite of the opinion of many, and given the increasing impoverishment of greater numbers of people excluded from the globalization process of the market's capital, liberation theology will continue to provide a critical function in the future. It will also be practiced in other parts of the Christian world, such as Africa and Asia,[49] and by theologians of other world religions.[50]

To be sure, liberation theology is a synthesis in which the contradictions of the theologies of the type of modernity I and II are overcome. This theological perspective emerges from a commitment to the poor of the South, that is, those who have been excluded from the present globalization modernizing process.[51] Thus this is a critical reflection leading to a transmodern hope, aimed toward an alternative of greater justice for the people at the periphery.

NOTES

Translated from the Spanish by Jose David Rodriguez.

1. For a bibliography on this topic see the following works written by this

author: Enrique Dussel, *Prophetie und Kritik: Entwurf einer Geschichte der Theologie in Lateinamerika* (Freiburg: Exodus, 1989); "Chronologische Darstellung der Entstehung und Entwicklung der Theologie der Befreiung in Lateinamerika (1959–1989), in *Theologiegeschichte der Dritten Weld* (Gütersloh: Taschenbücher, 1993), 263–362; short text in "Hinweise zur Entstehung der Befreiungstheologie: 1959–1972," ed. Raúl Fornet-B., in *Theologien in der Social und Kulturgeschichte Lateinamerikas*, vol. 3 (Eichstätt: Diritto Verlag, 1993), 302–34; new actualized version in *Teología de la liberación: Un panorama de su desarrollo* (México: Posterillos Editores, 1995). To explore its historical ecclesial context, see Enrique Dussel, ed., *The Church in Latin America, 1492-1992* (New York: Orbis Books, 1992), or the Spanish edition of this work: *Resistencia y esperanza: Una historia del pueblo cristiano en América Latina y el Caribe* (San José: DEI, 1995). These works refer to the sociopolitical, economic, and historical dimensions of the secular and political society and the church in particular, as well as to the specific history of liberation theology.

2. See the works of this author: "Eurocentrism and Modernity (Introduction to the Frankfurt Lectures)," in *The Postmodernism Debate in Latin America*, vol. 20, ed. John Beverley-José Oviedo (Durham: Duke University Press), 65–76, also in *Von Erfindung Amerikas zur Entdeckung des Anderen* (Düsseldorf: Patmos, 1993), 16–42; "Europa, Moderne und Eurozentrismus: Semantische Verfehlung des Europa-Begriffs," in *Das Geistige Erbe Europas*, ed. Manfred Buhr, Instituto Italiano vergli, Studi Filosofici 5 (Napoli: Vivarium, 1994), 855–967; "Sistema-Mundo, dominaçâo e exclusâo," in *Historia da Igresia na América Latina e no Caribe*, ed. E. Hoornert (Petrópolis: Voces, 1995), 39–80; also "El sistema-mundo como problema filosófico," in a future publication with the title *La ética de la Liberación ante el desafío de Apel, Taylor y Vattimo*.

3. I have given many reasons for this point in the studies mentioned in the last note.

4. Some of these territories were significantly larger than Europe itself. They were inhabited by millions of human beings, wealthy in gold and silver, first subjected to a mercantile system, then an industrial capitalist one, and lastly a system of slavery practiced with a prototypical inhumanity never equaled.

5. This unbalance had as a consequence the impoverishment of the Muslim world.

6. Greece had always been "Eastern" and was first recovered by the Muslim world by Al-Kindi (an Aristotelian philosopher of the ninth century C.E. in what is today Syria), much earlier than the Paris of the thirteenth century.

7. Including the North and Baltic Sea.

8. Nordic Europe followed this route until 1492.

9. As mentioned earlier, India was the farthest point from the "center" before the invasion of America.

10. Heirs of the Vikings and the Ansa of the North Atlantic.

11. And the slow conquest of all Latin America.

12. See Immanuel Wallerstein, *The Modern World System* (New York: Academic Press, 1974). For an exploration of modernity I, see vol. 1; for modernity II, vol. 2; and for England, vol. 3. From the same author, see *The Politics of the World Economy* (Cambridge: Cambridge University Press, 1984).

13. This expansion had included all Egypt since the ancient kingdoms of Mesopotamia, to the Sultanate of Delhi, following the Muslim merchants to Malacca and Mindanao.

14. Compare, for example, Lepanto twenty-five years after the discovery of the gold and silver mines in Potosi and Zacatecas by Spain.

15. Since the fourteenth century (and this becomes a relevant element for our topic), only Latin America constituted a practically exclusive Catholic Christendom of the type of the imperial modernity I. Since the seventeenth century, the Anglo-Saxon Protestantism of the properly bourgeois modernity II type established its dominance in the United States. By the end of the nineteenth century, and facing an increasing Islamic expansion, the missions in Africa became either Protestant or Catholic. In Asia, Christianity developed as a minority phenomenon, with the exception of the Philippines.

16. In contrast to the Christian presence in Africa and Asia.

17. Even Latin American Protestantism needs to take into account this "Catholic popular imagination," from the perspective of indigenous Indian religions, transformed in the colonial period. For this reason, Michael Novak argues that liberation theology is the product of a conservative preindustrial mentality, critical of capitalism. The understanding of "popular imagination" springs from a respect of the people's religiosity viewed from a progressive conscience, opened to technological, economic, politically democratic, autonomously cultural, and participative developing processes, as alternatives toward a better future for the greater majorities.

18. This was not a world war but a war for the hegemony of the center of world capitalism. This was one of the most violent, irrational, and numerically catastrophic conflicts ever experienced since the origins of humankind. This war was brought about by the "civilized" Europe.

19. The United Kingdom had been the center of world capitalism for the last two centuries.

20. As a means to establish its dominance as a world power, the United States used the Marshall Plan for the reconstruction of Germany and Europe against the Soviet Union of Stalin and its support of Japan against Mao's China.

21. These European colonies were liberated by the presence of the United States in Europe. The former European colonialism was modified by the "globalization" of the market and the capital in Asia and Africa since 1945. The postwar liberation in Asia and Africa was the transition from the European colonial domination to the new supremacy of the world market by the United States. This process of Americanization was the first step of today's "globalization."

22. This same type of pressure was practiced against Nazer in Egypt, the Nationalist Party in Iran, Sukarno in Indonesia, and so on.

23. This populist state pretended to be the product of a common agreement between the bourgeoisie, the working class, and the peasants to jointly rule the nation.

24. In Brazil, this took the form of *Vargismo*, in Mexico of *Cardenismo*, and in Argentina of *Peronismo*.

25. This took place in Guatemala in 1954 with Castillo Armas, in Argentina in 1955 with Videla, in Colombia in 1957 with Rojas Pinilla, and in the same year in Venezuela with Pérez Jiménez. However, in Cuba in 1959 there was an unprecedented turn of events with Fidel Castro.

26. The "Sorbonne Group" of Brazil's Military School under the leadership of Golbery do Coto e Sylva formulated the first paradigm.

27. It needs to be indicated that the paradigm would deepen without cracks, from the military governments of 1983 to the formal democracies of the present.

28. The popular repression produced by these military dictatorships, in both the political and ecclesial realms, had devastating effects.

29. This crisis hindered the support of the United States for its military allies in the continent.

30. This debt was acquired most irresponsibly by the private sector.

31. An example of this trend was the election of Raúl Alfonsín in Argentina (1983) or Tancredo Nêves in Brazil (1985).

32. This revolutionary process was initiated by the Cuban revolution in 1959 leading up to the electoral defeat of the Sandinistas in 1990. The latter was influenced by the ten-year war organized by the United States and the fall of the Berlin Wall.

33. This is the hope that presently drives the Mayan rebellion in Chiapas.

34. The notion of Christendom refers to the development of Christianity into a culture or empire since Constantine or Teodosio in the fourth century C.E.

35. There were many Christendoms—Iberian Catholic, Dutch Calvinist, British Anglican, Danish Lutheran,—with their respective national church, crown, confessions, and so forth.

36. Africa had a Coptic Christian presence in Ethiopia and Asia, and a St. Thomas Christian community in Kerala, before the installation of this world system in the fifteenth century. A sixteenth-century tradition in Latin America claimed that the preaching of the gospel by Thomas the Apostle from India (identified as Quetzalcoatl) and the virgin of Guadalupe dated from as early as the first century. Surely this was the effort of American-born Spaniards with liberation spirit who wanted to claim parity with Spain in terms of antiquity, even to the point of being unappreciative for her gift of Christianity.

37. This happened as a natural development of the "spirit" of the Catholic

Youth Workers' participation in deeply secularized and even militant atheist Marxist groups.

38. That is, the whole matter of "faith and politics."

39. This is where modernity or capitalism shows, in the misery of the numerous human sectors of society excluded from the globalization process, its most profound contradiction.

40. That is, the gospel, the Bible.

41. Jesus came to "evangelize the poor," and to judge with the following criteria: "I was hungry and was given food to eat." The poor of his context were in a colony ruled by the Roman Empire. Jesus was crucified by the religious and political powers of his time.

42. The event took place between 1968 and 1972 under the guidance of CELAM, the highest ecclesial institution in Latin America.

43. Formerly the opinion was that these struggles contradicted the gospel.

44. Liberation theology is a highly elaborated and novel perspective, which is also part of the most authentic traditional horizon, i.e., retrieves and transforms the Christian tradition.

45. Starting in 1972, this persecution was inflicted in Latin America by the Vatican, which restored its pre–Vatican II Council bureaucratic structures.

46. Military national security or conservative governments persecuted liberation theologians.

47. This takes place as students, militants, priests, members of various orders, and others increase their reference to this theological perspective in their writings, conferences, meetings, courses, books, articles, interpretations, and so on.

48. In this case, President Cardoso called on Christians committed to the "Movement of the Landless" to arrive at a solution to the crisis.

49. See my article "Existe-t-il une Théologie de la Libération en Afrique et en Asie?" *Recherches de Science Religieuse* 2 (April–June 1986): 165–78.

50. Therefore it will not be strange to find works of liberation theologians among the Muslims of Iran or Bombay, in India's Hindu beyond Gandhi's movement, or among the Buddhist of Sri Lanka or Thailand.

51. This is the territory where two-thirds of the entire population of the world is located.

EDUARDO MENDIETA

Society's Religion: The Rise of

Social Theory, Globalization, and

the Invention of Religion

One of the fundamental myths of modernity was its promise to abolish religion by sublimating it. To paraphrase Freud, where superstition and religion were, reason and science shall be. This myth went by the name of secularization. Modernity did not abolish religion. Society was not secularized. The converse happened. Religions proliferated, and secularization meant the institutionalization of religion within the social. Society itself became the site for the articulation of the religious. Modernity produced both the illusion of the end of religion and the birth of the religious proper. Before modernity there was no religion, just as there was no "society." The fact is that modernity could not have come about without the invention of religion.

Globalization has accelerated both this process of the creation of the religious and the increase in the awareness that religion itself was not, could not, and will not be abolished. In one reading, it could be affirmed that globalization is modernity become self-reflexive, and to this extent, it means that society has dispensed with the myth of secularization. In an opposite reading, globalization is a new social order, a new age, a new *saeculum*, in which the relationships between the parts that make the whole have not just been radically rearranged but have also undergone radical transformation: the state, civil society, the economy, culture, and so forth have taken on different dimensions just as they relate in new and unprecedented ways. Religion, inevitably, has also taken on a new character. It is not co-

incidental that globalization was partly heralded by global movements of religious revival and activism.[1] In this latter reading, therefore, globalization does not promise the end of religion, not even its
sublimation, but its reinvention, and reinception.

The question, therefore, is, Does religion occupy the same social
and theoretical place for both modernity and globalization? First, before discussing the place of religion within a global order, this essay
offers a typology of theories of globalization. Second, it examines the
relationship between modernity, sociology, and religion in terms of
a schematic discussion of the origins of social theory vis-à-vis the
invention of the religious. The essay closes with some general observations about the future of religion.

SOCIETY'S GLOBALIZATION, THE GLOBALIZATION OF SOCIETY

The scholarly production of analyses of globalization has reached
such a high level of differentiation and even specialization that we
have probably reached the stage in which we need to venture a typology of theories of globalization.[2] Furthermore, the kind of theory
of globalization one opts for in order to analyze the role of religion in
contemporary society is bound to produce particular effects. There
are theories of globalization that continue to perpetuate the myths
of modernity about religion and therefore have or make no place for
it within their analyses of globalization. In fact, we may infer that
a theory of globalization that makes no room for religion has major
theoretical flaws in its conceptual edifice. This essay is an argument
precisely about this internal conceptual linkage between religion
and social theory vis-à-vis its main contemporary preoccupation,
namely, globalization. The degree to which a particular analysis of
planetary integration dispenses with or incorporates a conceptual
reflection on the "religious" should be taken partly as a litmus test
of its appropriateness for the global age.

Theories of globalization can be divided into three types in accor-
dance with their (1) diffusionism or integrationism, (2) theoretical reflexivity, (3) degree to which they offer insights into the autonomy of
social subsystems without creating a hierarchy or teleological model
that may be merely a function of unanalyzed theoretical biases, and
(4) degree of empirical concreteness and theoretical complexity. The
more empirically detailed and textured a theory of globalization is,

the more it tends to emphasize the particular process or structure it analyzes.

1. *Mono-metastructural:* These are theories of globalization that explain the rise of globalization in terms of the expansion of one societal subsystem. In other words, these theories see world integration as having been catalyzed by the world expansion of one particular subsystem of social interaction. Every other subsystem develops and reconfigures under the pressure of the dominant, globalizing subsystem. Thus the political subsystem develops and globalizes under the pressure of the economic or cultural. In general, religion and culture, similarly, are seen as undergoing transformation under the "modernizing" pressures of the economy, or the globalization of certain modes of economic relations. To this extent, what we have is less an integrationist perspective that wants to rethink the new global order, and more a diffusionist perspective that sees globalization as the logical consequence of the "diffusion" of a particular "modernizing" agent.

In this sense, most of these theories of globalization are really just other versions of theories of modernity, that is, of the expansion of modernity. For these theories, globalization is just modernity pursued at a more accelerated pace. The difference between globalization and modernity is one of quantity and not of kind or type. Accordingly, they perpetuate the ethnocentrism and Eurocentrism of most of Western social theory. The critical options before these processes of catalyzation and accelerated modernity are of two kinds: euphoric celebration, or cynical rejection. The possibility for radical critique is undermined by the ineluctability with which the process is thought to have developed. Under this rubric, we can gather the theories of Amin, Wallerstein, Frank, Barber, Meyers, Barnet, and Cavanaugh.[3]

2. *Matrix Rearrangement and Differentiation:* Under this category fall theories of globalization that do not depart from the idea of the catalyzing function of one particular social subsystem. Nor do they depart from the idea that globalization ought to be understood in terms of subsystems that enter into new quantitative levels of deployment and differentiation. Instead, globalization is seen as a radically new order in which the fundamental building blocks of social interaction enter into radically new relations, sometimes me-

diated by new social subsystems that in many ways give entirely new meanings to these building blocks. These theories, in fact, are articulated at higher levels of generality and abstractness. Instead of trying to think world societies from the standpoint of a series of sometimes unique Western social structures and processes, this type of theory tries to circumvent such ethnocentrism by attempting to reach a different level of abstraction.

In this case, then, these theories are less about the diffusion of one particular type of social structure or process, and more about the conceptualization and visualization of the new social order in terms of an integrationist perspective. These theories therefore take issue with the debates concerning whether globalization is an extension of modernity. In the case of Robertson, for instance, modernity is seen as a consequence of globalization. There is a way in which the ideas of the differential expansion of modernity, the rise of "global modernities" or different paths through modernity, already presuppose the idea of a planetary whole. These theories also seem to be motivated by self-consciousness about Eurocentrism and ethnocentrism that would like to challenge the primacy of certain Western structures and modes of social development. Here we would include Arjun Appadurai, Roland Robertson, and Bryan S. Turner.[4] To varying degrees, some of these theories are plagued by a lack of clarity and reflection about their own theoretical standpoint. In other words, if the point is not to fall into Eurocentrism and ethnocentrism, why are these categories, and not others, used?

For instance, Robertson works on the givenness of the categories of self and humanity in his theory of the matrix of globalization, whereas Turner departs from a philosophical-anthropological perspective that takes for granted the idea of the exocentric character of human existence. In both cases, however, such categories are already detritus of globalization, and they are explaining the whole in terms of the parts that are in need of being explained in the first place. A self, and whatever content we assigned to this term, is already a function of a global order in which "individualities" must be discretely determined and differentiated. Hence the social order called globalization is prior to the "self" as a unity in the global matrix. One last point about this type of theory of globalization: they apparently are unable to answer the question, How is the particular theory of globalization being offered itself reflecting on its own globalization? Or more precisely, to what extent is a particular theory of globalization itself a necessary perspective on globalization?

3. *Metatheoretical Reflexivity:* Under this rubric, I gather the theories of globalization that see the new global order from an integrationist perspective. The global order is different not just in quantity and order but in kind from what has preceded it. The diffusion or expansion of one subsystem is seen by this type of theory as already a function of a global order. If the economy expands and extends to every corner of the planet, this is because we are already part of a planetary whole; similarly with the cultural and religious realms. Religious revolutions, reformations, and so-called regressive fundamentalisms are not just defensive or counterreactions to the effects of economic globalization. Instead, they are already aspects of a global culture. Similarly, if individuality, particularism, cultural diversity, and in general particularization become relevant and more pressing, it is because they are already part and parcel of a global order in which the new social system calls for such differentiations and distinctions.

From this theoretical perspective, then, global modernities are already forms of the world order, of a globalized social system. For these theories, the issue of globalization is not even an empirical issue; it is above all a conceptual and theoretical challenge that requires that we understand not just why a particular system seems to dominate but why such a subsystem is thought to be the agent of globalization at the very moment when we are able to see other sub-systems struggling for supremacy. In other words, this type of approach tries to think its object and subject at the same time. In Luhmann's terms, metatheoretical reflexivity requires that we observe the observer. For this reason, this type of theory of globalization is a second-order observation, in which we are trying to see ourselves looking at ourselves. These theories begin from the standpoint of theoretical self-reflexivity. This is to be understood as the observing of observers or as an analysis of who is observing what and for which reasons.

Put differently, globalization is a way in which society observes itself as an integrated system. From this perspective, namely, of society as a self-observing system, society itself can no longer conceive of itself as an aggregation of somewhat interrelated parts and elements, such as humans, selves, societies, cultures, and so forth. Were this to be the goal, the self-description and self-observation of society would become paradoxical and incomprehensible.[5] Consequently, to think globalization requires that we think the unity of society in different terms. In fact, we must think society anew. Under this rubric, therefore, I gather the theories proposed by systems theorists such as Niklas Luhmann[6] and Richard Münch.[7]

Social theory is the analysis of the means by which society reflects on itself—it is the observation of observation. Whether the images or conceptual totalities produced by social theory are true or false, ideological or ideal models, is itself part of the reflection that social theory performs. This issue arises only because social theory is already a reflection on society, a reflection that must give account of its relationship to society itself.[8] Reflexivity leads to the confrontation with contingency.[9] Once reflection is initiated, the question of alternative reflections, other possible self-images, becomes ineluctable. At the same time, it is clear that society has not always conceived itself in the same way. Viewed synchronically and diachronically, there is a plurality of ways in which society offers to itself an image of its unity. Simply put, there is a history of the ways in which society has conceptualized its unity as a totality.[10] Social theory itself therefore has a history. There are degrees of complexity and self-reflection within society's self-reflection that correspond to different levels of social differentiation. In this way, we have self-thematizations or self-presentations of society that vary historically in correspondence with the degree of social differentiation.

These rather abstract remarks are preliminary and necessary because I want to make explicit that to understand the relationship between social theory and religion, both under the epochal markers of modernity and globalization, it is necessary to make clear that there is a prehistory to the formalization of social theory, a stage of normalization, scientization, and a period of reconceptualization and reconsideration. These stages, in the evolution of social theory, must in turn be viewed in light of the very process of social transformation. Here, of course, I have in mind the major social transformations from ancient, to medieval, and then to modern society; from mercantile, to industrial, and then to finance capitalism. These transformations have been thought in tandem with the rise of different centers of social integration. Society comes to center itself around a different locus depending on the predominance of certain integrating social spheres of interaction: as in the "West," around the church, the state, the economy, and so on. These social transformations, similarly, were matched by changes in the sites for the production of self-reflections and self-thematizations of society. These sites of knowledge production, loci of social self-thematization, were and are accompanied by intellectual regimes.[11] Intellectual regimes are not just conceptual schemata but also, and perhaps most importantly, ways of interacting; in short, a habitus, a group of social practices that are enabled or disabled by social spaces.[12] *Reflection is a social habitus that inhabits a certain social space.*

To this extent, one can aver that social transformation is matched by evolution in the means for self-reflection. In light of this, we could tell the history of the self-thematizations of Western society as the histories of the social spaces for the production of those self-thematizations: the monastery, the cloister, the semiprivate, semipublic spaces of the salons and academies of the Renaissance and Enlightenment, the state-financed university, and the profit-driven "infotainment" (to use Benjamin Barber's term) networks of the information age. In sum, the story we wish to tell, schematically and propaedeutically, has the intention of demonstrating that "religion" —what we understand by this term and what social role we ascribe to it—is dependent on a series of factors that need to be properly put in our view.

INVENTING RELIGION

Whether we take religion to be a human constant or a variable dependent on social evolution, we inescapably face the question of the history of religion. If we turn to this history, we find a diversity of meanings for the term "religion" itself, not just across time within Western society, but also across cultures. For instance, it is extremely difficult to translate "religion" back into ancient Greek. One may use piety (*usebia*), in the sense meant by Socrates in the *Euthyphro*. It is, however, even more difficult to translate this term into other world languages. Sometimes the equivalences and overlappings match, but sometimes the overall sense of the corresponding cognate in another language has an entirely different connotation. Thus in Indian, religion is translated as *Dharma* (which may mean law, order, mores). In Chinese it may be translated as *Zong jia* (which may connote piety, lawfulness, respect, reverence, ritual), or it may also be translated as *li* (again rites, rituals).

What is significant about these comparisons is that they reveal to what extent religion remained undifferentiated from other aspects or dimensions of society.[13] Thus if we look at Socrates, we find a combination of ethics, religion, and civic duty. Two significant places where we are able to discern this integration of morals, religion, politics, and justice are the *Gorgias* and the *Apology*. In the former, Socrates affirms the correlation between knowledge and philosophy to refute the sophist's use of rhetoric to dispense of *doxa*. The vindication of philosophy's claim to true knowledge has the role of establishing philosophy as a moral arbiter: we can know the right and the wrong, the good and the bad. These distinctions are not arbitrary; nor are they a function of some irascible determining will. While the theme of the religious is tangentially addressed toward the end of the *Gorgias*, it is in the *Apology* where we encounter a more explicit thematization. There we find Socrates not just defending himself but actually turning the table on the Athenians who have just sentenced him to death. Socrates's trial turns into the indictment of Athens's own impiety. One of the main accusations leveled at Socrates by Meletus is that the former is impious, or an atheist. Socrates affirms his piety and in fact argues that his philosophical praxis is the way he lives out his divine calling. To philosophize is to be pious, to be reverent toward his own *daimonion*.

For Socrates, therefore, philosophy is as much the art of learning how to die, as he remarks toward the end of the *Apology*, as it is a way of living the holy life. The unexamined life is the unholy, impious life. Philosophy, in fact, is a holy voyage, a *Heilsweg*, a pilgrim's progress. Socrates thus offers an integration of *areté*, virtue (what Confucius calls *jen*), and *agathos*, the good, through philosophy, which is a form of piety.[14] Piety is a form of mindedness of the gods, a type of restraint measured by reverence and concern.

The lexical variation as well as conflation that is reflected so patently in Greek has partly to do with the fact that religion was imbricated with every other aspect of society. In addition, society for the Greeks was centered around the life of the polis. In fact, to be more precise, there was no society except the life of the polis. The social, as something separate, perhaps even above and in conflict with the political, had yet to appear, to be discovered. To this extent, the religious also could not be differentiated. Our story, however, will have to begin in the sixteenth century.

The sixteenth century marks a nodal point in the history of the evolution of human society in general, and religion in particular. The Reformation, the printing press, and the debates between Sepúlveda and de las Casas on the humanity of the Indians were key events and processes that altered the fabric of human relations in the so-called West first, but eventually throughout the entire world. But something perhaps more radical took place during this century, in 1492. For the first time in the history of humankind, humans were able to think the world as a whole from the perspective of a unified planet, a self-contained sphere.[15] Whereas the boundaries of the *ecumene* for the Greeks and Romans reached as far as their maps did, and for Christians the boundaries of creation were determined by God, the unity of the world after 1492 was surveyed from the standpoint of humanity. What allowed the world to be seen as a planet, as a *mundus*? Human activity and accomplishment.[16] The world is one not because God looks at it but because we ourselves can see it as one. Similarly, at the moment when humans begin to talk about the whole planet, humans discover themselves as members of a world system, a totality that is made up of human interaction and is observed from the standpoint of that human activity. At this moment, God is relativized. God is not the guarantor of the unity of the world; the planet is.

Interestingly, at the moment that the world is presented as a unity, as a planetary totality, human cultures are relativized. Some will claim for themselves supremacy and a higher status. But these claims will be ipso facto rendered questionable by the fact that they are offered as particular claims on a universality that no culture can claim for itself. Only humanity as such, and not one part of it, can make this claim. Perspectives become local; no one culture can claim a privileged point of view. All can ascend to the point of view sub specie terranus. It is this newly gained capacity to see the whole world as a unity of human activity that allows for the discovery of the social as such. When humans are able to visualize themselves as forming a unity that is more than a systems of nations, interactions between cultures, and economic exchanges, they are also able to conceptualize the social as sui generis. The social, in fact, unifies without subordinating all other spheres of human communication and interaction. The political, the economic, the cultural—all fall under the rubric of the social system.

Paradoxically, just as the social proper is discovered, humans discovered that society is made up of societies. Society itself is one and many. Society is simultaneously a system of subsystems of human interaction and societies across the planet. Society is a planetary system of world societies. What unifies the world is not a cosmic order, which was not as a whole observable. Nor is it a created order, which God alone could observe (this is the sub specie aeternitatis standpoint). The world is now its own subject. We are ourselves the observer, and our point of view is our sociality. In other words, where we look out from is society itself. Society produces its own unity. Society is its own society, so to speak.[17] And if society is its own totalizer, then where does religion fit in this picture? Religion is now seen as one of the subsystems of human interaction.[18] And a series of disciplines emerged dedicated to studying different parts of its internal structure and relationships to other subsystems of the whole. Sociology, however, as the science of the society, would have to deal with it as part of a whole.

Of course, it is not until the eighteenth century when social theory proper is formulated as a formal, self-conscious, fairly distinct endeavor. The kinds of epistemological convulsions brought about by the new perspective gained on humanity would have to be worked out through theology, state theory, moral theory, even economics, before they could reach their proper conceptualization in social theory, that is, sociology. From the standpoint of religion, of how religion comes to be conceptualized and localized within the new order of things, however, the story is as convoluted as the history that preceded the sixteenth century. It has become customary in certain circles to hold the notion that the modernity of our society has to do with the demise of the religious. In fact, it has become almost a sacred cow of contemporary social theory, and intellectual history in general, to affirm that Western society underwent a radical transformation after the sixteenth century, and that at the center of this transformation there stood the pushing out of the religious from society. This process of marginalization or pushing out came to be called secularization. Indeed, the standard view is that espoused by Peter Gay in his *The Enlightenment: The Rise of Paganism.*[19] For Gay, as for most Westerners, the Enlightenment, as well as the subsequent period, had to do with the rise of paganism, the challenge of Christianity, the secularization of all social systems. This view is no longer tenable.

As was already noted, society's self-thematization depends on the type of space from which a self-image and self-identity can be projected. In the case of Western society, such a space has varied significantly not just over the last two thousand years but also over the last five hundred years, the years that can be said to cover the period named as modernity. Since the so-called discovery of the "New World," Western societies have undergone accelerated and profound series of transformations. One of the central questions pertaining to these transformations is the degree to which they were either a rejection and abandonment of the religious spirit that characterized medieval Europe, or a further expansion, nuancing and unfolding the developmental logic of the spirit of Christianity. In essence, this is what underlies the debate concerning secularization. Is secularization to be understood as an exogenous process that acts on religion? Or is secularization a logical and necessary consequence of the unfolding of the spirit of Christianity? Another way of asking this question would be: Is the spirit of modernity inimical and antithetical to the spirit of Christianity? Social theory in its many guises and parts has had to confront these questions.[20]

Without attempting to be exhaustive or even systematic, let us examine a list of the most significant events and processes that unleashed the process of modernization that inaugurated modernity. Before there were nations, there were local languages. Thus one of the central processes of the transformation of Western culture was the development of secular or vulgar tongues.[21] This is a process that begins already in the early centuries of the second millennium with the formalization of local tongues into national languages with their respective national literatures. Thus we may see Dante not just as the last medieval theologian but also as the first modern.[22] He wrote in Tuscan, and wrote a treatise to defend his choice.

In tandem, the reurbanization and demographic recuperation that Europe underwent after the plagues of the last part of the medieval period began the rise of an urban and secular culture. These cultures flourished and developed under the aegis of the rising bourgeoisie, which wanted to challenge the power of the church. What has been taken as a revival of pagan hedonism was in fact the rise of a culture of individualistic sensualism that was less interested in pure pleasure and more in the exploration and affirmation of individuality. Romanticism, as well as all of its early modern precursors, like the baroque, and the sentimentalism and emotivism of some early critiques of the Enlightenment, were based on a celebration of individual conscience and carnality. These, again, are not foreign objectives to the spirit of empiricism and the scientific inclination of the moderns.

The individualism that underpins the sensualism, empirical bent, and autonomy of modern societies, however, could not have developed without the rise of urban centers, where individuals are required to develop this worldly orientation.[23] Cities, which developed under political and economic pressures, came to occupy more central places within the new world outlook. They became nodes of culture and germinals of both revolution and restoration. As Europe industrialized, cities became foci for mercantile exchange and mechanized production. The rise of capitalism, industrialization, and urbanization, all occurring at unprecedented speeds and without apparent planning, converged with the rise of nation-states and the consolidation of European imperialism.

Nation-states, in fact, are partly a result of pressures to formalize the legal and political systems that regulate economic exchange among European nations, but also to regulate the partition and allocation of parts of the globe. For instance, Napoleon's imperial quest in Europe during the early part of the nineteenth century resulted in the modernization of a substantial group of European social subsystems: bureaucracy was modernized, teaching was secularized, and the army, industry, and scientific community were rationalized and centralized and brought under the tutelage of the state.[24] There is no rise of the nation-state without some sort of imperial quest or question in the background.

These rapid, sometimes cataclysmic, processes of economic growth, coupled with the agglutination of illiteracy, superstition, and disease in cities, plus the increasing violence and destructive character of wars that often visited the very streets of major metropolises in the seventeenth, eighteenth, and nineteenth centuries, occasioned a profound phenomenological shock. It is this shock that is registered so well in the modernist literature that has come to characterize modernity. This literature both celebrated the individual and bemoaned the massification of society. Art, in general, became a battle zone: for or against the social. Art, like religion, in fact, also stands as witness to the institutional and structural changes that Western society underwent from the medieval to the modern periods. From being an extension of the church, to becoming a protégé of the nobility and bourgeoisie, to turning into just another "commodity" to be bought and enjoyed, art retraces some of the structural transformations that religion itself underwent.

Social theory developed partly in response to what appeared to be the threats of the mass, the crowd, the dehumanization, hedonism, consumerist paganism, and mechanization of humans that seemed so evident in the eighteenth and nineteenth centuries. It also developed partly as a response to inevitable transformations in the structure of the centers of cultural production in Europe. Thus, if we look briefly at France, the place that can be identified most easily with the laying down of the foundations of social theory, what we find is a series of stages in the development of what today is called social theory. First, there is a stage in which no distinct discipline has developed to deal with the social per se. The eighteenth century is the age of the Enlightenment, the age of the *philosophe*. It is an age in which a rising secular and bourgeois culture is being institutionalized in the forms that make up what Habermas has called the *Öffenlichkeit*, the salons, the newspapers, the serialized newspapers, even the personal and private confession.[25] The opposed centers of power are the church and the university—which through this period had not yet become a part of the nation-state, or a separate social subsystem. For this reason, most of the writings from this era are characterized by their "literary" qualities and their animosity toward "learning" or pedantry. Science or its methods have not yet become a major cultural contender.

A second stage begins with the French Revolution. This politicizes intellectuals, challenges the elitist culture of the salons, and inaugurates the secularization of the university, and the ascendancy of engineers, mathematicians, and natural scientists who seriously displace the hegemony of the *philosophe*. A third stage clearly begins with the Napoleonic revolution and the subsequent period of restoration. This period is characterized by the development of the intellectual as a university professor, which means that social analysis and social commentary have been professionalized. The mathematicians, physicists, and chemists have moved to center stage. The linkages between industry, the military, and the university have been formalized via government policies or through personal allegiances that date back to the revolution. Another significant aspect of this early-nineteenth-century stage in the evolution of social science is the expansion of learned societies and their respective journals.

In Heilbron's view, each stage can be personalized by a key figure or figures.[26] The first stage is personified by Montesquieu and Rousseau. In them, the preoccupation with the order of society is evident, but no clear term for it has been coined. In both of them, dissatisfaction with politics or economics is evident. The second is personified by Condorcet and Cabanis. Here the social makes its appearance, but its appropriate science is yet to be formulated. The third, finally, is embodied in the person of Auguste Comte. He is in many ways the true father of social analysis, the one who names the study of society, sociology. In him both the object and the method of analysis are formulated. Underlying all of their work, however, is a note of anticlericalism and an ambiguous relation to religion. Significantly, once the issue of counterhegemonic action against the church has disappeared, French intellectuals take up religion with less belligerence. This is the case of Durkheim, Mauss, and Lévi-Strauss in the twentieth century.

It needs to be remarked that this story would significantly alter were we to move to England or Germany, where state building either preceded or followed the development of French statehood. Similarly, in both England and Germany, the national elites had different relationships to the national religions. In England, for instance, the national church was already an ally and not a contender. In Germany, similarly, national religion was part and parcel of national identity. Therefore different dynamics were unleashed depending on local arrangements and responses to the national religions and established church.

The point of this historical journey is twofold. On the one hand, I wanted to gesture toward the cultural and institutional processes and transformations that created the conditions of possibility for social science to emerge. On the other, the aim was to make evident the extent to which "religion" was both a catalyst and a detritus. As the former, many of the processes that gave rise to the modern period would have been unthinkable without the presence of religion in society. The questions of language, individualism, even of bodily and subjective experimentalism and celebration, were made possible by the presence of Christian values and norms. Similarly, the rise of the state apparatus, its legal and constitutional norms, its principles of legitimation, were in one way or another derived from and rooted in canon law, church functions, and theological insights that necessitate their own relativization.

Social theorists' differing attitudes toward the religious, from Voltaire and D'Alambert to Comte and Durkheim, demonstrate less a generally shared rejection of religion and more an equivocal and heterogeneous concern with its conceptualizing under different social pressures and imperatives. These concerns and imperatives had to do with the development and formalization of national language, national secular cultures, urbanization, nation-state building, democratization, industrialization, war, and imperialism. To this extent, religion was invented by social theory in Western society to reflect what had been left behind, to bemoan what was lost, and to project on others what they had that we had overcome, or what they retained that might save us (the West).[27]

THE FUTURE OF RELIGION(S)

Modernity, to repeat a central thesis of this essay, constituted its identity vis-à-vis the invention of the "religious" as what it left behind or as what it had transformed and sublimated to give rise to a new social order. Today the cardinal points that oriented the self-reflection and self-thematization of society have been profoundly rearranged. The theoretical compass that social theory offered has been thrown off by the repositioning, demise, or re-creation of some, or even all, of our social systems and subsystems. Globalization at the very least can be understood as the creation of a new planetary social order in which the centrality of the state, in the form of both nationality and the rule-of-law state (*Rechtstatt*), the economy, as a system of hyperconnected interactions, and culture, as a new order of the production of world images, have been contested and repositioned. In turn, these now operate with what appears to be an unsurpassable limit and unassimilable risk: the environment.[28] What Marx and Engels wrote in *The Communist Manifesto* can be rephrased without doing violence to their insight:

The *new global order* cannot exist without constantly revolutionizing the instruments of production, and thereby the relations of production, and with them the whole relations of society. Conservation of the old modes of production in unaltered form, was, on the contrary, the first condition of existence for all earlier *modern* classes. Constant revolutionizing of the production, uninterrupted disturbance of all social conditions, everlasting uncertainty and agitation distinguish the *global age* from all earlier ones. All fixed, fast-frozen relations, with their train of ancient and venerable prejudices and opinions, are swept away, all new-formed ones become antiquated before they can ossify. All that is solid melts into air, all that is holy is profaned, and man is at least compelled to face with sober senses, his real conditions of life, and his relations with his kind.[29]

In light of the role that world religions have played in the globalization of the world, we must ask whether in fact everything has been profaned, and whether, in fact, we have truly reached an age beyond religion. Indeed, has globalization spelled the final end of religion, just as it has spelled, as it is argued by some, the end of the "state," "culture," and so on? Two answers can provisionally be ventured. First, the way we decide to theorize, conceptualize, and analyze globalization prejudges the place and function we allocate to religion. It is my contention that what I call "mono-metastructural" theories of globalization provide an ambiguous if not negative role for religion. They see religion as either reactively responding to the challenges of globalization or providing an exogenous antidote. In either case, religion is the supplement. The theories that conceptualize globalization as involving some type of societal matrix rearrangement try to give religion its due. Yet, as was pointed out, it is not clear why certain categories are picked as opposed to others. It could be argued that for instance, Robertson's selection of the "self" as a matrix category privileges a certain view of societal components, one that prejudices in favor of a "Western" way of looking at the world.

Finally, what I called metatheoretical reflexivity theories are avowedly self-conscious about not taking for granted the privilege or apparently self-evident character of any categories. In fact, they attempt to think the very theoretical place from which they think the global. In light of this, Luhmann's theory, in particular, profiles itself as highly promising. In this essay, I have merely discerned the place where his work may be located. I await a more detailed analysis of his work on religion and globalization.[30] In summary, the latter two types of theories make more conscious efforts to give religion its due. Whereas the mono-metastructural and the matrix rearrangement theories see religion as epiphenomenal and supplemental, the metatheoretical reflexivity theories see religion from a nonreductivist, nonsupplemental perspective.

At the very least, globalized society entails this much: the space that religion occupied somewhere in the interstices of culture, society, state, and personality structures has been reconfigured, necessitating religion's own reconfiguration.[31] Second, and from a more empirical perspective, it can be averred without much danger of being contradicted that part and parcel of globalization has been a serious revitalization of religion, sometimes positively, sometimes negatively. And the so-called modern nations have not remained unaffected by these "religious revivals." From this perspective, we can venture that religion will have a future, one in which it will figure differently in society, and in which future generations will be asking what their religions have to do with ours.

NOTES

1. See Roland Robertson and William R. Garrett, eds., *Religion and Global Order: Religion and the Political Order* (New York: Paragon House Publishers, 1991); Peter Beyer, *Religion and Globalization* (London: Sage, 1994); and Bryan S. Turner, *Religion and Social Theory*, 2d ed. (London: Sage, 1991).

2. See Ulrich Beck, *Was ist Globalisierung?* (Frankfurt am Main: Suhrkamp, 1997); see also the wonderful book by Malcom Waters, *Globalization* (London: Routledge, 1995).

3. Samir Amin, *Capitalism in the Age of Globalization: The Management of Contemporary Society* (New York: Zed Books, 1996); Benjamin R. Barber, *Jihad vs. McWorld: How Globalism and Tribalism Are Reshaping the World* (New York: Ballantine Books, 1995); Richard J. Barnet and John Cavanagh, *Global Dreams: Imperial Corporations and the New World Order* (New York: Simon and Schuster, 1994); Richard J. Barnet and J. Cavanagh, "A Globalizing Economy: Some Implications and Consequences," in *Conceptualizing Global History*, ed. B. Mazlish et al. (New York: Westview Press, 1993), 153–72; and Immanuel Wallerstein, *The Modern World System: Capitalist Agriculture and the Origins of the European World-Economy in the Sixteenth Century* (New

York: Academic Press, 1974), *The Capitalist World-Economy* (Cambridge: Cambridge University Press, 1979), *The Modern World-System II: Mercantilism and the Consolidation of the European World-Economy, 1600–1750* (New York: Academic Press, 1980), *Unthinking Social Science: The Limits of Nineteenth-Century Paradigms* (Cambridge: Polity Press, 1991), *Geopolitics and the Geoculture: Essays on the Changing World-System* (Cambridge: Cambridge University Press, 1991), and *After Liberalism* (New York: New Press, 1995).

4. Arjun Appadurai, *Modernity at Large: Cultural Dimensions of Globalization* (Minneapolis: University of Minnesota Press, 1996); Roland Roberton, *Globalization: Social Theory and Global Culture* (London: Sage, 1992); Bryan S. Turner, *Religion and Social Theory*, 2d ed. (London: Sage, 1991 [1983]), and *Orientalism, Postmodernism, and Globalism* (London: Routledge, 1994).

5. See Niklas Luhmann, "Deconstruction as Second-Order Observing," *New Literary History* 24 (1993): 763–82, esp. 774. See also his "The Two Sociologies and the Theory of Society," *Thesis Eleven* 43: 28–47; and "The Paradoxy of Observing Systems," *Cultural Critique* 31 (fall 1995): 37–55.

6. Luhmann has been dealing with the concept of the global society at least since the early seventies. For theoretical reasons, it stands at the center of his work. See Luhmann, "Die Weltgesellschaft," *Archiv für Rechts-und Sozialphilosphie* 57: 1–15, *Soziologische Aufklärung 2: Aufsätze zur Theorie der Gesellschaft* (Opladen: Westdeutscher Verlag, 1975); *The Differentiation of Society*, trans. Stephen Homes and Charles Larmore (New York: Columbia University Press, 1982); *Essays on Self-Reference* (New York: Columbia University Press, 1990); and *Die Gesellschaft der Gesellschaft*, 2 vols. (Frankfurt am Main: Suhrkamp Verlag, 1997).

7. See Richard Münch, *Sociological Theory*, 3 vols. (Chicago: Nelson-Hall Publishers, 1994); and *Globalen Dynamic, lokale Lebenswelten: Der schwierige Weg in die Weltgesellschaft* (Frankfurt am Main: Suhrkamp Verlag, 1998).

8. See Niklas Luhmann, "The Self-Thematization of Society: A Sociological Perspective on the Concept of Reflection," in Luhmann, *The Differentiation of Society*, 324–62.

9. See Niklas Luhmann, *Observations on Modernity*, trans. William Whobrey (Stanford: Stanford University Press, 1998), esp. chap. 3.

10. Niklas Luhmann, *Die Wissenschaft der Gesellschaft* (Frankfurt: Suhrkamp Verlag, 1992).

11. See Johan Heilbron, *The Rise of Social Theory*, trans. Sheila Gogol (Minneapolis: University of Minnesota Press, 1995), 13.

12. See Pierre Bourdieu, *Homo Academicus*, trans. Peter Collier (Stanford: Stanford University Press, 1988).

13. See the entry on "Religion" in Joachim Ritter and Karlfried Gründer, eds., *Historisches Wörterbuch der Philosophie*, vol. 8 (Basel: Schwabe, 1992), 631.

14. See Bruno Snell, "A Call to Virtue: A Brief Chapter from Greek Ethics," in *The Discovery of the Mind: The Greek Origins of European Thought*, trans.

T. G. Rosenmeyer (New York: Harper Torchbooks, 1960 [1948]), 153–90. For a discussion of the terms related to what we call religion in Greek, see Walter Burkert, *Greek Religion*, trans. John Raffan (Cambridge: Harvard University Press, 1985), 272–75.

15. See Walter Mignolo, *The Darker Side of the Renaissance: Literacy, Territoriality, and Colonization* (Ann Arbor: University of Michigan Press, 1995), esp. p. 3, "The Colonization of Space." See also Luhmann, *Die Gesellschaft der Gesellschaft*, vol. 1, chap. 1 ("Society as Social System"), sec. 10 ("World-society"). For critical perspectives on the idea of the planetarization of human consciousness see J. M. Blaut, *The Colonizer's Model of the World: Geographical Diffusionism and Eurocentric History* (New York: Guildford Press, 1992).

16. Marcel Gauchet, *The Disenchantment of the World: A Political History of Religion*, trans. Oscar Burge (Princeton: Princeton University Press, 1997).

17. This is both a cryptic and seemingly tautological iteration. I think, however, that this sentence captures Luhmann's intent in his magnum opus *Die Gesellschaft der Gesellschaft* (The Society of Society, or Society's Society).

18. See Peter Beyer, *Religion and Globalization*, 4–6. See also Niklas Luhmann, "Society, Meaning, and Religion Based on Self-Reference," in *Essays on Self-Reference* (New York: Columbia University Press, 1990), 144–64.

19. Peter Gay, *The Enlightenment: An Interpretation, vol. 1, The Rise of Modern Paganism* (New York: Alfred A. Knopf, 1973). For a counterposition see Carl L. Becker, *The Heavenly City of the Eighteenth-Century Philosophers* (New Haven: Yale University Press, 1932). For Gay's refutation of Becker, see Peter Gay, "Carl Becker's Heavenly City," in *The Party of Humanity: Essays in the French Enlightenment* (New York: W. W. Norton, 1971), 188–210. For a recent assessment of Gay's reading of the Enlightenment, see Martin Jay, "Modern and Postmodern Paganism: Peter Gay and Jean-François Lyotard," in *Cultural Semantics: Keywords of Our Time* (Amherst: University of Massachusetts Press, 1998), 181–96.

20. Talcott Parsons, "Christianity and Modern Industrial Society," in *Sociological Theory and Modern Society* (New York: Free Press, 1967), 385–421.

21. See Arno Borst, *Der Turmbau von Babel: Geschichte der Meinungen über Ursprung und Vielfalt der Sprache und Völker*, 6 vols. (München: Deutscher Tauschenbuch Verlag, 1995 [1957–1963]).

22. See *Encyclopaedia Britannica Online*, S.V. "Dante."

23. See Max Weber, *The City*, trans. and ed. Don Martindale and Gertrud Neuwirth (New York: Free Press, 1958); and Bryan S. Turner, "The Making of Sociology: The Early Sociology of the City," in *Social Theories of the City, vol. 1, Selected Essays*, ed. Bryan S. Turner (New York: Routledge/Thoemmes Press, 1997), 1–24.

24. See Hagen Schulze, *States, Nations, and Nationalism: From the Middle Ages to the Present*, trans. William E. Yuill (Oxford: Blackwell Publishers, 1996); and Heilbron, *The Rise of Social Theory*.

25. Jürgen Habermas, *The Structural Transformation of the Public Sphere*, trans. Thomas Burger (Cambridge: MIT Press, 1989).

26. Heilbron, *The Rise of Social Theory.*

27. See Talal Asad, *Genealogies of Religion: Discipline and Reasons of Power in Christianity and Islam* (Baltimore: Johns Hopkins University Press, 1993). See also Bryan S. Turner, *Weber and Islam: A Critical Study* (Boston: Routledge and Kegan Paul, 1974), as well as Turner, *Religion and Social Theory.*

28. Ulrich Beck, *Ecological Enlightenment: Essays on the Politics of the Risk Society*, trans. Mark A. Ritter (Atlantic Highlands: Humanities Press, 1994).

29. Karl Marx, *Selected Writings* (Indianapolis: Hackett Publishing, 1994), 161–62. I have removed certain words and added some that are in vogue.

30. Peter Beyer's wonderful first attempt. Note that Beyer does not really discuss Luhmann's *Funktion der Religion.* This essay was written before the author chould have known about or read the recently published work by Niklas Luhmann, *Die Religion der Gesellschaft* (Frankfurt am Main: Suhrkamp, 2000). This was one of Luhmann's last projects before he died.

31. See the insightful essay by Zygmut Bauman, "Postmodern Religion?" in *Postmodernity and Its Discontents*, by Zygmut Bauman (New York: New York University Press, 1997), 165–85.

MARK JUERGENSMEYER

The Global Rise of Religious Nationalism

If it can be said that the modernist ideology of the post-Enlightenment West effectively separated religion from public life, then
what has happened in recent years—since the watershed Islamic
revolution in Iran in 1978—is religion's revenge. After years of waiting in history's wings, religion has renewed its claim to be an ideology of public order in a dramatic fashion: violently. From Algeria
to Idaho, a legion of religious activists have expressed a hatred of
secular governments that exudes an almost transcendent passion,
and they dream of revolutionary changes that will establish a godly
social order in the rubble of what the citizens of most secular societies regard as modern, egalitarian democracies.[1]

Their enemies seem to most of us to be both benign and banal:
modern secular leaders such as Indira Gandhi and Yitzhak Rabin,
and such symbols of prosperity and authority as international airlines and the World Trade Center. The logic of their ideological religious view is, although difficult to comprehend, profound, for it
contains a fundamental critique of the world's post-Enlightenment
secular culture and politics. In many cases, especially in areas of the
world where modernization is a synonym for Westernization, movements of religious nationalism have served as liberation struggles
against what their supporters perceive to be alien ideologies and foreign powers.

"Palestine is not completely free," a leader of Hamas's policy wing
told me, "until it is an Islamic state."[2] The Hamas activist voiced
this opinion only a few months before the January 1996 elections,
an event that not only brought Yasir Arafat triumphantly into power
but also fulfilled the Palestinian dream of an independent nation.
Yet it was not the kind of nation that the Islamic activist and his

Hamas colleagues had hoped for. For that reason, they refused to run candidates for public office and urged their followers to boycott the polls. They threatened that the movement would continue to carry out "political actions," as the Hamas leader called them—terrorist attacks such as the series of suicide bombings conducted by a militant faction that rocked Jerusalem, Tel Aviv, and elsewhere in Israel in February and March 1996, threatening to destroy the peace process and Arafat's fragile alliance.

On the Israeli side of the border, Jewish activists have also attacked the secular leadership of their nation, and again a virulent mixture of religion and politics has led to bloodshed. Yigal Amir, who is accused of assassinating Israel's prime minister Yitzhak Rabin in Tel Aviv on 4 November 1995, claimed that he had religious reasons for his actions, saying that "everything I did, I did for the glory of God."[3] Amir has adamantly rejected attempts by his lawyers to assert that he was not guilty by reason of insanity. "I am at peace," he explained, insisting that he was "totally normal." His murder of Rabin, Amir argued, was deliberate and even praiseworthy under a certain reading of religious law that allows for a defense against those who would destroy the Jewish nation.[4]

A few weeks before the assassination, a conversation with Jewish activists near Hebron indicated that they shared many of Amir's views. They were still grieving over the killing of Dr. Baruch Goldstein by an angry Muslim crowd in February 1995, after he murdered thirty-five Muslims as they were saying their prayers in the mosque at the Cave of the Patriarchs, revered as the burial place of Abraham, Isaac, and Jacob. Goldstein's grave has now been made into a shrine. The militant Jews at the site explained that acts such as Dr. Goldstein's were necessary not only to protect the land but also to defend the very notion of a Jewish nation—one that for reasons of redemption and history had to be established on biblical terrain. Religious duty required them to become involved politically and even militarily. "Jews," one of them said, "have to learn to worship in a national way."[5]

This potentially explosive mixture of nationalism and religion is an ingredient even in incidents that might appear initially to be isolated terrorist incidents: the bombing of the federal building in Oklahoma City on 19 April 1995, for instance, or the 20 March 1995 nerve gas attack on a Tokyo subway station. In the Oklahoma City case, the Christian militia movements with which Timothy McVeigh and Terry Nichols have been associated have accepted a certain conspiratorial view of American politics: the nation is not free, they reason, because of a vast international conspiracy involving Jews and Freemasons. They believe that the nation needs to be liberated through an armed struggle that will establish America as an independent and Christian nation.[6]

Strangely, the same conspiracy was articulated by members of Aum Shinrikyo (Om Supreme Truth), the eclectic Buddhist-Hindu religious movement in Japan that has been accused of unleashing canisters of nerve gas in a Tokyo subway station, killing twelve people and injuring thousands. A young man who had been public affairs officer for the main Tokyo headquarters of the movement at the time said that the first thing that came to his mind when he heard about the attack was that the "weird time had come": the Third World War was about to begin. He had been taught by his spiritual master, Shoko Asahara, that Armageddon was imminent. He had also been taught that the Japanese government, in collusion with America and an international network of Freemasons and Jews, had triggered the January 1995 Kobe earthquake and then planned the nerve gas attack. He was surprised when Asahara himself was implicated in the plot—after all, the spiritual leader had portrayed himself as the protector of Japanese society and had begun to create an alternative government that would control the country after Armageddon had ended.[7]

In all these cases, the alleged perpetrators possessed worldviews that justified the brutality of such terrorist acts: they perceived a need to defend their faiths and held a heady expectation that what they did would lead to radically new social and political orders. The events they staged were therefore religious as much as they were political and provide examples of religious involvement and political change that might seem, at first glance, to be curiously out of step with the twentieth century.

But these religious rebels against modernity are becoming increasingly vocal. Their small but potent groups of violent activists represent growing masses of supporters, and they exemplify currents of thinking that have risen to counter the prevailing modernism—the ideology of individualism and skepticism that in the past three centuries has emerged from post-Enlightenment Europe and spread throughout the world. For that reason, and because of the rising tide of violence associated with movements of religious nationalism in the Middle East, South Asia, and elsewhere, it is important to try to understand what religious nationalists want: why they hate secular governments with such a virulent passion, how they expect to effect their virtually revolutionary changes, and what sort of social and political order they dream of establishing in their own vision of a coming world order.

THE IDEOLOGICAL DIMENSIONS OF RELIGIOUS NATIONALISM

Some forms of religious nationalism are largely ethnic—that is, linked to people and land. The struggle of the Irish—both Protestant and Catholic—to claim political authority over the land in which they live is a paradigmatic example. The attempts of Muslims in Chechnya to assert their independence from the rule of Russia, and other Muslims in Tajikistan to assert a cultural element to Tajikistan's resurgent nationalism, are examples that have emerged in the wake of the collapse of the former Soviet Union. In what used to be Yugoslavia, several groups of ethnic religious nationalists are pitted against one another: Orthodox Serbs, Catholic Croats, and Muslim Bosnians and Kosovars. In South Asia, the independence movements of Sri Lankan Tamil Hindus, Kashmiri Muslims, and to some extent the Khalistan supporters in the Punjab are also movements of ethnic religious nationalism. In these cases, religion provides the identity that makes a community cohere and links it with a particular place.

Ideological religious nationalism is attached to ideas and beliefs. In using the term "ideology," I mean a framework of values and moral positions. In the case of religious nationalism, the ideology combines traditional religious beliefs in divine law and religious authority with the modern notion of the nation-state.[8] If the ethnic religious nationalism *politicizes* religion by employing religious identities for political ends, an ideological form of religious nationalism does the opposite: it *religionizes* politics. It puts political issues and struggles within a sacred context. Compatibility with religious goals becomes the criterion for an acceptable political platform.

The Islamic revolution in Iran, for instance, was a classic example of ideological religious nationalism that turned ordinary politics upside down. Instead of a nonreligious political order providing space for religious activities—which in the West we regard as the "normal" arrangement—in Iran, a religious authority set the context for politics. In fact, the constitution of the Islamic Republic of Iran provides for a "just ruler," a cleric such as the Ayatollah Khomeini, who will be the ultimate arbiter in legislating the moral basis of politics. For that reason, the Iranian experience was a genuine revolution, an extraordinary change from the modern Westernized nation that the Shah prior to the Ayatollah had imagined for Iran. Because ideological religious nationalism embraces religious ideas as the basis for politics, national aspirations become fused with religious quests for purity and redemption, and religious law replaces secular law as the pillar of governmental authority. Although the enemy of ethnic religious nationalists is a rival ethnicity—usually the dominant group that has been controlling them—ideological religious nationalists do not need to look beyond their own ethnic community to find an ideological foe: they often loathe their own kind. As Yigal Amir dramatically illustrated when he shot Yitzhak Rabin, religious nationalists may target as enemies the secular leaders of their own nations. For that reason, tensions have been growing in nominally Muslim countries such as Saudi Arabia, Pakistan, and Turkey, where militant Islamic revolutionaries have identified their own moderate Muslim leaders as obstacles to progress. In the United States, it appears that this passionate hatred of secular government led to incidents such as Ruby Ridge and the bombing of the federal building in Oklahoma City. In India, a widespread disdain for secular politics has propelled the Bharatiya Janata Party (BJP) into becoming the largest movement for religious nationalism in the world. Buddhist movements in Sri Lanka, Mongolia, and Tibet have characterized their secular political opponents as being not just immoral and unprincipled but also enemies of dhammic (righteous) social order.

Some religious nationalists see their own secular leaders as part of a wider, virtually global conspiracy—one controlled by vast political and economic networks sponsored by European and American powers. For that reason, they may hate not only the politicians in their home countries but also these leaders' political and economic allies in lands far beyond their own national boundaries. Islamic militants associated with Egypt's radical Gamaa i-Islamiya (Islamic Group), for example, have attacked not only Egyptian politicians—

killing President Anwar Sadat and attempting to kill his successor, Hosni Mubarak—but also foreigners.

The Gamaa i-Islamiya literally moved its war against secular powers abroad when its leader, Sheik Omar Abdul Rahman, moved to New Jersey and became involved in a bombing attack on the World Trade Center on 26 February 1993 that killed six and injured a thousand more. The trial that convicted him in January 1996 of conspiracy in the attack also implicated him in an elaborate plot to blow up a variety of sites in the New York City area, including the United Nations buildings and the Lincoln Tunnel. Algerian Muslim activists have brought their war against secular Algerian leaders to Paris, where they have been implicated in a series of subway bombings in 1995. Hassan Turabi in Sudan has been accused of orchestrating Islamic rebellions in a variety of countries, linking Islamic activists in common cause against what is seen as the great satanic power of the secular West. In some cases, this conspiratorial vision has taken bizarre twists, as in the view shared by both the Japanese Aum Shinrikyo and certain American Christian militia movements that Jews and Freemasons are collaborating to control the world.

Often religious nationalism is "ethno-ideological," in that it is both ethnic and ideological in character. Such religious nationalists have double sets of enemies: their ethnic rivals and the secular leaders of their own people. Their efforts at delegitimization are "split" between secular and religious foes.[9] The Hamas movement in Palestine is a prime example. While waging a war of independence against Israel, they are simultaneously sparring with Yasir Arafat; often the attacks leveled at Israelis are also intended to wound the credibility of Arafat's fledgling Palestinian Authority. It is not a coincidence that the Hamas suicide bombings aimed at Israelis increased in the months immediately before and after the January 1996 elections—a poll that Hamas wished to discredit. The leaders of the movement believed, as their founder Sheik Ahmed Yassin said in a conversation several years ago, that "the only true Palestinian state is an Islamic state."[10] This means that the movement must simultaneously war against both Israeli leaders such as Rabin and Peres and secular Palestinian leaders such as Arafat.

Like the militant Muslims in Hamas, the Sikh separatists that flourished in Northern India until 1993 were both ethnic and ideological and, like their Palestinian counterparts, also had a double set of enemies. In the Sikh case, the Khalistani side of the movement aimed at creating a separate nation of Sikhs and tried to purge the rural Punjab of Hindus. But there was also a more ideologically religious side to the movement, the one led by Sant Jarnail Singh Bhindranwale, which aimed at establishing the Sikh religious tradition as authoritative in both secular and political spheres and targeted moderate Sikh leaders and secular politicians as foes. Followers of this wing succeeded in assassinating several important secular politicians including Prime Minister Indira Gandhi in 1984. A spectacular explosion that killed Punjab's chief minister, Beant Singh, on 31 August 1995, shows that some aspects of the movement are still potent threats to civil order.

Other movements of religious nationalism—even ones that appear to be primarily ethnic—may also have, at some level, an ideological component. This is so because religion, the repository of traditions of symbols and beliefs, stands ready to be tapped by those who wish to develop a new framework of ideas about social order. In the case of the former Yugoslavia, for example, the anger of Serbs— frequently described in the media as the residue of ancient ethnic rivalries—is also fueled by an imaginative religious myth. The Serb leaders are Orthodox Christians who see themselves as surrogate Christ figures in a contemporary political understanding of the Passion narrative. A drama and an epic poem have been invented to retell the New Testament's account of Christ's death in a way that portrays historical Serbian leaders as Christ figures, and Muslims in both Bosnia and Kosovo as Judases. This mythologized dehumanization of the Muslims allows them to be regarded as a subhuman species, one that in the Serbian imagination deserves the genocidal attacks of "ethnic cleansing" that killed so many in the darkest hours of the Kosovo conflict and the Bosnian civil war.[11] As these cases show, there is often a fine line between ethnic and ideological forms of religious nationalism.

In general, ethnic religious nationalism is easier for modern Americans and Europeans to understand, even though it may be just as violent as ideological nationalism. The London terrorist bombings by the Irish Republican Army after the cease-fire broke down in February 1996, and the Sri Lankan Tamils' suicide attacks that demolished downtown Colombo in January 1996, are examples. Yet these acts of violence are understandable because they are aimed at a society that the terrorists regard as exerting direct military or political control over them. The violence of ideological religious movements is focused on those who are ideologically different—secularists—and whose control over them may be cultural and economic, and therefore less obvious. But their impact on the changing shape of global politics is perhaps even more profound.

THE LOGIC OF IDEOLOGICAL RELIGIOUS NATIONALISM

Since the mid-1980s, I have been following movements of ideological religious nationalism in various parts of the world with the hope of discerning common patterns or themes within them. Although each movement is shaped by its own historical and social context, there are some common elements due in part to the massive economic and political changes of this moment in history, an experience that has been shared by many around the world. What follows, then, is an attempt to identify the stages in development of ideological religious nationalism that has resulted from this common experience, beginning with the disaffection over the dominance of modern Western culture and what is perceived to be its political ally, secular nationalism.

Despair over Secular Nationalism. The shifts in economic and political power that have occurred following the breakup of the Soviet Union and the sudden rise and fall of Japanese and other Asian economies in the past fifteen years have had significant social repercussions. The public sense of insecurity that has come in the wake of these changes is felt not only in the societies of those nations that are economically devastated by the changes—especially countries in the former Soviet Union—but also in economically stronger areas as well. The United States, for example, has seen a remarkable degree of disaffection with its political leaders and witnessed the rise of right-wing religious movements that feed on the public's perception of the immorality of government. At the extreme end of this religious rejection are the militant Christian militias and cults such as Waco's Branch Davidian sect. Similar movements have emerged in Japan, which is also experiencing disillusion about its national purpose and destiny. As in America, the critique and sectarian experiments with its alternatives often take religious forms, including new religious movements such as Soka Gakkai, Agon-shu, and the now infamous Aum Shinrikyo.

The global shifts that have led to a crisis of national purpose in developed countries have, in a somewhat different way, affected developing nations as well. Leaders such as India's Jawaharlal Nehru, Egypt's Gamal Abdel Nasser, and Iran's Riza Shah Pahlavi had once been pledged to creating versions of America—or a kind of cross between America and the Soviet Union—at home. But a new generation of leaders is emerging in countries that were formerly European colonies, and they no longer believe in the Westernized vision of Nehru, Nasser, or the Shah. Rather, they are eager to complete the process of decolonization. They want to assert the legitimacy of their countries' own traditional values in the public sphere, and to build a "postcolonial" national identity based on indigenous culture.[12] This eagerness is made all the more keen when confronted with the media assault of Western music, videos, and films that satellite television now beams around the world, and which threaten to obliterate local and traditional forms of cultural expression.

The result of this disaffection with the culture of the modern West has been what I have called a "loss of faith" in the ideological form of that culture, secular nationalism.[13] Although a few years ago it would have been a startling notion, the idea has now become virtually commonplace that nationalism as we know it in the modern West is in crisis, in large part because it is seen as a cultural construction closely linked with what Jürgen Habermas has called "the project of modernity."[14] Increasingly we live in a multicultural, postmodern world where a variety of views of nationhood are in competition, and the very concept of nationalism has become a matter of lively debate among scholars.[15] It has become even more important— a matter of political life and death—to leaders of nations that are still struggling to establish a sense of national identity, and for whom religious answers to these questions of definition have extraordinary popular appeal.

Seeing Politics in a Religious Way. The second step in the development of ideological religious nationalism is the perception that the problem with politics is, at some level, religious. This means "religionizing" politics, as I described it earlier in this essay, in two ways: by showing that political difficulties have a religious cause, and that religious goals have a political solution. If one looks at politics from a religious perspective, it may appear that secular nationalism has failed because it is, in a sense, religiously inadequate. As one of the leaders of the Iranian revolution put it, secular nationalism is "a kind of religion."[16] He went on to explain that it was not only a religion but one peculiar to the West, a point that was echoed by one of the leaders of the Muslim Brotherhood in Egypt.[17] Behind this charge is a certain vision of social reality, one that involves a series of concentric circles. The smallest are families and clans; then come ethnic groups and nations; the largest, and implicitly most important, are religions, in the sense of global civilizations.

Among these are to be found Islam, Buddhism, and what some who hold this view call "Christendom" or "Western civilization" or "Westernism."[18] Particular nations such as Germany, France, and the United States, in this conceptualization, stand as subsets of Christendom/Western civilization; similarly, Egypt, Iran, Pakistan, and other nations are subsets of Islamic civilization. From this vantage point, it is both a theological and a political error to suggest that Egypt or Iran should be thrust into a Western frame of reference. In this view of the world, they are intrinsically part of Islamic, not Western, civilization, and it is an act of imperialism to think of them in any other way. Those who hold this view would solve the problem of secular nationalism by replacing what they regard as an inappropriate religion, "Westernism," with Islam or some other religion related to the local population.

At the same time that religion is solving political problems, politics can help to solve religious ones. In the view of Messianic Zionists such as Dr. Baruch Goldstein and his mentor, Rabbi Meir Kahane, for example, the redemption of the world cannot take place until the Messiah comes, and the Messiah cannot return until the biblical lands—including the West Bank—are restored to Jewish control. "Miracles don't just happen," Kahane said in a conversation in Jerusalem a year before he was assassinated in New York City by Muslims associated with Sheik Omar Abdul Rahman's New Jersey mosque. Referring to the return of the Messiah, which he felt could only come after Jews had created the right political conditions, Kahane said, "Miracles are made."[19]

Some Messianic Jews think that the correct conditions for the return of the Messiah include the reconstruction of the Jerusalem temple described in the Bible on its original site—now occupied by the Muslim shrine, the Dome of the Rock. Some of these activists have been implicated in plots to blow up the shrine in order to hasten the coming of the Kingdom. One who served time in prison for his part in such a plot said that the rebuilding of the temple was a "national obligation" for the sake of redemption, a political position for which Israel should make "no compromise."[20]

Religious activists who embrace traditions such as Millenarian Christianity and Shiite Islam, which have a strong sense of the historical fulfillment of prophecy, look toward a religious apocalypse that will usher in a new age. The leader of Aum Shinrikyo, borrowing Christian ideas from the sixteenth-century French astrologer Nostradamus (Michel de Nostredame), predicted the coming of Armageddon in 1999 in the form of World War III, after which the survivors—mostly members of his own movement—would create a new society in the year 2014, led by Aum-trained "saints."[21] Activists in other religious traditions may see a righteous society being established in a less dramatic manner, but even Sunni Muslims, Hindus, and Buddhists have articulated a hope for a political fulfillment of their notions of religious society. They believe that "dhammic society can be established on earth," as one activist Buddhist monk in Sri Lanka put it, by creating a religious state.[22]

Identifying the Enemy. Perceiving politics in a religious way leads to the next step, identifying who or what religious power is at fault when things go wrong. In a religionized view of politics, the root of social and political problems is portrayed in religious terms. An opposition religious group—perhaps a minority group such as the Tamils in Sri Laṅka, or the Coptic Christians in Egypt—is sometimes targeted as the corrupting influence in public life. Or the foe of religion may be seen as irreligion—a force opposed to religion altogether. The secular state could fit either of those categories, depending on whether one sees it as the outcome of a "religious" tradition—"Westernism"—or as the handmaiden of those who are opposed to religion in any form. A great many religious activists regard anyone who attempts to curb the influence of religion—for example, by promoting a civil society shaped by secular values—to be opposed to religion. Hence anyone who encourages secularism is, in a sense, a religious foe.

The most extreme form of this way of thinking is satanization.[23] Some members of the Christian militia in the United States refuse to pay taxes in part because they feel that the government is controlled by an evil foreign power. During the early days of the Gulf War in 1991, the Hamas movement issued a communiqué stating that the United States "commands all the forces hostile to Islam and the Muslims" and singled out George Bush, who, it claimed, was not only "the leader of the forces of evil" but also "the chief of the false gods."[24] As this communiqué indicates, this line of reasoning often leads down a slippery slope, for once secular institutions and authorities begin to loom larger than life and take on a satanic luster, the conclusion rushes on that secular enemies are more than mortal foes: they are mythic entities and satanic forces.

Even in 1997, Iranian politicians, without a trace of hyperbole, could describe America as the "Great Satan." This rhetoric first surfaced in Iran during the early stages of the Islamic revolution when both the Shah and President Carter were referred to as Yazid (in this context an "agent of satan"). "All the problems of Iran," the Ayatollah Khomeini elaborated, are "the work of America."[25] By this he meant not only political and economic problems but also cultural and intellectual ones, fostered by "the preachers they planted in the religious teaching institutions, the agents they employed in the universities, government educational institutions, and publishing houses, and the Orientalists who work in the service of the imperialist states."[26] The vastness and power of such a conspiratorial network could only be explained by its supernatural force.

The Inevitable Confrontation. Once the enemy of religion has been identified, the fourth step follows naturally: the idea of cosmic war. There are parallels in many religious movements to the idea of the coming Armageddon that was feared by both Christian militia members in the United States and members of the Aum Supreme Truth in Japan. Rabbi Meir Kahane, for instance, spoke of God's vengeance against the Gentiles, which began with the humiliation of the pharaoh in the exodus from Egypt more than three thousand years ago and continues in the present with the humiliation of Arab forces that resulted in the creation of Israel, and would come to a head in what Kahane expected would be a great struggle against Arabs and other corrupting forces in Israel in the near future. "When the Jews are at war," Kahane said, "God's name is great."[27] Another Israeli activist explained that "God always fights against His enemies," and that militants such as himself "are the instruments of this fight."[28]

Elsewhere I have argued that the language of warfare—fighting and dying for a cause—is appropriate and endemic to the realm of religion.[29] Although it may seem strange that images of destruction often accompany a commitment to realizing a more harmonious form of existence, there is a certain logic at work that makes this conjunction natural. In my view, religion is the language of ultimate order and for that reason provides those who use it with some way of envisioning disorder, especially the ultimate disorder of life: death. Most believers are convinced that death and disorder on an ultimate scale can be encompassed and domesticated. Ordinarily, religion does this through images projected in myth, symbol, ritual, and legend. The cross in Christianity is not, in the eyes of the faithful, an execution device but a symbol of redemption; similarly, the sword that is a central symbol of both Islam and Sikhism is proudly worn by the most pious members of those faiths not as weapons of death but as symbols of divine power.

Thus violent images are given religious meaning and domesticized. These violent images are usually symbols—such as the cross, or historic battles, or mythical confrontations—but occasionally the image of symbolic violence is not a picture or a play but a real act of violence. The sacrifice of animals and, of course, human sacrifice are examples from ancient traditions. Today conceptual violence can be identified with real acts of political violence, such as firebombings and political assassinations.

These religious acts of political violence, although terribly destructive, are sanitized by virtue of the fact that they are religiously symbolic. They are stripped of their horror by being invested with religious meaning. Those who commit such acts justify and therefore exonerate them because they are part of a religious template that is even larger than myth and history: they are elements of a ritual scenario that makes it possible for people involved in it to experience the drama of cosmic war.

For that reason, it is necessary for the activists who support such acts of terrorism to believe that a confrontation exists, even when it does not appear to, and even when the other side does not seem to provoke it. When one visits Gaza, one can feel a tremendous sense of anticipation among many pro-Hamas activists that the real battle for freedom is yet to come, coupled with a deep disappointment over the superficial freedom resulting from the peace efforts of Yasir Arafat. It was as if the peace that Arafat was entering into had been pur-chased too cheaply: it had not come as the result of an extraordinary denouement. They expected—perhaps even wanted—that eschato-logical moment of confrontation: some great war that would usher in the beginning of their new age. The suicide attacks carried out by young and remarkably committed Palestinians in the months before and after the January 1996 elections were in some sense attempts to deny the very normalcy that elections imply. It is as if they wanted to precipitate a confrontation where none had existed, or rather—in their mythologized view of the world—to bring to public attention the fact that an extraordinary war, albeit an invisible one, was raging all around them. Their acts would bring this cosmic confrontation to light.

THE FUTURE OF RELIGIOUS NATIONALISM

In a strange way, the point of all this terrorism and violence is peace. Or rather, it is a view of a peaceful world that will come into being when the cosmic was is over, and when the vision of righteous order held by militant religious nationalists triumphs. The leader of the policy wing of the Palestinian Hamas movement told me that the bombings in Jerusalem, Tel Aviv, and elsewhere would ulti-mately "lead to peace."[30] The leader of Japan's Aum Shinrikyo—con-victed for his alleged masterminding of the subway nerve gas at-tack—prophesied that after a colossal global conflict around the year 2000 involving nerve gas and nuclear weapons, a thousand years of peace would be ushered in, led by the coming of a new messiah who would establish a "paradise on earth."[31]

What is common to these and virtually all other "terrorists"—as those of us who experience their shocking violent actions usually regard them—is their self-conception as peacemakers. They are sol-diers in a war leading to peace. What they do not agree on, however, is the kind of peaceful world they want to bring about. This difference in political goals is caused not only by a difference in religious back-grounds but by an uncertainty about what form of politics is most appropriate to a religiously defined nation.

Yet the prognosis for peace in a world increasingly filled with reli-gious nationalists is guarded. Ideological religious nationalism is a strident and difficult force in contemporary world affairs. As I have described in this essay, it follows a process that begins with a disaffection with secular nationalism, then moves to perceiving politics in a religious way, identifying mortal enemies as satanic foes, and envisioning the world as caught up in a cosmic confrontation, one that will ultimately lead to a peaceful world order constructed by religious nations. The result of this process is a form of global order radically different from secular versions of globalization, a difference so severe that it could usher in a new cold war, an ideological confrontation on virtually a global scale.

This process of religionizing politics, however, is still mercifully rare. Most forms of religion do not lead to religious nationalism. The reasons why the process begins and is nurtured are to be found in the social and historical contexts in which it emerges. That is to say that the religionizing process I have described is largely a response to social and political crises. This is certainly the case with the phenomenal growth of religious nationalism in recent years. The common geopolitical crisis experienced throughout the world explains why there have been so many movements of religious nationalism in such disparate religions and places within the last ten years.

In the present period of social turbulence and political confusion—which the collapse of the Soviet Union and the decline of American economic power have created around the world—it was inevitable that new panaceas would emerge that involved religion, sometimes perceived as the only stable rudder in a swirl of economic and political indirection. Moreover, as nations rejected the Soviet and American models of nationhood, they turned to their own past, and to their own cultural resources.

Politicized religious movements are the responses of those who feel desperate and desolate in the current geopolitical crisis. The problem that they experience is not with God but with politics, and with their profound perceptions that the moral and ideological pillars of social order have collapsed. Until there is a surer sense of the moral legitimacy of secular nationalism, religious visions of moral order will continue to appear as attractive solutions, and religious activists will continue to attempt to impose these solutions in violent ways, seeing themselves as soldiers in a cosmic drama of political redemption. Can these religious nationalists succeed? Certainly for a time. They may terrify political leaders, shake regimes to their foundations, and even gain the reigns of power in unstable states such as Iran. But it remains to be seen whether nations can long endure with only the intangible benefits that religious solutions provide.

NOTES

1. These and other ideas in this essay are also explored in my book *The New Cold War? Religious Nationalism Confronts the Secular State* (Berkeley: University of California Press, 1993); my essay "The World-Wide Rise of Religious Nationalism," *Journal of International Affairs* 50, no. 1 (Summer 1996); and *Terror in the Mind of God: The Global Rise of Religious Violence* (Berkeley: University of California Press, 2000).

2. From my interview with Imad Saluji, Hamas journalist and leader of the policy wing of the movement, 19 August 1995, at his home and office on the outskirts of Gaza City, near the Jabailya refugee camp. I appreciate the research assistance of Aaron Santell and Antony Charles for this and other cases mentioned in this article.

3. Yigal Amir, quoted in news services used in the article "Rabin Assassin's New Version," *San Francisco Chronicle,* 14 January 1996, A6.

4. Yigal Amir, quoted in Barton Gellman, "Rabin Assassin Shocked in Court," *Washington Post,* reprinted in *San Francisco Chronicle,* 30 January 1996, A8.

5. From my interview with Yochay Ron, a volunteer guard at the grave of Dr. Baruch Goldstein at the Kirya Arbat settlement near Hebron in Israel, 18 August 1995.

6. For the ideology of the Christian Identity Movement and other forms of right-wing Christian militancy in the United States, see James Aho, *The Politics of Righteousness: Idaho Christian Patriotism* (Seattle: University of Washington Press, 1990), 83–104.

7. From my interview with "Takeshi Nakamura" (a pseudonym), former information officer of the Tokyo office of Aum Shinrikyo, 12 January 1996, in Tokyo with the translation assistance of Prof. Susumu Shimazono and his graduate students. My information on the movement comes from interviews with present and former members, and articles by (and conversations with) Professors Shimazono and Ian Reader.

8. I expand on this idea further in the chapter "Competing Ideologies of Order," in *The New Cold War,* 26–41. The term "religious nationalism" in that book refers to ideological religious nationalism.

9. See Ehud Sprinzak, "Right-wing Terrorism in a Comparative Perspective: The Case of Split Delegitimization," in *Terror from the Extreme Right,* ed. Tore Bjongo (London: Frank Cass, 1995).

10. From my interview with Sheik Ahmed Yassin in his home on the outskirts of Gaza City, 14 January 1989, shortly before he was placed under arrest by the Israeli authorities.

11. I am grateful to Michael Sells, *The Bridge Betrayed: Religion and Genocide in Bosnia* (Berkeley: University of California Press, 1997).

12. For a forceful statement of this thesis, see Partha Chatterjee, *The Nation and Its Fragments: Colonial and Postcolonial Histories* (Princeton: Princeton University Press, 1993).

13. Juergensmeyer, *The New Cold War*, 11–25.

14. Jürgen Habermas, "Modernity—an Incomplete Project," in *Interpretive Social Science: A Second Look*, ed. Paul Rabinow and William M. Sullivan (Berkeley: University of California Press, 1987), 148.

15. The academic literature on nationalism has become a veritable growth industry in the last several years. The journal *Nations and Nationalism* was launched in 1995 to appeal to this interest, and several other journals have devoted special issues to the topic: for example, "Reconstructing Nations and States," *Daedalus* 122, no. 3 (summer 1993); "Ethnicity and Nationalism," *International Journal of Comparative Sociology* 33, nos. 1–2 (January-April 1992) (Anthony D. Smith, guest editor); and "Global Culture," *Theory, Culture, and Society* 7, nos. 2–3 (June 1990). See also these recent books: Harumi Befu, ed., *Cultural Nationalism in East Asia* (Berkeley: University of California Press, 1993); Gidon Gottlieb, *Nation against State: A New Approach to Ethnic Conflicts and the Decline of Sovereignty* (New York: Council on Foreign Relations, 1993); Liah Greenfeld, *Nationalism: Five Roads to Modernity* (Cambridge: Cambridge University Press, 1992); Dawa Norbu, *Culture and Politics of Third World Nationalism* (London, 1992); William Pfaff, *The Wrath of Nations: Civilization and the Fury of Nationalism* (New York, 1993); Yael Tamir, *Liberal Nationalism* (Princeton: Princeton University Press, 1993); and Crawford Young, ed., *The Rising Tide of Cultural Pluralism: The Nation-State at Bay?* (Madison: University of Wisconsin Press, 1993). I am indebted to Darrin McMahon for research assistance on the contemporary crisis of nationalism.

16. Abolhassan Banisadr, *The Fundamental Principles and Precepts of Islamic Government*, trans. by Mohammad R. Ghanoonparvar (Lexington: Mazda Publishers, 1981), 40.

17. From my interview with Dr. Essam el Arian, member of the National Assembly, Cairo, 11 January 1989.

18. From my interview with Prof. Ibrahim Dasuqi Shitta, Professor of Persian Literature and adviser to Muslim students at Cairo University, 10 January 1989.

19. From my interview with Rabbi Meir Kahane at the Sheraton Hotel in Jerusalem, 18 January 1989; he was assassinated in a meeting room in the Marriott Hotel in midtown Manhattan in November 1990. My thanks to Prof. Ehud Sprinzak for arranging the interview. For a description of Kahane's position in

political and historical context, see Ehud Sprinzak, *The Ascendance of Israel's Radical Right* (New York: Oxford University Press, 1991).

20. From my interview with Yoel Lerner, member of a new political party, Yamini Israel, in the old city in Jerusalem, 17 August 1995. My thanks to Prof. Gideon Aran of Hebrew University for his help in arranging the interview.

21. Interview with "Nakamura." See also Shoko Asahara, *Disaster Approaches the Land of the Rising Sun: Shoko Asahara's Apocalyptic Predictions* (Tokyo: Aum Publishing Company, 1995), 300.

22. From my interview with Rev. Uduwawala Chandananda Thero, member of the Karaka Sabha, Asgiri chapter, Sinhalese Buddhist Sangha, in Kandy, Sri Lanka, 5 January 1991.

23. In this and the next two sections of this essay, I repeat ideas first expressed in my book *The New Cold War*, 22–23, 173, and 197.

24. Hamas communiqué, 22 January 1991, quoted in Jean-Francois Legrain, "A Defining Moment: Palestinian Islamic Fundamentalism," in *Islamic Fundamentalisms and the Gulf Crisis*, ed. James Piscatori (Chicago: Fundamentalism Project, American Academy of Arts and Sciences, 1991), 76.

25. Ayatollah Khomeyni, *Collection of Speeches, Position Statements*, translations from "Najaf Min watha'iq al-Imam al-Khomeyni did al-Quwa al Imbiriyaliyah wa al-Sahyuniyah wa al-Raj'iyah" (From the Papers of Imam Khomeyni against Imperialist, Zionist, and Reactionary Powers), 1977, in *Translations on Near East and North Africa*, no. 1902 (Arlington: Joint Publications Research Service, 1979), 3.

26. Imam A. Khomeini, *Islam and Revolution: Writings and Declarations*, trans. Hamid Algar (London: Routledge and Kegan Paul, 1985), 28. Originally published by Mizan Press, Berkeley, 1981.

27. Rabbi Meir Kahane, "Speech on the Announcement of the Creation of the Independent State of Judaea," Jerusalem, 18 January 1989 (from my notes taken on that occasion).

28. Interview with Yoel Lerner, Jerusalem, 20 January 1989.

29. Mark Juergensmeyer, "The Logic of Religious Violence," in *Essay: Inside Terrorist Organizations* (London: Frank Cass, 1988); and "Sacrifice and Cosmic War," in *Violence and the Sacred in the Modern World*, ed. Mark Juergensmeyer (London: Frank Cass, 1992).

30. Interview with Saluji, 19 August 1995.

31. Asahara, 302.

LOIS ANN LORENTZEN

Who Is an Indian?

Religion, Globalization, and Chiapas

My morning cup of *café con leche* in the plaza of San Cristóbal de las Casas in Chiapas, Mexico. As always, I enjoyed
watching the square come to life—boys and girls running wildly through the plaza, indigenous women with bright rib-
bons woven through long braids, men selling newspapers, and the
occasional gringa or gringo like me, stumbling through the plaza,
tour book in hand. My cherished daily routine of the morning's
news, café con leche, and soaking up sights and sounds was soon
disrupted by three enormous buses descending on the plaza. Disappointed, I imagined tourist crowds overwhelming the peaceful scene
in which I was immersed. I watched as people poured out of the
buses, moving quickly and purposefully, in contrast to the slower
pace generally required by the plaza. I noticed that they were all
wearing identical bright, fluorescent, lime green vests with black
lettering on them. In bold letters I read *"Todos Somos Indios de el
Mundo,"* which in bad Spanish means "We are all Indians of the
World." The Italian observers had come to town.

Over the next two weeks, I watched the actions of these 150-odd
international observers, as well as reactions to them. In the process,
and because of other experiences and research in Chiapas, I came to
question concepts I had once fervently espoused, such as the ability
of globalization theories to provide adequate explanations for oppression. This essay explores basic principles in globalization theory
as applied to a specific context, that of Chiapas, and a particular
crisis, that of southern Mexico's indigenous peoples.[1]

Fernando Mires begins his book *El discurso de la Indianidad: La cuestión indígena en América Latina,* by asking the question "Who is an Indian?"[2] He concludes that *"indios"* to this day remain the products and imaginations of their "discoverers." The indigenous throughout history were repeatedly "discovered," first by negation (Columbus depicting Indians as an extension of nature), by death and genocide, by slavery, by evangelizing, by modern philosophy, and finally by affirmation. The modern rediscovery of the indigenous, according to Mires, is done in the name of the defense of the indio: "The naturalizing of the Indian revives the image of the 'savage' with the difference that now it is framed positively."[3] In this modern version, the indigenous is discovered by the state, in this case Mexico, as the bearer of, and symbol for, nationalism. Latin American leftists look to the indigenous to represent resistance against imperialism, whereas increased interest in ecology has led to a "rediscovery" of the indios, who are somehow more "natural" than the rest of us, for environmentalist purposes. And as Chiapan women who protest what they call "official indigenous discourse" tell us, in the process, the real indigenous disappears, "assassinated by the functions they've been assigned within an ecosystem or by reactionary idealizations."[4] In a remarkable twist, my Italian observer friends had again rediscovered the indio. We are *all* indigenous, it turns out — discoverers and rescuers of the oppressed, naturalized Other, now becoming ourselves the indigenous.

The lime green clad neoindigenous observers are probably too easy targets for my point. Using this example, however, what I came to question was the term "globalization," seeing it as a similar invention. I had embraced the term and its principles and then "discovered" its power in far-flung contexts, agreeing with Peter Beyer when he writes:

> If we want to understand the major features of contemporary social life, we have to go beyond local and national factors to situate our analyses in this global context. More pointedly, we must make the primary unit of analysis the global system and not some subunit of it, such as the nation, the state, or the region.[5]

The "extravagant images of globalization," to use Michael Veseth's language, are especially seductive in Chiapas, which many claimed was the site of the first "postmodern revolution."[6] The image of the guerrilla in the forest with a rifle in one hand and a laptop in the other captured the imagination as revolution went "on-line." Yet the history and roots of Mayan resistance, its current manifestation, and the role religious groups play involve multiple actors, processes, and contradictions, not all of which can be explained by considering the world as a "single place."[7]

CHIAPAS: CONTEXT AND CRISIS

Rich in resources including oil, natural gas, forests, and farmland, the southern state of Chiapas is also one of the poorest regions in Mexico. Eighty-five percent of its population is considered "highly marginalized" as compared to 48 percent nationally.[8] One-half of the population lacks access to potable water, and two-thirds are without sewage. In rural areas, most people have little or no income, and 54 percent of the population is considered malnourished. One-half of the population is illiterate, and with .2 clinics for every 1,000 people, most Chiapans lack access to medical services.[9]

The 1 January 1994 uprising of the Ejercito Zapatista de Liberación Nacional (EZLN), or the Zapatistas, was but the most recent of indigenous rebellions in the region, beginning as early as the 1500s, when exploitation of indigenous labor for mining and agriculture resulted in frequent indigenous resistance. As in much of Latin America, the control of land use rights has been a central political issue in Mexican history. The roots of the current version of the indigenous crisis in Chiapas, as well as the resistance movement, run deep and are explained in part, but only in part, by globalization theory.

There are three primary ways in which globalization and the global economy affect the lives of Chiapan indigenous peoples: through tourism, increased telecommunication, and the impingement of global markets as represented by the North Atlantic Free Trade Agreement (NAFTA). All are more complicated than they seem at first. Globalization is evidenced by a shocking increase in tourism since the Zapatista uprising. This has occurred, in part, because of the Mexican government's *Mundo Maya* (Mayan World) tourism campaign. Paradoxically, although real indigenous people are often undervalued by the state, the rescue of cultures and customs is also necessary and seen as a source of resources. The exoticizing of the indigenous, and especially the indigenous woman, is necessary for tourism. Thus the government globally promotes tours of Chiapas and the Mundo Maya. For some, the Mundo Maya campaign fits George Ritzer's description of the "McDisneyization" of postmodern tourism. For Ritzer, signs or signifiers are central to contemporary tourism.[10] For those living in Baudrillard's contemporary "world plagued with disenchantment," Chiapan tourism may signify a search for authenticity in the form of the "true" indigenous of the Mundo Maya.[11] This "imperialist nostalgia" demands that the indigenous exist for us to visit, and that they not change.[12]

There are many good reasons to criticize tourism's impact on a place like Chiapas. However, in an odd twist, increased tourism has allowed Chiapan women to continue in their roles as bearers of indigenous culture. Indigenous women are seen as bearers of traditional culture, given their roles in weaving, pottery making, and fruit collecting. Women save the language, rituals, and traditions. Men, more likely to leave their villages to seek paid employment, often symbolize compromise with outsiders, especially with the hated *ladino*. Indigenous women, through textile and artisan cooperatives, through selling in the markets of San Cristóbal de Chiapas, have been able to bring in needed income to households while practicing their traditional skills.

Brenda Rosenbaum claims, following extensive fieldwork in San Juan Chamula, Chiapas, that a certain level of tourism in Chiapas actually serves to preserve indigenous culture. Women's providing income through weaving or pottery making is seen as preferable to serving as a maid in a ladino home or leaving home to work in a factory.[13] And what the Mexican president Ernesto Zedillo Ponce de León scornfully termed "revolutionary tourism," when referring to the influx of international observers to Chiapas, has provided international support, solidarity, and visibility to the Zapatista cause and to the plight of the Chiapan indigenous peoples. To overly criticize tourism, even the imperialistically nostalgic tourism of the Mundo Maya campaign, is to argue implicitly that "the society or culture being impacted is a static, ahistorical, agencyless, solidly bounded, noninteractive object, whether conceptualized (imagined by social scientists) as an organism, a system, a structure, or a text."[14] Residents of San Juan Chamula thus charge their tourists fees to view their church, disallow them from taking photographs, and kick them out at night.

What of the criticism offered by some theorists that the increased globalization of technology results in the spreading of U.S. mass culture and the eroding or damaging of particular cultural identities? In his essay earlier in this volume, Eduardo Mendieta accurately lists Amin, Barber, and Greider as mono-metastructural theorists of globalization who view globalization as "modernity accelerated." Responses to this acceleration are, according to Mendieta, either "euphoric celebration or cynical rejection," although rejection and fears related to the destruction of particular cultural constructions seem to be more common.

Yet in Chiapas, globalization as represented by information technologies actually aided the Zapatista cause, allowing for a high level of international support and solidarity. Transnational pressure was applied on the nation-state on behalf of a particular and localized culture. In this case, "global consciousness," to use Robertson's term, was created through the use of information technologies. Global consciousness was self-consciously created to intensify attention and focus on the particular. As Walter Mignolo notes, "One of the paradoxes of globalization is that it allows subaltern communities within the nation-state to create transnational alliances beyond the state to fight for their own social and human rights."[15] Globalization, according to Mignolo, is thus able to provide the conditions for "barbarian theorizing": theorizing from and of the Third World.[16] Consequently in the case of the Zapatista uprising, globalization, as represented through information technologies, was celebrated by some as the global in service of the particular and the local.

Lest we get carried away, however, with this "extravagant image of globalization" offered by the Zapatista on-line, let us remember that two out of every three people in the world have never used a telephone. The much-touted information highway is both actual *and* imaginary or mythic. Walking through Chiapan jungles and villages, one will be hard-pressed to find a telephone, much less a computer, in this desperately poor part of the world. And as Gossen notes, this "postmodern mesh" of EZLN strategy including "armed confrontation, massive and carefully orchestrated media coverage, World Wide Web sites, e-mail, faxes, wooden guns, and poetically crafted communiqués" reflects continuity rather than discontinuity for the Maya peasant composition of the EZLN. Given "the power of Maya-derived cyclical time-reckoning to absorb otherness in an ever-evolving historical matrix that consistently yields new end points and renewed identities," we should not wonder at this actual *and* imaginary Mayan information highway or automatically consider it discontinuous with Mayan identity.[17] It is not just that the global (symbolized here by the computer) is supporting the local (the static Maya community) but that the Maya community has appropriated the global for itself and its own dynamic cultural reconstruction.

Certainly if we look to the global economy and NAFTA as a symbol of dominant global systems seeking economic profit, the picture would seem to become more clear and less paradoxical. It is clearly the case that NAFTA, with its attendant erosion of *ejidos* (communal lands) and communal ownership patterns, as well as its encouraging of export crops, is destructive in Chiapas. Numerous books and articles already exist on the topic.[18] The neoliberal policies of NAFTA called for, for example, the deregulation of commodities including corn, resulting in less-stable prices for this staple of the indigenous Chiapan diet. Coffee production is also affected by deregulation, thus jeopardizing the seasonal labor and income on which many indigenous Chiapans rely. The move toward privatization and away from agrarian reform, moreover, affects *ejido* (communal) indigenous landholdings. Some claim that responses to these changes, initiated by global as well as national forces, include further growth in Protestantism, additional social activism on the part of the Roman Catholic Church, as well as a wide appeal for the reforms proposed by the EZLN.[19]

The impact of NAFTA-initiated policies and the further deterioration of social and economic conditions in southern Mexico are real. However, the primary oppression still remains rooted in internal rather than external logics. As Gossen notes, Chiapas has a "centuries-old pattern of symbiotic collusion among Indian *caciques* (local indigenous elites), local white elites and the Mexican state."[20] By 1847, the Mexican government decreed that indigenous peoples had to live in pueblos, thereby forcing them to work for *patrones*. This initiated an economic system in Chiapas that was essentially feudalistic. Internal markets and control by the wealthy landholding elite minority shapes the primary logic up to the present.

The basic questions to ask are, Who owns the land? And, Where do the products and profits go? As Subcomandante Marcos notes, "A handful of businesses, among them the Mexican state, take the wealth of Chiapas."[21] Nearly all the oil fields of Chiapas are run by PEMEX, the Mexican oil company. Thirty-five percent of Mexico's coffee production is from Chiapas, with roughly one-half going to the national market, and one-half for export. Chiapas provides 55 percent of Mexico's hydroelectric power and 20 percent of its electrical energy. Nearly all of the Chiapan precious woods are sold outside Chiapas, but within Mexico. One-half of Chiapan corn is sold on the national market. Ninety percent of its tamarind leaves Chiapas, but not Mexico. Sixty-nine percent of Chiapan cocoa is sold nationally, and 31 percent internationally. Chiapas provides 5 percent of Mexico's oil and 12 percent of its natural gas.[22]

The point is, this resource-rich yet desperately poor area does indeed suffer from exploitation. Yet the resources extracted from Chiapas are primarily for use by Mexico's central and southern states, while indigenous laborers live in the most marginalized conditions of the country. By 1911, ladinos had taken most of the land in Chiapas. Thus it is that in Highland Chiapan stories and rituals, a common theme of ladino domination of indigenous peoples exists. During fiestas and rituals, ladinos are often ridiculed. Chamulan ideology, according to Rosenbaum, depicts the "Earth Lord" as a supernatural ladino with light hair, fair skin, and great wealth, who seeks workers. The Earth Lord's wife seeks servants, and both the Earth Lord and his wife try to capture the souls of Chamulans. Chamulans who envy their neighbors are said to have struck a deal with the Earth Lord. In the realm of the Earth Lord, Chamulans work as peons and servants. Those who adopt ladino values risk eternal damnation.[23] These powerful rituals directly identify ladinos, who may or may not be part of the circuits of the global economy, as the cause of indigenous pain, suffering, and poverty. When John Watanabe asked his Maya friend the most important thing to write about his pueblo, Santiago Chimaltenango, Guatemala, his friend answered, "I would write about Indians and Ladinos."[24]

I am not saying that the imperatives of the global economy do not make life worse for many Chiapans. It is clear from Zapatista analysis that the global market has a destructive impact on indigenous peoples. However, to leave it at that level of abstraction does little to illuminate the ongoing ladino-indigenous struggle and the particular forms it takes. I agree with Watanabe that we must "reject notions of easy presumption of global determinism."[25] Here we have intertwined but separate histories, multiple levels of oppression that may or may not be connected. There are oppressions internal to indigenous communities, the ladino-indigenous struggle (which for most Chiapans is primary), the state-indigenous struggle, and the ever increasing demands of the global economy. In terms of day-to-day life, however, I suspect that most indigenous would still rather work in a *maquila* (factory) than in the hacienda of a ladino patrón.

RELIGION, GLOBALIZATION, AND CHIAPAS

What of the relationship between religion and globalization in Chiapas? Again, the situation is complicated. We first encounter the problem with which the essay begins, the problem of discourse about the indigenous. Mires begins his book by asking, "*Quien es un indio?*" [Who is an Indian?], and he suggests that indio has become a homogenizing concept signifying the "not European," expressed not as an affirmation of identity but as a negation.[26] Alberto Huerto claims that "*en México los indios son los naturales*" [in Mexico, the indigenous are the "natural" ones].[27] This "imaginary" Indian, according to Mires, emerges from a "romantic naturalistic vision of history" reflecting the rediscoverers more than the actual indigenous community.[28] In the case of Chiapas, traditionalists most closely resemble Mires's "imaginary" Indian.

Traditionalists. Chiapas has one of the largest of Mexico's indigenous populations and also one of the most conservative or traditional. Yet not all indigenous peoples of Chiapas are traditionalists. Three main religious groups exist in Chiapas: traditionalists who practice a blend of Mayan and Catholic practices; evangelical Protestants, who are predominantly Pentecostal; and Catholic Action groups, who follow the liberation theology espoused by Bishop Samuel Ruíz Garcia. Identity strongly corresponds to these categories. Intergroup tensions and conflicts are not uncommon. Conventional wisdom would suggest that traditionalists are the most "authentic" indigenous people, reflecting greater continuity with their Mayan roots, shaped less by forces of globalization, with an ability to mount resistance to such forces given their religio-cultural roots and resources. And there is indeed truth in these claims, although contradictions exist.

Traditionalists claim, for example, that Protestants threaten traditional ways of life. Virginia Garrard-Burnett, in her excellent analysis of religious change in Chiapan and Guatemalan Mayan communities, quotes the police chief of San Juan Chamula: "We are a traditional people. . . . These Protestants want to forget tradition, and anyone who forsakes tradition is not welcome here."[29] Yet contemporary traditionalists are distinguished by beliefs and practices developed by combining Mayan and Catholic practices to yield indigenous community identity. As Garrard-Burnett notes, writing of the *cofradia* (cargo system), "Indigenous people were able to adapt what was, even in 1800, a fundamentally Iberian, colonial, and well-established institution into a locus of ethnic identity and even resistance. They accomplished this adaptation in less than three-quarters of a century."[30] In highland Chiapas, local communities such as San Juan Chamula and Zinacantán severed ties with Roman Catholic clergy and took over the local Roman Catholic churches for "traditional" practices. These popular religious practices, according to Garrard-Burnett,

> focused more on local beliefs and practices, fiestas which permitted (and affirmed) full community participation, and which, importantly, were garnished with the accoutrements of ritual celebration such as fireworks, horseback riding, alcohol, and brass bands, that could only be purchased from ladino venders in cash or credit in anticipation of future earnings. While the economic reality of this arrangement simply shifted debt from Spanish clergy to ladino merchants, the local perception was altogether different: that is, that cash and community mobilization had replaced colonial dependency with authentic community autonomy, at least in the religious sphere.[31]

For ancient Mayans, blood symbolized the life force. Contemporary traditionalists substitute alcohol for blood, rum in San Pedro de Chenalhó, for example, or *pox*, the local liquor made from sugarcane, in San Juan Chamula. Alcohol carries great symbolic weight in the fiestas of contemporary traditionalists in Chiapas.[32] Rum, crucial for ceremonies, is produced and often sold by ladinos, however, thus reinforcing their economic power even in service of "tradition." As Rosenbaum notes, dramatic income differences exist in these communities, in part due to monopolies on liquor and soft drinks used in rituals. Protestants, as we will see, often protest that these practices are not obligatory for claiming strong indigenous identity, and will resist forced participation in rituals, especially those involving alcohol.

The point is, traditionalists seem to embody most clearly a "pure" indigenous identity, less tainted by religious imports such as Catholicism and, more recently, Protestantism. And this is the case in many ways. As Eber comments:

> Traditionalists say that what is wrong with Protestants and Catholic Action members is that they don't follow the path the ancestors walked. Specifically this means that Protestants no longer serve ritual cargos; they no longer visit sacred places in the township to leave offerings of rum to the earth; they no longer garnish graves with yellow marigolds on the Day of the Dead; nor decorate altars with candles, flowers, meat, and tamales.[33]

Yet today's traditionalists practice a religion that blends Catholicism and preexisting Mayan practices. The practices both preserve cultural identity and continue to tie them to ladinos and to unequal economic structures. Traditional religious practices are sites, then, of both resistance and accommodation.

Gossen further complicates the picture we've painted of traditionalists. He notes that few heroic figures in Chamulan folklore are ethnically Indian. For Gossen, simple models of hybridity or syncretism are inadequate to explain beliefs and practices of the traditionalists; rather, he claims that this absorption of otherness is typically Maya.[34] He writes that "Chamulas live in a constructed matrix that actively incorporates us, our object, and our religions into their world," and this is consistent with "Maya-derived cyclical time-reckoning."[35] Incorporating elements from Catholicism and deities with light skin thus makes these traditionalists not less traditional but more Maya.

Roman Catholics. One can look to the Iberian Catholic Church for an early example of "hyperglobalization." Following 1492, transnational religious organizations such as the Society of Jesus (Jesuits) and the Franciscans met with remarkable success in permanently altering the cultural landscape of Latin America. As Daniel H. Levine and David Stoll note:

> In remarkably little time, they implanted a network of missions, churches, schools, and related ecclesiastical institutions (including the Inquisition), attacking indigenous religious practices and aggressively spreading the gospel. Conversion to Catholicism was an integral part of the whole experience of domination. The monopoly they established has only lately been challenged, this time by the aftereffects of another wave of transnational religious activism, which not only attacks the religious monopoly laid down over these five hundred years but also a series of cultural assumptions and political practices that have grown up around it.[36]

During hundreds of years of Catholic dominance in Latin America, little seemed to challenge the church's power. The church generally enjoyed close ties with the government and a religious monopoly. The Catholic Church during most of this period was not noted for being a defender or promoter of indigenous ethnic identity. Following the Second Vatican Council (1962–1965) and the Latin American Bishops conferences in Medellín, Colombia, in 1968 and Puebla, Mexico, in 1979, however, an increased emphasis on lay participation resulted in new spaces opening up for democratization and social and political action. In the case of Chiapas, Acción Católica (Catholic Action) began in the highlands of Chiapas in the early 1960s under the guidance of Bishop Samuel Ruíz Garcia. Espousing liberation theology, more than seven thousand indigenous lay leaders have been trained to organize and teach in Chiapan communities.[37]

Throughout the 1970s and 1980s, catechists and missionaries sponsored literacy programs and lobbied for improved health care and new farming techniques. As Eber indicates, the Chiapan church also encouraged "fiestas, music, and expressions of ethnic identity."[38] The Chiapan Catholic Church and liberation theologians, through numerous organizing efforts, also helped to create relatively autonomous political and social space for the growth of other nongovernmental organizations, including women's groups. The Diocesan Women's Committee, for example, made possible other women's organizations. In the report produced by the Human Rights Center – Bartolomé de Las Casas concerning the 1997 massacre in Acteal, women informants claimed that they first learned of the concept of the rights of women in their catechism classes.[39]

In spite of attempts to encourage ethnic identity, relations between traditionalists and Roman Catholics have often been strained. Liberation theologians have criticized the power of local caciques, as well as the close relationships between local caciques, the Mexican state, and Mexico's ruling party, PRI.[40] The use of alcohol at religious festivals and fiestas and in rituals has also been questioned at times by Catholics. In the most famous local conflict, the civil and traditional religious leaders of San Juan Chamula withdrew from the Roman Catholic Church following a dispute concerning religious instruction for children.

Protestants. Relations between traditionalists and the *evangélicos*, or evangelical Protestants, are even more conflictual than those between Catholics and traditionalists. Often condemning it as an "alien cultural invasion,"[41] some scholars view the growth of Protestantism in Latin America in general and in Chiapas in particular as a result of global forces (e.g., missionary efforts of North Americans, neo-Weberian attempts to assimilate to capitalism through religious ideology, Western notions of progress as expressed in Protestantism, etc.) and as a response to social and economic disruption brought about by globalization. In general, academics who write about the growth of Protestantism view conversion as threatening ethnic and cultural identity. Eber concludes, after an overall positive portrait of Protestantism in San Pedro Chenalhó, for example: "But in the long run I believe that Protestant groups undermine traditional Pedrano values of community and service."[42]

The Protestant missionaries of the nineteenth century, most of them from mainline denominations in the United States and Europe, gained few converts. The new wave of Protestant missionaries following World War II tended to come from evangelical and fundamentalist denominations. Yet they alone were not responsible for the current rapid growth of converts in Chiapas. Throughout Latin America, and Chiapas is no exception, churches are pastored by locals. Support and control is local, and congregations are Pentecostal (unlike most evangelical United States congregations).

Protestants have tended to be dissident voices in many traditional communities, and this dissidence has resulted in conflict and the charge that conversion is destructive to indigenous identity. Eber reports that in San Juan Chenhaló, in which one-third of the residents have converted, Protestants complain that religious festivals are costly and time-consuming and that alcohol abuse is common. Eventually, Protestants stopped performing religious cargoes and offering feasts to their ancestors.[43] In Zincantán, Protestants and Catholics together attempted to pressure traditionalists to change the way fiestas were conducted. And in San Juan Chamula, Protestants refused to pay taxes to local religious leaders for festivals and alcohol.[44] Furthermore, Protestants claim that conversion results in less drinking, better health, and increased prosperity.

This dissidence has at times resulted in religious persecution, including violence. In 1957 a traditionalist assassinated a Protestant in San Juan Chenalhó, and in 1965 traditionalists tried to expel Protestants.[45] In the last fifteen years, Protestants have been jailed and beaten, have had their homes burned, or have been expelled from their communities. Roughly 25,000 *expulsados* have been exiled and now live in the slums surrounding San Cristóbal de las Casas or in the Lacandón jungle.[46]

Not all scholars, or Maya for that matter, interpret conversion as a threat to ethnic and cultural identity. As Levine and Stoll observe, most converts are Pentecostal, and practices such as speaking in tongues, prophecy, and healing may draw on both folk Catholic and shamanistic traditions.[47] Furthermore, evangelicals tend to be linguistic conservatives. Pedrano Protestants, for example, contacted the Summer Institute of Linguistics to have the Bible translated into Tzotzil.[48] And according to Garrard-Burnett, Maya Protestant theology draws heavily from "native cosmology."[49] Thus for Garrard-Burnett, Protestantism serves not as a "broker between encroaching modernization" but as a "contemporary means of asserting ethnic identity."[50] She concludes:

> For the Maya, identity conflates such varying elements as language, locality, dress, social relations, livelihood, and religion into what some simply call "the way of being." That any one of these elements might change, even dramatically, does not necessarily negate the "essentialness" of the whole for those who subscribe to the "way of being," as disappointing as this

may be to those of us on the outside who continue to yearn for the exotic and the antique.[51]

For the Chiapan convert, to be Protestant does not mean to be "Western" or less Maya. Rather, through strategies of accommodation, ethnicity is defined and redefined.

The Zapatistas and Pan-Indianness. Given the attention I have paid here to religious conflict, one might be surprised at the diversity within the Zapatista movement. The composition of the EZLN is predominately Maya, yet it is diverse in terms of religious, linguistic, and ethnic background. There are evangelical Protestant Zapatistas (who agree on, among other things, the destructiveness of alcohol in indigenous communities), Catholic Zapatistas, and traditionalist Zapatistas. At the 1996 National Indigenous Forum, all indigenous communities were invited, in a mostly successful attempt to promote Pan-Indianness and indigenous rights to cultural autonomy and ethnic heritage. For Gossen, the seeming contradiction of many diverse Indian communities (with their separate dialects, customs, beliefs, etc., claiming a shared identity) is in itself very Maya. Religious pluralism, according to Gossen, was part of the ancient Mayan world as well as the contemporary one. So Zapatistas, like their forebears, include "competing and overlapping cults."

> Therefore, what I have identified above as the apparently anomalous and peculiar link of the Zapatistas to foreign alliances and symbolic affiliations—including Marcos, white foreign martyrs, the paladin of Zapata and the Mexican revolutionary ideology that he embodies—is not at all strange to the Maya imagination. In fact, such alliances appear to have been a centrally important strategy for Maya cultural affirmation and political legitimacy since well before the contact period.[52]

Thus the Zapatistas, following Maya tradition, are highly adaptive, borrowing symbols from local communities, Mexican nationalism, the white Other, and even the technologies of the "new," globalized, postmodern world.

CONCLUSION

"Globalization can apparently destroy democracy, create it, and be used by political entrepreneurs to manipulate democracy. This globalization must be a terrible, wonderful thing."[53] Does this terrible, wonderful thing (i.e., globalization) illuminate religious practices, construction of ethnic identity, social change, and the bleak living conditions of indigenous peoples in Chiapas, Mexico? Is globalization the most important dynamic to consider—more important than intergroup conflict, the power of local caciques, the Mexican government, regional inequities, ladino-indigenous dynamics, or more important than the characteristics of Maya religion and cosmology, with its capacity to absorb and re-create itself? Clearly, given the numerous paradoxes emerging for globalization theories, religious practices, and ethnic identity in the case of Chiapas, I am reluctant to jump too quickly to macrodeterminants. Even those theorists who stress the constant interplay and creativity between the "global" and the "local," the "particular" and the "universal," may leave out too many layers.

Clearly the global is important. The case of Chiapas is not complicated at all. The indigenous suffer and are victims of the global economy, the Mexican state, and local prejudice. The Mexican military and paramilitary groups have committed atrocities against indigenous peoples. A resource-rich area is sucked dry while local indigenous people remain desperately poor. This is deeply wrong. The macroforces we see at work in Chiapas are real, not imaginary. As Garrard-Burnett notes, many places in southern Mexico

> barely survived the assault of "modernization" . . . the community as an integral social unit has been besieged by land incursions, tourism, migration, growing disparities of income even within the *municipio*, a population surge, and divisions within the Catholic church.[54]

However, internal differentiation, complexity, and agency exist as well. Gossen reports that the result of a yearlong international project of coordinated research on the encounter of Native American and African practice and discourse with the constructs and practices of Europeans was the following:

> In essence, the only unanimity that emerged from scholarly examination of dozens of case studies . . . was the *absence* of any easily generalizable pattern of ethnic formation and expression even among those communities—such as those of

Highland Chiapas—that spoke dialects of the same language and were subject to the same state policies. In all cases, local knowledge, local politics, and local actors seem to have had the last word in determining the form and expression that "belonging to a group" and "acting in history" would assume.[55]

Local actors have the last word in these case studies of ethnic identity formation. We return to our opening question, "Who is the Indio?" The "traditionalist" selling her Zapatista dolls to U.S., French, and German tourists in the plazas of San Cristóbal de las Casa, buying his rum and coke from ladinos, burning candles in a Catholic church in San Juan Chamula in which priests are not allowed? The catechist promoting social justice in the face of neoliberalism's policies and cataloging human rights abuses against the indigenous people? The evangelical Protestant conducting worship services in Tzotzil and constructing a theology using elements of Maya cosmology? The point is, the Maya have always had a complex relationship with other religions, whether they are competing sects within Maya traditions, Catholicism, or Protestantism. This history of transformation may be exacerbated by globalization in some ways, but it is not new. The Maya in Chiapas are again transforming religious traditions and indigenous beliefs and making them their own.

This indio, then, is agent. This indio is not just the "discovered" indio. The ideology or discourse of Indianness, to which Mires objects, is a true product of globalization. If as Baudrillard suggests, the developed world is demystified, then those who are *not* indios are precisely those who cling to the idea of a pure and untouched Indian. The "West" first invents and then discovers this "authentic" indio who isn't Catholic, isn't Protestant, is ecologically pure, and practices centuries-old rituals.

And while protesting this ideology of *indigenismo* with its demand for homogeneity, paradoxically, heterogeneous contemporary Maya deploy Pan-Indianness to secure their rights, to protect cultural autonomy, to fight for land, to survive. They are traditionalists, Catholics, Protestants, and all Maya. Maybe we should take our cue from the Maya themselves, who believe that as part of the human condition, we are "never to have easy access to the true scheme of things."[56]

Thanks to Eduardo Mendieta for his careful reading of this article and helpful comments. Also, thanks to the University of San Francisco, whose sabbatical funding made research time in southern Mexico possible. I am indebted to Fernando Mires for the title. He begins his excellent book *El Discurso de la Indianidad: La cuestión indígena en América Latina* (The Discourse of "Indianness": The Indigenous Issue in Latin America) with the question "Who is an Indian?" See Mires, *El discurso de la Indianidad: La cuestión indígena en América Latina* (San Jose: Editorial Departmento Ecumencio de Investifaciones, 1991).

1. I realize there are many types of globalization theories and little consensus about how to define globalization. Eduardo Mendieta, in this volume, provides a helpful typology of globalization theories. See also S. O'Riain and P. B. Evans's excellent overview of globalization theories ("Globalization and Global Systems Analysis," in *Encyclopedia of Sociology*, ed. Edgar F. Borgatta [New York: MacMillan Publishing, 2000]). What global theorists seem to hold in common, however, is that global connectedness, whether economic, political, or cultural, is the single most important process forcing localities to adjust and react to global demands. The primary unit of analysis for these theorists, then, must be the global system. Sean O'Riain and P. B. Evans, "Globalization and Global System Analysis."

2. Mires, 11.

3. Mires, 37.

4. Mires, 37.

5. Peter Beyer, *Religion and Globalization* (Thousand Oaks: Sage Publications, 1994), 1–2.

6. Michael Veseth, *Selling Globalization: The Myth of the Global Economy* (Boulder: Lynne Rienner Publishers, 1998), 157.

7. Roland Robertson, *Globalization: Social Theory and Global Culture* (London: Sage Publications, 1992).

8. Tracy Konstant, "The Social Factors Influencing Forest Use in Chiapas, Mexico" (*M.Sc. diss*, University of Edinburgh, 1997).

9. Subcomandante Marcos, "Chiapas: The Southeast in Two Winds, a Storm and a Prophecy," in *The Geopolitics Reader*, ed. Gearoid O. Tuathail, Simon Dalby, and Paul Routledge (New York: Routledge, 1998), 296.

10. George Ritzer, *The Thesis* (Thousand Oaks: Sage Publications, 1998), 143.

11. Jean Baudrillard, *Symbolic Exchange in Death* (London: Sage Publications, 1993).

12. Quetzil Castaneda, *In the Museum of Maya Culture: Touring Chichen Itza* (Minneapolis: University of Minnesota Press, 1996), 37.

13. Brenda Rosenbaum, *With Our Heads Bowed: The Dynamics of Gender in a Maya Community* (Albany: State University of New York Press, 1993).

14. Castaneda, 9.

15. Walter Mignolo, "Globalization, Civilization Processes, and the Reloca-

tion of Languages and Cultures," in *The Cultures of Globalization*, ed. Fredric Jameson and Masao Miyoshi (Durham: Duke University Press, 1998), 44.

16. Mignolo, 51.

17. Gary Gossen, *Telling Maya Tales: Tzotzil Identities in Modern Mexico* (New York: Routledge, 1999), 248, 25.

18. Tom Barry, *Zapata's Revenge: Free Trade and the Farm Crisis in Mexico* (Boston: South End Press, 1995); and Elaine Katzenberger, *First World, Ha Ha Ha! The Zapatista Challenge* (San Francisco: City Lights, 1995).

19. Gossen, 264.

20. Gossen believes, however, that this collusion is threatened by NAFTA policies (Gossen, 265).

21. Marcos, 294.

22. Marcos; Phillip Howard and Thomas Homer-Dixon, "Environmental Scarcity and Violent Conflict: The Case of Chiapas, Mexico," *Occassional Paper, Project on Environment, Population, and Security* (Washington, D.C.: American Association for the Advancement of Science and the University of Toronto, 1996).

23. Rosenbaum.

24. John M. Watanabe, *Maya Saints and Souls in a Changing World* (Austin: University of Texas Press, 1992), 24.

25. Watanabe, 10.

26. Mires, 11.

27. Alberto Huerta, "Otra Vez 'el Indio': Chiapas," *Religion y Cultura* 64 (1998): 388.

28. Huerta, 122.

29. Virginia Garrard-Burnett, "Identity, Community, and Religious Change among the Mayas and Chiapas and Guatemala," *Journal of Hispanic/Latino Theology* 6, no. 1 (1998): 71.

30. Garrard-Burnett, 65.

31. Garrard-Burnett, 67.

32. Christine Eber, *Women and Alcohol in a Highland Maya Town: Water of Hope, Water of Sorrow* (Austin: University of Texas Press, 1995).

33. Eber, 245.

34. Gossen, xxiii.

35. Gossen, 25, 28.

36. Daniel Levine and David Stoll, "Bridging the Gap between Empowerment and Power in Latin America," in *Transnational Religion, Fading Sates*, ed. Susanne Hoeber Rudolph and James Piscatori (Boulder: Westview Press, 1997), 68.

37. Eber, 223.

38. Eber, 223.

39. Rosalva Aida Hernandez Castillo, ed., "Antes y Despues De Acteal: Voces, Memorias y Experiencias desde las Mujeres de San Pedro Chenalho," in *La Otra*

Palabra: Mujeres y Violencia en Chiapas, Antes y Despues de Acteal (Centro de Derechos Humanos, 1997).

40. Gossen, 82.
41. Levine and Stoll, 85.
42. Eber, 246.
43. Eber, 216.
44. Garrard-Burnett, 70.
45. Eber, 245.
46. Garrard-Burnett, 70.
47. Levine and Stoll, 85.
48. Eber, 216.
49. Garrard-Burnett, 72.
50. Garrard-Burnett, 61.
51. Garrard-Burnett, 78.
52. Gossen, 184.
53. Veseth, 12.
54. Garrard-Burnett, 72.
55. Gossen, xxiv.
56. Gossen, 254.

PART TWO / CASE STUDIES

LAMIN SANNEH

The African Transformation of

Christianity: Comparative Reflections on

Ethnicity and Religious Mobilization in Africa

RACE AND ETHNICITY IN WESTERN HISTORY

In an article entitled "The Diversity Myth: America's Leading Export," Benjamin Schwartz, a historian and foreign policy analyst, speaks of the "diversity myth" that frames America's perception of, and prescription for, the world.[1] Although it is a distortion and an oversimplification, the myth constitutes "America's leading export." He says that the immigrant populations that flocked to the United States were subjected to a cultural process that did not so much cleanse America of its ethnic minorities as cleanse those minorities of their ethnicity. The American melting pot, he points out, "celebrated not tolerance but conformity to a narrow conception of American nationality by depicting strangely attired foreigners stepping into a huge pot and emerging as immaculate, well dressed, accent-free 'American looking' Americans—that is, Anglo-Americans." Sinclair Lewis recognized the melting pot, in *Main Street*, as a means by which "the sound American customs absorbed without one trace of pollution another alien invasion."[2]

In 1786 John Jay, one of the Founding Fathers, wrote in his second *Federalist* paper that "Providence has been pleased to give this one connected country to one united people; a people descended from the same ancestors, speaking the same language, professing the same religion . . . similar in their manners and customs."[3] In 1916, the liberal writer Randolph Bourne reflected in a similar manner on what makes America unique: "English snobberies, English religion, English literary style, English literary reverences and canons, English ethics, English superiorities"—these are what held America together, a cultural tutelage that made mashed potatoes of non-Anglo ethnic groups. A popular guide for Jewish immigrants advised them to "forget your past, your customs, and your ideals."[4]

When America as a new nation confronted the issue of ethnic and national difference (the issue, that is, of Native Americans and of national communities belonging to Britain, Spain and France), it adopted a policy of forcible assimilation. Thus were created present-day Texas, California, New Mexico, Arizona, Nevada, Utah, and parts of Colorado and Wyoming. Schwartz contends that America was involved in a three-hundred-year-long ethnic conflict with Native Americans in which one of two solutions was acceptable: extinction of the Native races or permanent quarantine in native reserves. It led a congressman from Georgia, Richard Wilde, to declare in 1830 concerning the destruction of Native Americans, "What is history but the obituary of nations?"[5]

All this historical evidence is indispensable background to understanding ethnicity and what came to transpire in the radical transformation of Christianity in Africa. Africa was colonized on the basis of the race theory, in particular on the basis of white hegemony. As Hannah Arendt pointed out, however, in contrast to the whites, Africans "do have a genuine race origin, they have made no fetish of race, and the abolition of race society [in South Africa] means only the promise of their liberation."[6] When used for Africans, "race" and "tribe" carry the meaning of a people without history or a knowledge of history. Race or tribe is not a self-applied designation: it is imposed in all its dense meaning. It entails the cultural meaning of a people with no historical record, specimens of nature unrefined by discipline, struggle, and self-control.

It also means geographic regions where nature is particularly hostile, as reflected in the wild habits of the natives. Cribbed and confined by nature, the natives lost out in the struggle from which only can develop a specifically human character and a moral temper. Instead, the natives perceived nature as their enchanted master and abandoned themselves to its mindless gyrations with awe and incomprehension. This was the view of Hugh Trevor-Roper, at that time the Regius Professor of Modern History at Oxford University. In a widely quoted remark, he insisted that there is no African history, properly speaking, because "there is only the history of the Europeans in Africa. The rest is darkness ... and darkness is not a subject of history. Please do not misunderstand me," he pleaded, "I do not deny that men existed even in dark countries and dark centuries, nor that they had political life and culture, interesting to sociologists and anthropologists; but history, I believe, is essentially a form of movement, and purposive movement, too. It is not a mere phantasmagoria of changing shapes and costumes, of battles and conquests, dynasties and usurpations, social forms and social disintegration." Trevor-Roper cast his remarks in a global frame, contending that "the history of the world, for the last five centuries, in so far as it has significance, has been European history." This being so, he concluded, Western scholars cannot afford to "amuse ourselves with the unrewarding gyrations of barbarous tribes in picturesque but irrelevant corners of the globe."[7]

Thus lacking the intelligence and purpose denoted by a historical sense, Africans were classified under "race" and "tribe" and given an objective status in anthropology. The classification acquired economic meaning: Africans were "drawers of water and hewers of wood." Then the political idea of domination and control merged all these meanings with the argument that the white race had attained through struggle the progress that separates human beings from nature, and so elected race inheritance established the hereditary genius of whites vis-à-vis nonwhite peoples. And then, in the nineteenth century, "race" was employed by writers such as J. A. Froude in his *Short Studies on Great Subjects* (1867–1882), Charles Dilke in his *Greater Britain* (1869), J. R. Seeley in his best-selling *Expansion of England* (1883), and Cecil Rhodes, the arch-imperialist, as a political symbol of white power and black subordination. Symbols are anchored in what one holds to be true, in values, and as such are liable to change and shift, depending on circumstances and context. Thus, in the high imperial era, say, between 1890 and 1940, aspiring blacks would compete for attributes of white power, knowing it was the only way to advancement and status, and in that competition they were sometimes among the staunchest defenders of a race society.

On this reading, Africa was afflicted with a double jeopardy. It served as an outpost of Europe's mastery, exploitation, and world dominance, and while thus repressed, it was held to standards of freedom and progress it lost under European hegemony. The central question became whether, given the extent of Africa's absorption into the Western political scheme, categories such as ethnicity, plural languages and dialects, and tribal fragmentation held in check under foreign overlordship left any room to African initiative, left any room for a distinctly African solution to emerge.

ETHNICITY AND THE MODERN MISSIONARY MOVEMENT

Through the modern missionary movement, Africa was offered a chance to answer the intellectual assault of the West, because the same missionary movement that identified itself with colonialism in terms of establishing schools, modern clinics and architecture, scientific agriculture, the emancipation of women, a bureaucratic state, town planning and modern means of transport and communication also identified itself with indigenous societies by fostering the use of mother tongues in Bible translation and literacy. Many European and American writers were inclined to a form of Trevor-Roper's argument that the history of Africa was the history of Europeans in Africa. These writers insisted that in instituting mother tongue development and literacy, missionaries extended European hegemony over oral cultures, with the superior technology of writing and systematic documentation overrunning the backward values of oral tradition. Besides, we were told, missionary motives were in any case suspect, being in turn hostile to native cultures and bigoted in doctrine. Consequently, any work or interest in African languages represented unwarranted interference.

This is not the place or time to pick through this line of reasoning, so provocatively stated by Trevor-Roper. But suffice it to say that it oversimplifies a complex theme and overlooks the point of so-called native victims being able to turn to their own account the things to which Europeans introduced them, including mother tongue literacy. For that, European motives could be discounted. Furthermore, African societies, insofar as they were living societies, were no more immune to change than other societies, and to condemn them to lost authenticity from having encountered Europeans seems particularly harsh, and without ground. Africans are not like children, fixed for life from the first white impressions. Thus you do not have to deny the presence of Europeans in Africa to believe that African history abides by its own internal logic, that African agency is authentic, that African themes are original, and that an African outlook on life shapes people's historical and moral consciousness. I make those and similar assumptions in my work generally, and here specifically.

Let me present the subject in this way. The missionary sponsorship of Bible translation became the catalyst for profound changes and developments in language, culture, and ethnicity, changes that invested ethnic identity with the materials for a reawakened sense of local identity. It is that theme I would like to expound with historical and theological materials.

In approaching Africa through the fruits of European science and literature, the West was dealing with a version of its own identity, with what was recognizable and acceptable in terms of the West's ascendant values. African doctors, African nurses, African clerks, lawyers, mechanics, engineers, teachers, and factory workers were such agents and mediators of Western medicine, law, engineering, education, and manufacturing. As long as Europeans were willing to accept Africans as equals, so would Africans be allowed to compete on Western terms. As Diedrich Westermann observed, "it is fortunate that the Africans are patient and intelligent enough to meet these requirements: in the case of Togo and part of Kamerun, the Natives had, within one generation, first to learn English, then German and now French."[8] But there would come a time when such equality would be denied, and those Africans who had gained their qualifications in those more favorable times would find they had become the victims of affirmative action of the quota kind; senior-level jobs would be taken and reserved for whites without regard to qualification. Africans were restricted to subordinate positions and kept in their place by virtue of their race, not because they were unqualified. The race policy of the colonial empire was the most wholehearted preferential quota program ever undertaken in history, and it was blacks who paid the price for it.[9]

Much of the policy was motivated by a benign paternalism, by the attitude that, as members of an inferior race, Africans were required to be placed under white oversight and grudgingly given promotion on the scale of civilization. That was the white man's burden, in Kipling's memorable phrase, the responsibility destiny had placed on superior races everywhere. The racism of apartheid is very different from this race policy, but only in degree, not in kind. Separate development is the answer to uppity black pretensions that spatial proximity with whites was apt to encourage. As long as Europe remained physically separate from Africa, there would be no need to introduce separate-but-equal policies. However, once Europe and Africa shared a common physical space, as happened with white settler communities in Northeastern, Central, and Southern Africa, then race and ethnicity became tools of political and administrative policy.[10] Thus race and ethnicity, folk and tribe, were constructed to capture and distribute dislocated Africans, to entrap unsuspecting hinterland populations, and to punish the recalcitrant among mission-educated natives for being inclined to step outside their place in the scheme of things. There is little debate that Western missions in general aligned themselves accordingly on this political fault line, adding to the drama of race politics in Zimbabwe and South Africa, for example, the moral passion of a Manichaean duel between good and evil, light and darkness, between the messengers of God and the dupes of the devil, between medical and development experts and the incubus and succubus of witchcraft. Similarly, the French *mission civilisatrice* was launched in this spirit to level the *native feudalities* and to abolish ethnic wisdom.

BIBLE TRANSLATION AND THE ETHNIC CAUSE

The exception, at least in unintended consequences if not in deliberate design, to this wholesale Western assault on the Africa of ethnic classification was the mother tongue projects of Bible translation that shifted the ground to African languages as things of native origin for which Africans had only God and the ancestors to thank and not the whites who gave the languages written form. In retrospect, it is hard for us to imagine what might have happened to Africans, and to the dark races in general, had Europeans as the master race gone through with the grim logic of domination and control to which they felt entitled by their technology and power. Let us remember, for example, that the invention of the science of eugenics, of genetics as social policy, coincided with Europe's complete mastery of the nonwhite races. And through the writings of Madison Grant, America promoted the race theory.[11] However, two important forces intervened to avert universal ethnic genocide. One was the growth and influence in the eighteenth century of the evangelical and humanitarian movement in Europe, in Scandinavia, France, and

Britain especially a movement that spawned the antislavery movement. The other was the contemporary missionary movement, if not in its rhetoric and ideology, then certainly in its field policy of mother tongue development.

Accordingly, in the language projects of modern missions, Europe confronted the native character of non-Western races in its irreducible profundity, in its core self-understanding, rather than as space to be filled with European speech forms and habits only. In that confrontation, only two responses were possible for Europeans. One was for them to say that blacks were too different from Europeans to belong to the same category of *Homo sapiens*, and may accordingly be excluded from the privilege of civilized company. The second was to say that given this difference as a mark of human diversity, there was no basis for saying that one race was superior or inferior to another, but only that the human condition was deeply marked by variety and difference, as Herbert Spencer maintained, and that given the uncontrived nature of the ethnic spirit, Africans might possess by that fact an advantage for the gospel that Europe had chosen to abandon. Both attitudes were prevalent, although the second was much truer to the facts and more attuned to field experience than the first. Consequently, the tribes and ethnic groups of Africa came to be furnished with the necessary cultural and linguistic apparatus for mother tongue development, and that gave them confidence not only in who they were but in what they were here for.

I have argued in *Translating the Message* (1989) that the "central and enduring character of Christian history is the rendering of God's eternal counsels into terms of everyday speech. By that path believers have come to stand before their God."[12] Bible translation has marked the history of Christianity from its very origins: the Gospels are a translated version of the preaching and message of Jesus, and the Epistles a further interpretation and application of that preaching and message. Christianity is unique in being promoted outside the language of the founder of the religion. Having abandoned the mother tongue of Jesus, Christians were freed to promote a Gentile religion, the religion of the uncircumcised and the non–Chosen People. Consequently, Christianity through Bible translation offered to the world a genuine share in the heritage of Jesus, however inferior in cultural attainment ethnic groups might be, or might be deemed to be. Similarly, with regard to those languages and cultures that had attained the highest levels of civilization and thus transcended tribal life, Christianity by virtue of its open policy on Bible translation would not surrender to them as an exclusive right the heritage of Jesus.

In Bible translation, hitherto taboo ethnic groups and their languages and cultures were effectively destigmatized while at the same time superior cultures were stripped of their right to constitute themselves into exclusive standards of access to God. In affirming weak and stigmatized languages and cultures, Bible translation bade fair to Western cultural prerequisites for membership in the human family. Bible translation breathed new life into local languages and equipped local populations for participation in the emerging new world context. This action results from Bible translation being based on the idea that all languages are equal in terms of their value and right in mediating the truth of God. By the same token, they are all equally inadequate in relation to that truth. No one language can claim exclusive prerogative on the truth of God, just as, conversely, no language is intrinsically unworthy to be a language of faith and devotion.[13] The message of God and the language of ordinary human communication shared the same moral universe, though no human language in any combination is identical completely with that message. The quest for divine meaning is not exhausted by any one historical approximation, even though such approximations are inseparable from such a quest or its results.

To reinforce this point, Bible translation looked to the common forms of local expression in all their rich diversity and paradox and by so doing enfranchised the language and speech of ordinary people rather than the elitist forms. There were corresponding implications for the affected societies and cultures. Where it happened, such indigenous social and cultural revival often set off mass social change.

Thus it was that indigenous religious and cultural categories received validation by their being adopted in translation. In few fields was this principle more important than in the matter of adopting the names of what were essentially ethnic deities as the God of Scripture, for in those names was contained not only the religious worldview but the rules of property, social structure, and personal identity. Almost everywhere in the mission field, missionaries and local agents had to confront three fundamental questions: (1) How else can we transmit the faith except in the language and experience of the ethnic groups to whom the message is being brought? (2) How may such ethnic groups connect with the message unless there is in the message itself a point of contact? (3) Finally, how best can we ascertain that contact point except through systematic attention to ethnic specificity as revealed in language, usage, and culture? Even missionaries who confined themselves deliberately to the development and technical side of mission could not entirely escape the repercussions of theological engagement with the local communities in which they lived. The striking mark of Christianity in its mission is its confidence that because God spoke to us all, then all human speech in its concrete ethnic diversity is hallowed for our ordinary and consecrated use. Therefore missionaries plunged into hitherto neglected languages and cultures to engage their immense potential for the message and to bring that potential into public harmony with the values of choice and ethnic fulfillment. Through mother tongue translation, Christianity would crystallize, not into a cultural confectionery as such, but into a power that can make God sound as sweet music to ethnic ears.[14] It conforms to the insight of the incarnation, namely, not that diversity is a human loan word but that humanity is the chosen language of divine self-expression.

The general principle of Christianity succeeding as ethnic fulfillment rather than as ethnic self-rejection has been well expressed by Professor Diedrich Westermann of Berlin, a former missionary to Africa. He argued that in each people, the mental life has evolved to produce an individual shape and a proper mode of expression. He went on, giving a striking illustration of what today we would call *inculturation:*

> In this sense we speak of the soul of a people, and the most immediate, the most adequate exponent of the soul of a people is its language. By taking away a people's language we cripple or destroy its soul and kill its mental individuality. . . . We do not want Christianity to appear in the eyes of the Natives as the religion of the white man, and the opinion to prevail that the African must become a pseudo-European in order to become a Christian, but we want to implant the Gospel deep into the soil of the African mind, so that it may grow there in its own African form, not as a gift of the white man but as the gift of God. . . . If this is to be effected, the Gospel and the

whole Christian education must take root in the mother soil of the vernacular. Only in this way will it enter into the African mind and become the medium of a new life—not of new forms of life—and of a regeneration of the people's soul. . . . If the Christian Church in Africa is to be really African and really Christian. It must be built upon the basis of the indigenous peculiarities and gifts of the people, it must become part of the African genius, and these will forever be embedded in the mother language. A people without a language and a tradition of its own is individually dead, it has become part of a mass instead of being a living personality. . . . If the African is to keep and develop his own soul and is to become a separate personality, his education must not begin by inculcating him with a foreign civilization, but it must implant respect for the indigenous racial life, it must teach him to love his country and tribe as gifts given by God which are to be purified and brought to full growth by the new divine life. One of these gifts is the vernacular, it is the vessel in which the whole national life is contained and through which it finds expression.[15]

THE THEOLOGICAL DIMENSION

The field dimension of Bible translation came to grips with this language issue and, in so doing, activated a profound religious process in African societies. James Green, the Church Missionary Society agent in South Africa, wrote that the issue concerning the word that the church should use to instruct the Zulu about God the Creator belongs directly to the task of theology. He did not wish to minimize questions of philology and other technical features of language work, but he was convinced that at the heart of the enterprise is the theological question: Has God been known to the Zulus in former times, and if so, how can we ascertain that? To answer that question, the only reasonable course was to embrace the terms that the Zulus, in God's own providence, had been accustomed to employ. It is the Zulu frame that would shape what missionaries brought, or thought they were bringing, for in the Zulu way of receiving the message, missionaries would awaken to the God who had preceded them among the Zulus. That was the first order of business. It was a necessary step. It had to be taken, and taken willingly and without delay. Yet in taking that step, the missionary committed himself or herself to the next step, namely, the natural developments in the Zulu worldview that Christian translation would have stimulated but that belonged with Zulu self-understanding, and therefore lay well beyond the power of the missionary to control. That further step many missionaries were unwilling to take, or allow to be taken, though there was little they could do to stop it.

Green saw the problem clearly and moved courageously to confront it. Thus he spoke of the phases of God's instruction of the human race. "God," he said, "revealed Himself to men by degrees; adding to that knowledge, from time to time, as they were able to receive the increase. We find, in addition, that God, in His ineffable love, when He began to raise fallen man to dwell in His Presence, humbled Himself to the level of man's ignorance, as witness the wording of the First Commandment. Those words, 'Thou shalt have none other gods but Me,' would be received by those on whose ears they first fell, as admitting that there were other gods besides the Lord, God of Abraham, and of Isaac, and of Jacob."[16]

By seeking to penetrate ethnic cultures and societies with the message of the Bible, translators found a paradox of the need to reconcile opposites. Green concluded that in the nature of the case, "we must look into the heart and mind of the Zulu, ascertain the principal features in his character, and denote God in the Zulu tongue by a word related to that distinguishing characteristic."[17] The task as Green described it would be very different from that of seeking to transmit the Western intellectual tradition, since, as colonial governments insisted, that was viewed as beyond the ability of "natives." Consequently, Bible commentaries, Bible dictionaries, and lexicons as the fruits of the Western intellectual tradition were left out of the work of translation. In that ironic way, African societies were shielded from Western intellectual domination. The only exception was in the field of theological training, where a relatively few Africans were educated in the Western tradition of commentaries, exegesis, and systematic thought; but even they would have to deal with the mass of Christian Africans weaned on the mother tongue.

As such, scriptural translation pointed in a different direction, toward the discovery of Zulu ways of thought and patterns of life as the functioning frame for Christianity. Thus the sort of proficiency required for receiving the message had its roots in mother tongue affirmation, for "the law which holds the earth in its orbit and regulates the fall of a pin, is the same law which has directed the Greek to call God *theos* [and] has guided the Zulu to speak of Him as Unkulunkulu. And that law we must accept with its consequences."[18] Scriptural translation turned the *ethnoi* into primary mother tongue agents, though many in addition acquired literacy in Western languages, which, in the case of English, did not remain unaffected.

A corresponding double effect attended the work of missionaries themselves, for by translating the Bible into the mother tongue, missionaries, with the assistance and leadership of local language experts, learned the vernacular and so made the strategic shift from the familiar Western idiom to a totally new system. Bible translation in its consequences affected ethnic sensibility, gave it material expression, moral affirmation, and a historical vocation, even if at the same time it mediated the spread of European cultural ideas.[19] In so many places in Africa, from the Ashanti of Ghana, the Kaka of Cameroon, the Gikuyu of Kenya, to the Ndebele and Shona of Zimbabwe and the Zulu of South Africa, we find in Bible translation work this ethnic theme being taken up, not in a cruel design to foment intertribal bigotry, but in the critical historical effort to reclaim and refocus the race instinct. Hence, in his *Schism and Renewal in Africa*, David Barrett described the many examples of Bible translation work and fellowship helping to break down interethnic barriers and overcome the cumulative residue of tribal grudges. John Taylor also gave theological voice to that theme in his suggestive book *Primal Vision* (1963). But he was hampered and diverted into empty speculation by the scholastic rules he had learned to follow, rules that did not allow him to grasp fully the potential of the ethnic force in the transformation of Christianity.[20] And what is equally curious in the copious historical literature on the subject is how historians are still dominated by ethnicity and tribe as subcategories of European race theory. Ethnicity and tribe are construed as colonial and missionary ploys of victimization, or—and no better—as examples of negative agency, of primitive tribes acting from malice toward their neighbors. Therefore, whether in victimization or in negative agency, the view persisted that what whites thought and intended had normative valence for what blacks did and practiced. Here the connection of white history with black history is one of

superimposition and capture. Edward Said has made this point bril-
liantly in his *Orientalism.*

However, vernacular Bible translation offers a more complex picture. On the face of it, missions did impose a written form on oral cultures and thereby interfered with internal morphological processes.
Yet in the logic of the case, mother tongue literacy freed up mother
tongue reserves for creative adaptation, as Albert Gérard has shown.[21]
Consequently, as students of culture, we can profit from understanding the theological nature of the missionary engagement with non-
Western cultures because, where it was the case, in their systematic
and successful cultivation of the mother tongue for translating the
Scriptures, missionaries went right to the heart of living cultures. In
this respect, James Green was convinced that in looking for the right
Zulu concept to adopt for God, missionaries should resist their own
scholastic bias and reject any rigidly abstract terms and instead settle
on those terms that have within them the idea of personality. Our
conception of God as infinite, unconditioned, and absolute, though
justified, should nevertheless not be allowed to obfuscate the idea
of personality. Biblical theology, Green insisted, warranted having
the paradox of these two contrasting conceptions of God, that is to
say, the paradox of God as an unconditioned infinity and God as a
personal deity. True knowledge of God demanded the concurrent va-
lidity of these two apparently contradictory ideas, so that what in
strict logic could not be predicated of God as Spirit and Architect became in the reality of religious life a necessity. The scholastic tenor
of the question of whether human beings first believed in an infinite deity and then by faith ascribed to such deity personality, or
whether human beings first knew God as the personal God and then
went on to acknowledge his infinity, was resolved by the historical
nature of biblical faith. That is to say, the whole debate about whether
monotheism or polytheism was the first or final stage of religious
development was not as illuminating as the discovery of the concrete terms by which the first dim awareness of God was signaled to
people, whether in Africa or among the ancient Hebrews. Moreover,
Green insisted, we had the warrant of the Bible for this view, because
in it the divine was revealed as a person, not just as an idea.

The question of whether, in using personal attributes for God,
we have not incurred too great a risk for any reasonable and proper

notion of God's infinity is at heart really a religious question. In other words, it was awe of the religious mind that prompted it to veer toward a sense of human inadequacy before divine transcendence, a human inability, for example, to unite infinity with personhood, to reconcile an incomprehensible transcendence with the human celebration of a personal God. Modern philosophy, Green objected, took infinity as a principle of speculative thought and, in so doing, sundered it from its religious roots to claim it as the perfection and crown of the system of human cognition. Thus philosophy of religion ended, as it began, in rootless speculation, speaking to the elite few of an abstraction, rather than to flesh-and-blood humanity of a progressive relationship founded on divine instruction. Thus, if we started from the religious roots of knowledge, we should see that the impulse to understanding was grounded in the encounter with a personal God, with a God who had spoken and acted and, as the source of living and meaning, was graciously available to us in the habits and languages of human community, in fact in ethnic particularity, if you will. In philosophy it was the accepted custom to speak of God as the Supreme Being; in religion the divine was spoken of as the living God. As long as we kept close to the soil, we would not split God between an abstract form and a personal deity. That was the spirit in which Green and his colleagues approached their work.

In the mission, this split, which has been such a fateful mark of modern Western thought, was not made, or made with the same effect.[22] Green cited a remark on this point to the effect that "all ancient religion, as distinguished from the primitive, labored under the total inability of even conceiving the idea of the *worship of God*. It split and went to pieces upon that rock; acknowledging, in a speculative sense, one God, but not applying worship to Him. The local, the limited, the finite, was, as such, an object of worship; the Infinite, as such, was not. The one was personal; the other impersonal. Man stood in relation to the one; he could not place himself in relation to the other.[23] In that formulation, the particular and the concrete merely functioned as idolatrous diversion, while the general and universal were emasculated of any specific content or power. That procedure sat poorly with experience and tradition. The question for religion at this point was how the conception of a universal God could be reconciled with worship of God in all the particularity and concreteness necessarily involved in worship as such, notably in the particularity and concreteness of language, symbol, ritual, aesthetics, music, dance, and art. It turns out, however, that these were not opposite conceptions but different levels of apprehending the real. The truth, of which ethnic particularity became a concrete hypostasis and a representation, was still capable at a different level of thought of more general, conceptual expression. It is a matter of the 'One and the Many,' of the *one* God and the *many* representations.

Thus could Johannes Christaller, the great missionary-linguist, urge Africans, especially Christian Africans, "not to despise the sparks of truth entrusted to and preserved by their own people, and let them not forget that by entering into their way of thinking and by acknowledging what is good and expounding what is wrong they will gain the more access to the hearts and minds of their less favored countrymen."[24] Thus, too, could Edwin Smith inveigh against foisting an artificial culture on Africans. He concluded that the African "cannot be treated as if he were a European who happened to be born black. He ought not to be regarded as if he were a building so badly constructed that it must be torn down, its foundations torn up and a new structure erected on its site, on a totally new plan and with entirely new materials."[25]

On the issue of colonial authorities imposing European languages such as English, Smith was cogent, saying, "to insist upon an African abandoning his own tongue and to speak and think in a language so different as English, is like demanding that the various Italian peoples should learn Chinese in order to overcome their linguistic problem."[26] Westermann, agreeing with Smith, appealed for mother tongue literacy. "If the African is to keep and develop his own soul and is to become a separate personality, his education must not begin by inoculating him with a foreign civilization, but it must implant respect for the indigenous racial life, it must teach him to love his country and tribe as gifts given by God which are to be purified and brought to full growth by the new divine life. One of these gifts is the vernacular, it is the vessel in which the whole national life is contained and through which it finds expression."[27] Both Westermann and Smith knew of the contrary policy adopted for India by Alexander Duff, and they were determined there would be no repeating of that in Africa.

Nor, for that matter, did the history of the northern peoples of Europe and North America entirely support Duff in the Indian case. Walt Whitman, in his *November Boughs*, spoke for his and other generations when he insisted: "I've said nothing yet of . . . the Bible as a poetic entity, and of every portion if it. . . . How many ages and generations have brooded and wept and agonized over this book! . . . Translated in all languages, how it has united the diverse world! Not only does it bring us what is clasped within its covers. Of its thousands there is not a verse, not a word, but is thick-studded with human emotion," human emotion that is the fuel of artistic and cultural creativity.[28] And thus did critics credit Tyndale with having "created the glories of English prose" in his translation of the Bible: "Though I speak with the tongues of men and of angels, and have not charity, I am become as sounding brass, or a tinkling cymbal": such are common, homely figures Tyndale employed that have survived as pearls in many of our versions. It is hard to imagine the scandal this caused to the cultural proprietors of the day. Sir Arthur Quiller-Couch, in his Cambridge lectures on the subject, reminded us that the idioms we assume to be original are not in fact so. Isaiah did not, he challenged, write the cadences of his prophecies as we know them; Christ did not speak the cadences of the Parables or the Sermon on the Mount as we know them. "These have been supplied by the translators. By all means let us study them and learn to delight in them; but Christ did not suffer for the cadences invented by Englishmen almost 1600 years later."[29] The story of the Bible in the West is the story of the soul of the West itself, according to Quiller-Couch. The sentiment is echoed in the words of the Catholic man of letters Hilaire Belloc, who testified that the English Bible in Tyndale's translation "created the glories of English prose," its spirit moving through the majestic cadences of the language.[30] Quiller-Couch concluded that our translated Bible haunts and moves us because "it is everything we see, hear, feel, because it is in us, in our blood."[31] You could not put the truth of cultural origin and practice into truer, more succinct, and more intimate words. The biographer of the Jesuit missionary to India Robert de Nobili takes up this theme of cultural intimacy and speaks of de Nobili's commitment in that regard, saying he "was aware that no amount of learning could replace the deepest springs within the soul, fed by blood, tradition and climate, and crystalized in a mother tongue."[32]

Pursuing this theme of the "native" impulse of the Bible, Whitman cites De Sola Mendes, who makes the point eloquently with respect to the Jewish roots of the Bible, the particularity of its ethnic ethos. Dr. Mendes wrote: "The fundamental feature of Judaism, of the Hebrew nationality, was religious; its poetry was naturally religious. Its subjects, God and Providence, the covenants with Israel, God in nature, and as reveal'd, God the Creator and Governor, nature in her majesty and beauty, inspired hymns and odes to Nature's God. And then the checker'd history of the nation furnish'd allusions, illustrations, and subjects for epic display—the glory of the sanctuary, the offerings, the splendid ritual, the Holy City, and lov'd Palestine with its pleasant valleys and wild tracts."[33]

It is this ethnic theme that has resounded in the tongues of countless African tribes, too. Thus here too the story of the Bible, of Bible translation, became the story of the tribes. The history, biography, and narratives of the Bible became weighted with local duplicates. Whatever the different or alternative narrative idioms, the whole range served to indicate the thread of the divine original: "the metaphors daring beyond account, the lawless soul, extravagant by our standards, the glow of love and friendship, the fervent kiss—nothing in argument or logic, but unsurpass'd in proverbs, in religious ecstasy, in suggestions of common mortality and death, the spirit everything, the ceremonies and forms of the churches nothing, faith limitless, its immense sensuousness immensely spiritual—an incredible all-inclusive non-worldliness and dew-scented illiteracy (the antipodes of our Nineteenth Century business absorption and morbid refinement)—no hair-splitting doubts, no sickly sulking and sniffling, no 'Hamlet,' no 'Adonais,' no 'Thanatopsis' no 'In Memoriam.'"[34] It is the special power of the Bible clothed in the mother tongue thus to bring together individuality and universality, with tribal yearnings, the strains of illiterate speech and the impulse of youthful life prevailing on God, and not just on the myriad of ethnically constructed angels and the other heavenly messengers.

As an intellectual matter, we are familiar with the dilemma that theology has rightly construed as the incompatibility of idolatry and worship of God, of self-moralization and trust in God. Yet we have not noticed, or not noticed to the same extent, the operative theology of Bible translation acting as a solvent on the race or ethnic problem by responding to its enduring yearning for messianic consolation and giving it the central figure of the New Testament, the figure of Nazareth, a tribal Jewish figure. In the historical record of the missionary encounter with African societies, this Jesus, born of Mary in Bethlehem, this man who grew up in Hebrew society and culture and was marked with all the Jewish characteristics of time, space, and blood, became the African's brother, example, and savior. The cosmic Christ, by contrast, stripped of the inconveniences of his tribal Jewish heritage, equipped with standardized toneless gestures, and refined in the astringent essence of rational formalism, never took root among the tribes. As Edward Wilmot Blyden noted, "Voltaire, who denounced the god brought to his country, was condemned as an infidel. But he could not recognize in the Christ brought from Rome the Jesus of Nazareth, of Bethlehem, of Bethany, of the Mount of Beatitudes or the Sea of Galilee, and in the rush of patriotic impulse exclaimed, 'Dieu n'est pas Français.' "[35]

Alexander Fraser reported in the *Church Missionary Review* (February 1908) the objection of an Indian, Keshub Chunder Sen, "that the Christ that we to-day preach in India is an English Christ, an Englishman, with the customs and manners of an Englishman about him, and the acceptance of whose message means denationalization, and who, therefore, must raise hostility in every true son of India."[36] Thus could my adopted Creole grandmother, Cecilia Moore, for example, say of the Jesus of Nazareth, the Jewish Jesus, "Na we yone" [He is our own], but not of the cosmic Christ we study in philosophy of religion.

As Blyden insisted, Christ's cosmic transformation tribalized him for Europeans whose intellectual elites harmonized him with the Western philosophical ideal, thereby evading the inconvenient facts of their own history. The Western quest for the historical Jesus ended up being a quest for the primacy of critical method, for what will conform to the West's rational scruples and cultural tastes. Accordingly Jesus was constructed as a fictional character who reflected prevailing agendas.[37] New discoveries outside the accepted idiom were ruled out, and so was the possibility that an African Christianity, founded on mother tongue affirmation and expressed in ethnic accent, could rise to take its place in the universal human quest for transcendence. The courageous if forlorn career of Albert Schweitzer of Franco-German Alsace, latterly translated into Gabonese Lamberene, for example, is testimony of this. His creed of "reverence for life" left little room for African ideas of God or for Africans themselves, whom Schweitzer kept at arm's length though he lived among them. Schweitzer has become an icon of the West, an Enlightenment hero who forsook a lucrative, secure career in Europe for a life of danger and deprivation in the jungles of Africa. Yet the Western adulation of Schweitzer contrasts with African attitudes to him. He thus represents a strange contradiction. Europeans honor him for not preaching to Africans, but Africans resent him for his aloofness, his condescension. Schweitzer did not believe in evangelizing Africans, only in doing good for them and being entitled to their gratitude. In his view, Africans lacked the cultural qualifications presupposed in Christianity. It was the duty of Europeans to remedy that cultural deficiency without requiring Christianity. The race matter was thus transmuted into a cultural matter, but even in that cultural guise, it was still a matter of race. Who would thus have suspected that the ideology of the cosmic Christ, and the Enlightenment dalliance with the historical Jesus, would create cultural barriers with African Christians? Or how Africans who flocked almost by herd instinct to the Jewish Jesus in preference to the enlightenment Christ would end up paying their ethnic homage in mother tongue hymns, songs, and prayers to the ruler of the universe?

THE EXAMPLE OF SAMUEL AJAYI CROWTHER
OF SIERRA LEONE AND NIGERIA

There are too many examples of such convergence between mother tongue affirmation and the appeal of the figure of Jesus of Nazareth to fit into the restricted space of an essay. The foundation was laid with the pioneering work of African agents, of whom Bishop Samuel Ajayi Crowther (1806?–1891), of Sierra Leone and Nigeria, was an outstanding example. Crowther was the chief architect of the plan to open up West Africa to the antislavery movement. Born around 1806, the year before the abolition of the slave trade, Crowther (the name was adopted from his missionary benefactor) came from the Yoruba town of Oshogun, from where he was captured by invading Yoruba Muslim forces who sold him to a Portuguese slave ship in Lagos. By a series of remarkable coincidences, he was eventually rescued in April 1822 by the British naval squadron and brought to Freetown, where he came under instruction.

Crowther was all too conscious of the danger of Britain imposing its cultural habits on the rescued Africans as the price for their emancipation, thereby offering the hapless refugees the choice of civilization at the expense of indigenous self-respect. Accordingly, under the terms of British suzerainty, Crowther looked for room to promote what he was as the necessary African transformation of Christianity. Here is his testimony with regard to his own mother tongue, the context being the newly created recaptive settlements in Sierra Leone. He is describing an event that occurred in Freetown in 1844, where Yoruba was used as the language of liturgy, the first such use. (The first celebration of the Christian ritual among the Yoruba took place in Abeokuta in 1842 under Thomas Birch Freeman, who was normally based in Cape Coast. But that celebration was not in the Yoruba language.)

> A large number of Africans crowded thither to hear the words of prayer and praise for the first time in their own tongue in an English church. "Although it was my own native language," says the Rev. S. Crowther, "with which I am well acquainted, yet on this occasion it appeared as if I were a babe, just learning to utter my mother-tongue. The work in which I was engaged, the place where I stood, and the congregation before me, were altogether as new and strange, that the whole proceeding seemed to myself like a dream. . . . At the conclusion of the blessing the whole church rang with *ke oh sheh*—so be it so let it be!"[38]

With his linguistic and ethnographic inquiries, Crowther formulated terms for Christianity as an African religion, with the use of African languages in Scripture, prayer, worship, and study to provide the new anthropology required for inculturation. It became a central plank of his vocation. Thus when he came under pressure to submit to missionary directives from London, Crowther responded by pleading African priority, saying the time was near when he should retire from the Niger Mission altogether and turn his attention to his linguistic work and the translation projects that he had neglected on account of the heavy demands of travel and administering stations on the River Niger. When the time was right, Crowther pleaded, "I should like to spend the remainder of my days among my own people, pursuing my translations as my bequest to the nation."[39]

Yet if Crowther was wary of harmful Western assimilation, he was no less mindful of the mischief of romanticizing traditional Africa, and so he launched a public campaign to scrutinize political structures and native institutions in the light of the new ethic of antislavery. Crowther's moral commitment to antislavery, sharpened by the events of his own personal history, sprang nevertheless from much wider principles. Africans were no exception to the rule of righteousness, a rule opposed to any compromise with slavery and its supporting chiefly and priestly structures. Crowther would not denounce or applaud indigenous institutions and native authorities merely for their being African. Rather, he demanded of them an unyielding, stringent compliance with the credo that slavery "is a great abomination in the sight of God." Pledging his total commitment to the cause, he wrote "for Zion's sake will I not hold my peace, and for Jerusalem's sake will I not rest, until the righteousness thereof go forth as brightness, and the salvation thereof as a lamp that burneth."[40] He would not spare tainted institutions and customs or exempt them from the purifying pains of critical historical scrutiny. The African transformation of Christianity demanded no less of Africa itself. Crowther's view of Christianity carried this historical perspective of the religion, not as a neat doctrinal package draped in approved Western forms and imposed on Africans in the interests of preserving religious dogma, but as a mediated teaching that must run its African course.

Crowther had encountered more militant alternatives to his policy of accommodation. There was first the view of those we may call cultural prescriptivists, who believed that a ready-made, one-size-fits-all imported template should be imposed on Africans, if need be at the tried and trusted hands of civilized West Indians, but in any case under imperial tutelage. Another was the evangelical pietism that, with its gnostic tendencies, eschewed worldly arrangements, including primitive cultures, and trusted instead in the preaching of the word to effect the wholesome moral and social emasculation necessary for salvation.

Sir Richard Burton, a founding officer of the Royal Anthropological Institute, who trumpeted his ideas of race supremacy throughout the length and breadth of Africa, was a cultural prescriptivist very much in the tradition of Madison Grant and Randolph Bourne. In that position, Burton attacked Crowther's work as pretentious, as a delusory view of Africa's civilized capacity. He derided the recaptives as "half-reclaimed barbarians clad in dishclouts and palm oil," and cankered with ethnic malice. For Burton, Africans, whether native or Creole, were a setback for "the ruling race" and for progress.[41] Such recaptives and their evangelical allies, Burton charged, were an obstacle to the real interests of Africa, whose people would be better off under firm colonial control. Instead, Burton lamented, the evangelicals and the humanitarians had succeeded only in combining with free enterprise advocates to transfuse imperial doctrine with "homoepathic doses of scientific political economy."[42] Aiming a barb at Crowther and his campaign to expand the cause to Nigeria, Burton declared, "No one is more hopeless about the civilization of Africa than the semi-civilized African returning to the 'home of his father.' "[43]

As for the evangelicals of the period, they were at one with the cultural prescriptivists in rejecting any agency role for Africans or for African culture, convinced that only Europeans could achieve the objectives of true conversion in Africa. Thus Crowther's work was deemed inadequate in the light of a reawakened sense of colonial and evangelical paternalism. Andrew Walls describes the general historical background and context as follows:

European thought about Africa had changed . . . the Western powers were now in Africa to govern. Missionary thought about Africa had changed since the days of Henry Venn; there were plenty of keen, young Englishmen to extend the mission and order the church; a self-governing church had now seemed to matter much less. And evangelical religion had changed since Crowther's conversion; it had become more individualistic and more otherworldly. A young English missionary was distressed that the old bishop who preached so splendidly on the blood of Christ could urge on a chief the advantages of having a school and make no reference to the future life.[44]

The answer Crowther gave to the cultural prescriptivists, the answer, that is, of the need for receptivity to African culture, was similar to the answer he gave to evangelical pietism. Christianity, he said, did not come into the world to undertake to alienate or destroy national culture. Even where it sought to correct false and oppressive ideas and structures, Christianity must still do so "with due caution and with all meekness of wisdom."[45] The system of mutual aid that might be found in African society should not be condemned or despised but appreciated for the example it offered Christians entering the culture for the first time. Even aspects of traditional culture that might strike the foreigner as puerile amusements that excluded the ideas of the spiritual and eternal, such amusements as stories, fables, proverbs, and songs, said Crowther, were actually a storehouse of knowledge and original thinking, as Christaller's investigations in Ghana proved. Africa did not have to become Black Europe to be Christian, for salvation was neither a matter of producing a breed of sanitized, blow-dried citizens nor a matter of putting to rout local systems of ideas and practice. Consequently, Africa's encounter with the West required separating Christianity from the West's political project and uniting it with Africa's own cultural priorities.

In looking to Africa's own cultural priorities, Crowther was drawn to African languages—it is scarcely possible to think of living cultures without a language—and their indispensable role in the historical development of traditional societies. Yet Crowther was also drawn in particular to African religious and moral ideas as the index of cultural priorities. For this reason, combining the techniques of field ethnography and the methods of moral reasoning, Crowther made extensive observations during his explorations of the Niger on people's ideas of God. Thus, although he noted somber aspects of their customs and traditional practices, Crowther was nevertheless enthusiastic about what he learned of religion among, for example, the Igbo people. He found that they had concise, clear ideas about God, ethics, and moral conduct. He said he heard references to such things among the Sierra Leoneans of Igbo background but had refrained from stating them as facts "before I had satisfied myself by inquiring of such as had never had any intercourse with Christians. . . . Truly God has not left Himself without witness!"[46] The idea that premodern Africa had anticipated in all relevant respects Christian teaching was stated by Crowther with such natural conviction that it marked him as native mouthpiece, not just as a foreign agent. His views had none of the collateral safeguards of planned economic developments as a Christian prerequisite.

Crowther credited the Igbos with crucial theological advantage. On this point, his journal is worth citing at some length:

> The Ibos are in their way a religious people, the word "Tshuku" [Chukwu], God, is continually heard. Tshuku is supposed to do everything. When a few bananas fell out of the hands of one into the water, he comforted himself by saying, "God has done it." Their notions of some of the attributes of the Supreme Being are in many respects correct and their manner of expressing them striking. "God made everything. He made both white and black," is continually on their lips. Some of their parables are descriptive of the perfections of God, when they say, for instance, that God has two eyes and two ears, that the one is in heaven and the other on earth. I suppose the conception that they have of God's omniscience and omnipresence cannot be disputed. It is their common belief that there is a certain place or town where Tshuku dwells, and where he delivers his oracles and answers inquiries. Any matter of importance is left to his decision, and people travel to the place from every part of the country.
>
> I was informed today that last year Tshuku had given sentence against the slave trade. The person of him is placed on a piece of ground which is immediately and miraculously surrounded by water. Tshuku cannot be seen by any human eye, his voice is heard from the ground. He knows every language on earth, apprehends thieves, and if there is fraud in the heart of the inquiring he is sure to find it out, and woe to such a person, for he will never return. He hears every word that is said against him, but can only revenge himself when persons come near him. . . . They sincerely believe all these things, and many others respecting Tshuku, and obey his orders implicitly; and if it should be correct that he has said that they should give up the slave trade, I have no doubt that they will do it at once.[47]

In Onitsha, Crowther took notes on what he and his party observed of the cult of Tshi, a deity with power to preserve people from witchcraft. A goat was sacrificed to the deity, the blood allowed to run into a bowl, and an invocation made over the victim: "I beseech thee, my guide, make me good; thou hast life. I beseech thee to intercede with God the Spirit, tell Him my heart is clean. I beseech thee to deliver me from all bad thoughts in my heart; drive out all witch-crafts; let riches come to me. See your sacrificed goat; see your kola-nuts; see your rum and palm wine."[48]

Race theory or colonial tutelage offered little scope or indication for the kinds of adaptations that characterized Christianity's introduction and inculturation in Africa. For that matter, Africa's own repressive chiefly structures and native authorities offered little scope, either. In the end, a society of recaptives was established to institute changes in the old political morality and to overthrow the old ethics of enslavement. Evangelical Christianity, freed of ideological denominationalism and fired by a Franciscan-like passion for social justice, made a pivotal alliance with antislavery to pursue in Africa a dual mission of emancipation and evangelization, a mission at first entrusted to Africans but later taken out of their hands.

In spite of serious political and cultural obstacles, African leadership remained crucial for the course and final outcome of Africa's encounter with the West in its colonial and missionary phase. Ultimately, mother tongue affirmation would complicate the logic of continued foreign overlordship, an affirmation that Bible translation and literacy did a lot to advance. In Africa and elsewhere, the boundaries of Christianity's cultural frontiers were expanded and deepened rather than being merely repeated, resulting in a shift of key and scale to local initiative, local enterprise, and local paradigm. Western forms of the religion, being themselves transformations of an earlier commensurate vernacular process, were scrambled within the African setting by the process of reappropriation and adaptation.

Another issue relates to the liberating and empowering effects of Bible translation in the native idiom. We need not insist here on an original affinity between a translated and translatable Christianity and the infinite series of complex indigenous adaptations and idioms arising from that. What remains a fact was the novel and empowering response on the ground, a response that the native idiom inscribed into the thoughts and habits of millions of people. The spectacle of a translated Bible, being at the same time novel and patriotic, empowered victim and marginal populations to take charge of their lives.

In closing, let me return for the final time to race and empire. It is a paradox of the West's missionary expansion in Africa that it should make the close link that it did with the antislavery movement in the strategy for developing native leadership. The antislavery movement established free settlements along the African coastline, and those free settlements opened the way for the intrusive impulse of colonial rule, but also for colonialism's nemesis with the rising aspirations of a resurgent class of receptives. It shows something of the deeper significance of the antislavery campaign that the movement, bolstered by the liberating effects of mother tongue mobilization, should produce the new African mobile classes, whose demonstrated ability would question colonialism's hegemonic claims. From Africa's complex engagement with Europe's presuppositions about non-Western cultures, then, a distinctly African Christianity eventually emerged, admittedly bearing all the marks of the West's exploits, of the West's machinery of literacy and the authority of the text, certainly, but still sufficiently endowed with mother tongue assurance to indicate viability for the power of old narratives. As I had occasion to write elsewhere, "What subsequently distinguished African Christianity was its being invested with the idiom of mother tongue translation, and its emerging from its indigenous transformation as a mass movement, fluent in the native Scriptures, untrammeled by Western borrowings, and able to respond to local life and values with inborn confidence."[49]

NOTES

1. Benjamin Schwartz, "The Diversity Myth: America's Leading Export," *Atlantic* (May 1995): 57–67.

2. Schwartz, 62.

3. Schwartz, 62.

4. Schwartz, 62.

5. Cited in Schwartz, 64.

6. Hannah Arendt, *The Origins of Totalitarianism* (Cleveland: Meridian Books of the World, 1964), 205.

7. Reported in *The Listener* (a BBC publication), 28 November 1963. The occasion was a series of BBC television lectures entitled *The Rise of Christian Europe*, delivered at the University of Sussex. Trevor-Roper's break with Arnold Toynbee was over this issue, because Toynbee, for Trevor-Roper, was too inclined to minimize or even reject the assured ascendancy of modern Europe over the non-Western world.

8. Diedrich Westermann, "The Place and Function of the Vernacular in African Education," *International Review of Missions* 14 (1925): 31.

9. Hannah Arendt says that the Boers in colonial South Africa discovered that British colonialism was not detrimental to their interests, and so "they demanded and were granted charity as the right of a white skin, having lost all consciousness that normally men do not earn a living by the color of their skin" (194). In that scheme, Africans passed from slavery to hired cheap labor and the dumping ground of mine and urban reservations.

10. Hannah Arendt comments that the philosophy of Thomas Hobbes "provided political thought with the prerequisite for all race doctrines, that is, the exclusion in principle of the idea of humanity which constitutes the sole regulating idea of international law. With the assumption that foreign politics is necessarily outside of the law of contract, engaged in the perpetual war of all against all, which is the law of the 'state of nature,' Hobbes affords the best possible theoretical foundation for those naturalistic ideologies which hold nations to be tribes separated from each other by nature without any connection whatever, unconscious of the solidarity of mankind and having in common only the instinct for self-preservation which man shares with the animal world. If the idea of humanity, of which the most common conclusive symbol is the common origin of the human species, is no longer valid, then nothing is more plausible than a theory according to which brown, yellow, or black races are descended from some other species of apes than the white race" (157).

11. Madison Grant, *The Passing of the Great Race, or The Racial Basis of European History* (New York: Charles Scribner's Sons, 1916).

12. Lamin Sanneh, *Translating the Message: The Missionary Impact on Culture* (Maryknoll: Orbis Books, 1989), frontispiece.

13. Such a favorable view of indigenous languages was not universally shared. Saul Bellow's famous attack on African languages as unworthy of great literary merit is a case in point. Some ethnographers expressed similar sentiments, as in the example of Sayers, who wrote on Sierra Leonean language: "Limba is a very fourth-rate language in which, so far as my experience goes, it is almost impossible to get any fine shades of meaning expressed." E. F. Sayers, "Notes on the Native Language Affinities in Sierra Leone," *Sierra Leone Studies* 10 (1927). In contrast, speaking of vernacular Bible translation, Westermann remarks: "No African languages have hitherto been found into which the Bible could not be translated" (28).

14. In his preface to his Zulu dictionary, R. C. A. Samuelson, the interpreter to King Cetywayo, affirms, "It is the mother-tongue which is sweet." *The King Cetywayo Zulu-Dictionary* (Durban: Commercial Printing, 1923).

15. Westermann, "The Place and Function of the Vernacular in African Education," 26–28.

16. James Green, *An Inquiry into the Principles Which Should Regulate the*

Selection of a Word to Denote "God" in the Language of a Heathen Race: With Special Application to the Case of the Zulus (n.d.), 4–5.

17. Green, 24.

18. Green, 41.

19. "The missions have realized from the beginning that if they wanted to reach the heart of the Africans and to influence their inner life, they could do so only through the medium of their own language and they have kept to this principle; even where a considerable section of the people know a European language. Church work is with rare exception done in the vernacular, and it is characteristic that most African books and periodicals deal with religious subjects. Only in this way was it possible and will it be possible in the future to build up an indigenous African Church." See Diedrich Westermann, *The African To-day and To-morrow*, 3d ed. (London: Oxford University Press for the International African Institute, 1949), 124.

20. The following statement is typical of what is suggestive and at the same time distracting in terms of ethnic meaning: "The genealogies in the gospel linking Christ himself with the unnumbered myriad of the dead are a symbol of the unbroken cord with which God will finally draw Adam back to paradise." See John V. Taylor, *The Primal Vision* (London: SCM, 1963), 171. Elsewhere Taylor draws on Greek examples to argue that Africans lack a sense of sin and guilt except where it is induced by external crisis and despair, and even there, Africans would seek remedy in projecting their feelings (176). Cf. Hendrik Kraemer: "Theology is the effort to reflect in a system of coherent thinking the religious apprehension of existence" (*The Christian Message in a Non-Christian World* [London: Edinburgh House, 1938], 111).

21. Albert S. Gérard, *Four African Literatures: Xhosa, Sotho, Zulu, Amharic* (Berkeley and Los Angeles: University of California Press, 1971).

22. Westermann stressed this as one of the most important effects of education in the mother tongue: "The teaching of the vernacular is by many considered as a waste of time; this may be true for the pure rationalist and for those who regard knowledge of a European language and education as two almost identical things. But if education in Africa means the full development of personality and of the organic growth of a new society, it cannot lose sight of the soil out of which the existing society has grown and the human values it has produced. The medium for studying and appreciating these things and for assigning them their due place in the new order of things is the Native language, and from this point of view it is one of the important means of education" (*The African To-day*, 128).

23. Green, 10.

24. Cited in J. B. Danquah, *The Akan Doctrine of God* (London: Lutterworth Press, 1944), 186.

25. Edwin W. Smith, *The Golden Stool: Some Aspects of the Conflict of Cultures in Modern Africa* (London: Holborn Publishing House, 1926), 295.

26. Smith, 303.

27. Westermann, "The Place and Function of the Vernacular in African Education."

28. Walt Whitman, "The Bible as Poetry," in *November Boughs: Complete Poetry and Collected Prose* (New York: Library Classics of the United States, 1982), 1141–42.

29. Sir Arthur Quiller-Couch, *On the Art of Reading: Lectures Delivered in the University of Cambridge* (Cambridge: Cambridge University Press, 1920), 137.

30. Hilaire Belloc, *Cranmer: Archbishop of Canterbury, 1533–1556* (Philadelphia: J. P. Lippincott, 1931), 193.

31. Quiller-Couch, 156.

32. Vincent Cronin, *A Pearl to India: The Life of Robert de Nobili* (London: Rupert Hart Davis, 1959), 173.

33. Whitman, 1140.

34. Whitman, 1140.

35. Edward Wilmot Blyden, *The Three Needs of Liberia: A Lecture Delivered at Lower Buchanan, Grand Bassa Country, Liberia, January 26, 1908* (London: C. M. Phillips, 1908), 31.

36. Cited in Blyden, 31.

37. For a summary of such treatment, see Charlotte Allen, *The Human Christ: The Search for the Historical Jesus* (New York: Free Press, 1998). Allen, for example, writes of Renan's *Life of Jesus* that it was a wishful self-portrait. In Renan's hands, Jesus was reduced to "a matinee idol, handsome and languorous, with perfect manners and winning ways, whose attractiveness to women added a sexual frisson to the traditional gospel stories." See also the review in the *Wall Street Journal*, 26 May 1998, A16.

38. Modupe Oduyoye, "The Planting of Christianity in Yorubaland: 1842–1888," in *Christianity in West Africa: The Nigerian Story*, ed. Ogbu Kalu (Ibadan: Daystar Press, 1978), 251–52. A similar contemporary story is told of an elderly Tartar who was given the first translation of the Scriptures in his own language. He "fell on his knees . . . and with tears in his eyes thanked God for having vouchsafed to him at least once in his life to pray as he should." See James J. Stamoolis, *Eastern Orthodox Mission Theology Today* (Maryknoll: Orbis Books, 1986), 26.

39. Cited in J. F. Ade Ajayi, *Christian Missions in Nigeria, 1841-1891: The Making of a New Elite* (Evanston: Northwestern University Press, 1969), 184. Crowther's journal entries show him in impressive form engaging matters of language and translation. See Jesse Page, *Samuel Crowther: The Slave Boy of the Niger*, London edition, n.d. 108; New York edition, *Samuel Crowther: The Slave Boy Who Became Bishop of the Niger*, n.d., 91.

40. Samuel Crowther, 30 September 1851, citing Isaiah 62:1 in a personal inscription in *The Church Missionary Intelligencer*, 1850. Isaiah 62:2 goes on to

speak about God's righteousness being extended to the Gentiles and rulers, a thought that would have been very much in Crowther's mind.

41. Richard F. Burton, *Wanderings in West Africa*, 2 vols. (London: Tinsley Brothers, 1863; reprint, New York: Dover Publications, 1991), vol. 1, 217. Burton returned to the subject among recaptives in Cape Coast, Ghana (vol. 2, 72–73).

42. Burton, *Wanderings*, vol. 2, 48.

43. Burton, *Wanderings*, vol. 1, 210.

44. Andrew F. Walls, "The Legacy of Samuel Ajayi Crowther," *International Bulletin of Missionary Research* (January 1992): 19–20.

45. Cited in Ajayi, *Christian Missions*, 224.

46. Ajayi, 57.

47. Rev. James Frederick Schšn and Samuel Crowther, *Journals*, 2d ed. (London: Frank Cass, 1970), 50–53.

48. Page, London ed., 127; New York ed., 107.

49. Lamin Sanneh, "Missionary Enterprise, Christianity," in *Encyclopedia of Africa South of the Sahara*, vol. 1 (New York: Charles Scribner's Sons, 1997), 288–97.

LINDA E. THOMAS

Macroeconomy, Apartheid, &

Rituals of Healing in an African

Indigenous Church

This essay explores how apartheid in South Africa was a bridge between the macropolitical economy of globalization and the microrituals of healing deployed by St. John's Apostolic Faith Mission Church (a black South African Indigenous Church). In response to the everyday exigencies of apartheid, I will analyze, as a case study, the acts of survival and resistance of the members of this congregation, which embodied a novel spiritual resilience.

Apartheid existed as an economic, political, and cultural system from 1948 (the election of the National—Afrikaner—Party) to 1994 (the first ever democratic election in South Africa). During this period, and even before, international global financial capital (especially from the United States) helped to sustain a profound racial asymmetry. Consequently, poor black South Africans have suffered immensely and, at the same time, have created a spiritual foundation for maintaining a sense of their humanity in face of material deprivation.

Though political apartheid has been voted out of power, still the legacy of economic apartheid, backed by U.S. financial capital and others, continues to affect poor blacks in a systemic and critical way.[1] In a word, the dynamic of global capital and the continued reality of racial economic dislocations will demand the necessity for rituals of healing for some time. Thus St. John's Church signifies the rapid growth of South African Indigenous Churches that attempt meaning making from their own sacred sources.

African Indigenous Churches (AICs)[2] have been established all over Africa as well as on other continents,[3] and yet their proliferation has been most apparent in the Republic of South Africa. Myriad theories abound about the reasons for their rapid and concentrated growth at the tip of the African continent, but there is no singular cause for their ascendancy.[4] The literature suggests that sociocultural, political, and religious variables played a key role in their emergence. These factors include, but are not limited to, racial intolerance in "mission" churches that negatively affected African cultures,[5] losses related to urbanization and Westernization,[6] and hardships connected with economic, social, and emotional stress.[7] Texts written by members of AICs underscore their ritual life, the role of the Spirit (umoya), and its power to heal.[8]

While an immense volume of literature has been written about AICs in South Africa generally, to my knowledge, no research has been published specifically about healing rituals practiced by members of AICs in the Western Cape in relation to Cape Coloured Preference Policies.[9] That such a study has not been published leaves a gap in our knowledge about AICs, since black South Africans in the Western Cape lived under special oppression because these government policies privileged Cape Coloureds.[10] Indeed, because of the Cape Coloured Preference Policies, black South Africans in the Western Cape experienced an additional layer of repression within the context of the oppression of apartheid.[11]

This essay examines (1) globalized macroeconomic support for apartheid as a context for the special oppression experienced by black West Capetonians, who are members of St. John's Apostolic Faith Mission Church located in Guguletu, (2) the testimonies they gave about issues that affected their lives, and (3) healing rituals they performed four times daily as a source of restoration.[12]

St. John's, like many AICs, brings together a community of people whose cosmology arises from the synthesis of precolonial African religion and Protestant Christianity.[13] I carried out research for this study from June 1991 through January 1992, July and August 1992, July and August 1994, and 1996. While participating in church services, being a part of the daily activities of several families, and conducting in-depth interviews, I sought to understand the ways that members singularly and collectively designed adaptive systems of support to oppose degrading social conditions that resulted from race discrimination and an economic scheme that created conditions of perpetual poverty for many black South Africans.[14]

Healing rites played a central role in creating a ritual process in which individual members who experienced *ukugula* (sickness/pollution) participated in dramatic presentations that ameliorated their afflictions. Healing at St. John's confronted ukugula directly. Such spiritual and physical "medicinal" rituals fought off types of sickness/pollution that encompassed anything that was a threat to one's wellness or health as it related to an assortment of issues varying from violence, unemployment, marriage, infertility, to family problems. In St. John's cosmology, to be sick or subjected to impurity (ukugula) included any one or all of these problems, since they compromised the well-being of a person and the community to which he or she was attached. Healing performances affected participants' minds, bodies, and spirits positively, so that they shared a mutual sense of accountability for each other's well-being.

Individual members, consequently, were less likely to be overwhelmed by social difficulties. When a member told the congregation about an ailment or adverse condition (ukugula) that he or she experienced, whether it was physical, social, or mental, the performance of healing rituals brought a degree of resolution for the individual and reliance on a faith community. With this as background, this essay will demonstrate that healing rituals performed at St. John's Church were a proactive communal theo-political device that enhanced the quality of life for Western Cape blacks living under intense apartheid structures supported by the globalization of finance capital.

GLOBAL POLITICAL ECONOMY

U.S. financial capital, along with similar investments from most of the European countries, backed apartheid South Africa throughout its history.[15] Without the presence and aid of American transnational corporations and banks, apartheid would not have been able to continue the economic, political, and cultural domination of its black majority population. Despite opposition to this racial system (e.g., from countries throughout the world, citizens within the United States, and the outcries from within South Africa), the primary incentives for investing in an international outlaw country, during this period of apartheid South Africa, were enormous rates of profit return, cheap and abundant labor, low taxes, and a favorable economic climate.

During the apartheid era, some of the earliest financial support came from banks. The First National City Bank of New York opened in 1958; a year later, Chase Manhattan Bank started its business. Though these financial institutions initiated activities in South Africa, they often hid their lending operations by coalescing with other bank branches. For example, Chase merged its enterprises with British Standard Bank.

Perhaps the clearest instance indicating the reinvigoration of apartheid South Africa by global capital occurred between 1960 and 1966. In March 1960 the Nationalist government massacred black demonstrators protesting nonviolently against mandatory identification passbooks (the Sharpeville Massacre). The international community mobilized worldwide condemnation against this atrocity, and global investments began a massive retreat out of South Africa. In fact, many suspected that the political system would finally collapse without its international loans and investments from transnational banks and corporations.

Instead, for the next six years, the First National City Bank of New York, along with nine other U.S. banks, infused massive loans and credit lines into the apartheid government. Similarly in this six-year period, American direct investments doubled. Previously, U.S. transnationals had focused on mining industries, but now they shifted to manufacturing, which was the fastest-growing sector of the apartheid domestic economy. Thus not only did the racial system not collapse, but it now became stronger and more self-sufficient.

By 1984, U.S. monopoly capitalist corporations held 60 percent of all foreign holdings on the Johannesburg Stock Exchange. And 350 to 500 American companies were conducting direct business; indirect operations (e.g., through shareholdings and loans) further increased their presence and impact. Throughout the apartheid era, American businesses focused on strategic industries. Caltex and Mobil Oil accounted for 40 percent of South Africa's oil during the 1970s. With a loan from the U.S. Export-Import Bank and technological know-how from the U.S. Department of Energy, the National Party successfully created a synthetic oil extraction process. And Esso acquired offshore drilling rights to pursue a diverse oil supply alternative. All these efforts moved apartheid toward self-sufficiency from numerous international boycotts.

Throughout the 1970s, Ford, Chrysler, and GM intensified their production of cars and accessories and, in fact, cornered 60 percent of the South African auto market. Between 1980 and 1982, the combined loan packages of the United States and the International Monetary Fund equaled the exact military expenditures of the apartheid government. Moreover, the United States became the apartheid state's leading trading partner for both exports and imports in 1981.

One can surmise the strategy of U.S. multinational corporations from their concentration in the areas of oil (45 percent of the market was controlled by Exxon, Caltex, and Mobil), automobiles and trucks (for civilian and military use), and computer technology. By the 1980s, American companies represented 44 percent of the petroleum market, 70 percent of computer activity (led by IBM), and 23 percent of automobile sales. General Electric produced the most electrical equipment under apartheid—equipment used for military electronics, atomic and nuclear energy, and aerospace.

Clearly, the apartheid state apparatus maintained its intransigence over and against overwhelming domestic and international pressures partly because of globalized finance capital. With this backing and confidence, particularly from U.S. multinational monopolies, apartheid intensified its grip on the daily lives of poor black Africans. The emergence of black African Indigenous Churches served as one form of opposition against the deleterious effects created by this intermixture of globalization and political-economic separation of the races. By focusing on the at-risk status of black South Africans in the Western Cape regarding the Cape Coloured Preference laws, the following section will add texture to what a globally backed apartheid system meant for one case study.

THE CAPE COLOURED PREFERENCE POLICY
AND BLACK SOUTH AFRICANS

The South African government officially announced the Cape Coloured Labour Preference Policy in 1954. However, through enforcement of the Black Urban Areas Consolidation Act, No. 25, of 1945,[16] influx control of Africans was even more meticulously regulated in the Western Cape than in other parts of the country. The Cape Town City Council, the South African government, and various Western

Cape employers acted together to ensure labor preference for Coloured people.[17] In 1946 more than nine thousand Africans were expelled from the region, and regulations were rigorously applied to keep others from entering the area.[18]

The victory of the National Party in 1948 meant a radical shift in the quality of life for both Coloureds and Africans in the Western Cape. Yet the downward turn in each group's quality of life was relative to the degree of subjugation each experienced and therefore must be considered in light of the way each group was treated by the government. Some Nationalists believed that the future strength of their party and its philosophy could be connected positively to Cape Coloureds,[19] while "Natives" were considered a threat and associated with the demise of the party and its control of the country. Thus, though both Coloureds and Africans were disenfranchised and subjected to the Group Areas Act of 1950, the Reservation of Separate Amenities Act of 1953, and other apartheid legislation, the National Party executed a "damage control" plan for Cape Coloureds. They performed this political maneuver to cultivate a group consciousness or identity[20] in the Coloured community that was both appreciative of the National Party and radically separate and decidedly different from that of African people who were even more rudimentarily and callously oppressed than Coloureds. Many "divide and rule" tactics on the part of the government created a chasm between Africans and Coloureds.

For instance, Coloureds were not required to carry passbooks, nor were they subjected to influx control.[21] Although the 1954 announcement by the South African government (that Coloured laborers in the Western Cape would be given preference) was a statement of that which was already effectively taking place, it also signaled more overt and aggressive action against Africans and African women in particular. An assault was launched immediately; indeed, African women in the Western Cape were the first people in the country forced to carry passbooks in mid-1954.[22] By the end of that year, twenty thousand African women were cataloged and forced to have a permit for their jobs and tenancy.[23]

The National Party sought even more clarity in its policy of appeasing the Coloureds in the face of a growing opposition movement on the part of the latter.[24] Several governmental agencies[25] advised the enactment of a Cape Coloured Labour Preference Policy that would elevate the conditions of Coloureds in the Western Cape.[26] Therefore in January 1955, Dr. W. M. M. Eiselen, secretary of native affairs, reported the establishment of a "Coloured Labour Preference Area" that would oust all Africans from the region.[27] Eiselen explained that such an area was being created because Coloureds had an honorable prerogative to seek job protection or work preference over Africans, the Western Cape was the "natural *lebensraum*" of Coloureds, and relations between these two groups needed to be curtailed because it was destructive to both.[28] To reinforce Eiselen's announcement, Dr. H. F. Verwoerd, the minister of native affairs, also in 1955, stated in a House of Assembly speech that

> the Western Province [is] the area where, due to a whole series of circumstances, the policy of apartheid in regard to the Bantu can be applied with the greatest ease and where it is most essential to take certain steps.[29]

Africans in the Western Cape continued to be harshly affected by influx control until the 1986 abolition of influx control bill. However, with so many Africans in the Western Cape having faced the chaos associated with the effects of influx control, it seems appropriate to ask a series of questions. How did black South Africans in the Western Cape deal with the difficulties to which they were subjected? What strategies did they develop to offset their anguish? What effects did influx control have on succeeding generations who lived in the Western Cape after influx control was abolished in 1986?

The answers to these questions will be difficult to ascertain. People, of course, had various ways of dealing with the challenges of influx control in the Western Cape. The members of St. John's (in the Guguletu township of Cape Town), who migrated to the Western Cape during the period of rigorous influx control implementation, articulated their own responses to such queries.

ST. JOHN'S MEMBERS AND INFLUX CONTROL

In 1991 the membership of St. John's consisted of forty-eight persons. Sixteen of the eighteen members (fourteen women and four men) whom I interviewed migrated to the Cape Peninsula from the Eastern Cape between 1942 and 1991.[30] Of the remaining two, one person was born in Cape Town, and the other was born in the Northern Cape Province. Out of the entire group of informants, four women talked explicitly about being arrested for not having passes; one of the four was arrested three times. All four were not defended for their infraction of the law, and all were kept in jail overnight in Langa after their arrest.

Mama Myira Zotwana,[31] who was apprehended two weeks after she came to Cape Town in 1952, told me about what happened when she was arrested:[32]

> I was called by my brother to come to Cape Town to take a look for a job at St. Monica's Home, but we were not given a permit to stay in the Cape. They gave me about two weeks. The next time I went to the office to ask for some more days, they arrested me saying I ought to have gone back to the Transkei. They put me in the office there by Langa; to sleep there that night. My sister-in-law came to Langa to fetch me the following day. She had to pay for me.
>
> I didn't go back to Transkei. I was staying in the home of my aunt and uncle. After that they [the officials] didn't meet me on the way going up and down. I did stay in Cape Town. I never had a job. Then I just got a husband and stayed here in the location.

When I asked Mama Zotwana why she was arrested, she responded:

> It was because we were not to come into the Cape. The Cape was for the Coloureds. That was the only reason they told us.

Mama Zotwana's story duplicates the experiences of others who came to the Western Cape looking for work and attempted to escape the harsh life of the rural areas.[33] When people arrived in the city, however, there were many deleterious challenges.

Several topics emerged, during structured interviews, as informants told me their life histories.[34] Because these conversations were conducted in June 1991, immediately following the abolition of the Population Registration Act and the Group Areas Act, the effects that apartheid had on the lives of informants and their families were discussed. Those discussions, outlined hereafter,[35] included issues about work, violence, and education as it related to apartheid. Six informants made explicit comments about apartheid. One man who had worked in the mines was extremely articulate about the ways apartheid affected his life. Women commented about apartheid's restrictions (e.g., segregated trains, marriage) and its relation to education and violence. Some informants talked about whether the repeal of apartheid legislation would bring authentic change to their lives.

Nozipo, age fifty-one, who was employed as a "tea girl" at a hotel in Bellville, said the following about apartheid:

> It is still very difficult to talk about apartheid, because there's so many things that don't encourage us;[36] that don't give us hope. Apartheid is slowly, slowly going away. But still you can see it's difficult to die. It doesn't die. It still exists.
>
> As for me, what I can explain is that I don't see any changes at the moment. There are places where they don't allow us to enter, even our wages are not the same with Coloured people. I don't want to say anything about it.[37]

While it was difficult for Nozipo to talk about apartheid or the lingering effects of the Cape Coloured Preference Policies and what she perceived to be inconsistent wage earnings between Coloured and blacks, she finds her voice and speaks about these issues. The cardinal point is that apartheid did not make her feel encouraged (a quality of life issue). She admitted that things were changing, but the ramifications of a racialized political economy and culture were still present.

Sixty-eight years old, Mama Mazibula talked about apartheid with some hesitation:

> I don't know how to explain apartheid, because most of the time I am working in the house, but I can say this. Sometimes you go and get on a bus. Then they say, you can't get in this carriage because it's for whites only. You can't go to this place because it's for whites only. You can't go on the bus, and even in the train, you can't get in first class unless it's first class that is for blacks only. There is a special first class for whites only on the trains. If you are late, you have to go to your own class on the train. They make a special third class for blacks. These are some of the things I see with my own two eyes. I don't see that apartheid has ended as de Klerk says. I haven't seen any action to end it. I just see that things are as they were before.

I might see a white person sitting next to me, but with other things there is no movement. It is still the same.

Mama Mazibula articulates the ambiguity of social transformation, a reality altered more in form than in substance.

Banzi worked in the mines in Johannesburg because he could not find work in the Cape. He was forthright in his conversation about apartheid and the consequences that it had had on his life and members of his family.

The violence here in South Africa happens because we are under pressure. The pressure is like this: black people don't get what they want. Apartheid divides black people. People are living in a terrible way. For example, the Group Areas Act divided us in our place.

Apartheid affected me very much because some members of my family are in jail. Some members of my family died, so it is something that affects my life. It has been very bad for me. For example, when I went to Johannesburg looking for work, there was a time when we were in the train and the soldiers and policemen came and hit us and shot us. I used to pray very hard because every day when I went to work I didn't know if I was coming back. So I prayed and God helped me a lot because I'm still alive.

Banzi associates apartheid with violence, black people's needs not being met by the white government, and oppressive structures such as the Group Areas Act. He is impatient with slow change. Apartheid has affected his family because loved ones had been jailed and killed.

Thobeka, age twenty-three, who followed her husband, a migrant laborer, to Cape Town, also made comments about violence, lack of food, and unemployment. She asserted the following:

We are hungry and we are pulling hard. It is so difficult for us. The violence in the townships is because the white people don't give us jobs. We haven't seen any action that apartheid has ended. If de Klerk says this is so, it is only in his mind. He lies. Apartheid laws are changed only in the minds. Even if I'm working, I don't get the same wages as white people. If you are looking for a job, you don't get a job. The cause of the taxi war is money.

"Pulling hard" is an expression that Thobeka and other black South Africans used to express an extreme sense of challenge as it related to an outside force's effect on them. The violence in townships, unemployment, and underpayment created stress for Thobeka, who even associated the taxi war with issues of money.

Forty years old, Thozama, who lived in a one-room shack behind St. John's Church, talked about the negative impact that violence had on children in townships. She worried that they would not have a future.

> I don't want to talk about the future because I'm just waiting to die. Even the future of the children is uncertain because of what's happening outside. I don't believe there is a good future for them. Already they have seen so much wrong in front of their eyes. So much killing. There's no future for our children.

Children were very much on the minds of those I interviewed in 1991 and 1992. Nozipo, whose testimony we read earlier, was concerned about her school-age daughter not being able to attend classes in Cross Roads because of violence. Nozipo was not only concerned about her daughter's schooling but had fears about the future in general because of the culture of violence that was a part of their everyday lives. She continued:

> Our own future is a problem. It's a problem, because you go out and you wait for death. You go into the train and you wait for death. You go into the bus and you wait for death. You go to sleep and you're afraid somebody will shoot you. Somebody will burn your house. Somebody will just shoot you. So, you just pray for the day that God will come.
>
> That's why now there's no hope for us. Now the only thing we can do is pray while we are in our houses. As you go out of your house, you get a bullet. You don't know where to go to be safe. So, the only way to be safe is to come to God, and pray and wait for your day to die. We only keep on working, trying to earn a little money to get what we need. The little things that we can get. If you get the chance to put away R2 [2 Rand,

South Africa's currency], you put it away, but you never know what's going to happen tomorrow.

One can conclude that there is a relationship between the documentation about the special oppression of blacks in the Western Cape from the 1940s to 1991 and narratives from those who were the victims of the harsh treatment that negatively impacted their quality of life. I argue that these statements (concerning violence, unemployment, underpayment, and children's futures) are connected to the ruthless years of apartheid and, more particularly, to the consequences of life controlled by influx laws. Informants' testimonies exhibit the worldview of low-paid, unskilled black Capetonians, whose lives, along with those of their families, were entwined and controlled by the production needs of the state.[38] That the government applied apartheid through influx control and other measures is unquestionable, as is the fact that these measures contributed adversely to the quality of life of black South Africans.[39]

If influx control and other apartheid measures negatively affected the intellectual, physical, and psychosocial aspects of those most harshly subjected to its oppression, how did they cope? I suggest that healing rituals performed at St. John's Church in Guguletu were one avenue to assuage the challenges of life in an apartheid city. The symbols and meanings encoded in these sacred "cures" denoted deep salvific and medicinal responses to the congregation's conception of sickness/pollution and restoration.

Furthermore, I argue that St. John's healing rituals were a proactive device practiced in a religious setting and may be viewed as a liberative theo-political tool in the context of oppression. Among grassroots people, healing performances and narratives offered alternative meaning structures, forged sacred space, and established moral and social stability in the midst of the hardships of township life.

HEALING AT ST. JOHN'S CHURCH–GUGULETU

St. John's Church began conducting services in Guguletu in 1958; however, before that time, religious meetings were held in Kensington under the leadership of Mama Shenxane. A new leader, a Reverend Xaba, became the minister at St. John's–Guguletu in 1979. Twelve years later, Reverend Xaba taught me about the significance of healing rites and gave me permission to interview church members. Commenting often on healing as the central work of St. John's, Reverend Xaba explained: "This church is a hospital (*isibhedlele*) and there are doctors and nurses here." My interviews with informants agreed with this assessment. They came to the church because they were sick (ukugula) and wanted to be healed or because they were related to someone who had been healed.

Sickness (ukugula) was a broad category that included anything that caused disharmony or discord in a person's life or the lives of their family members. For St. John's members, sickness/pollution (ukugula) included the negative impact of the influx control laws and the Cape Coloured Preference Policies. Consequently, when they performed rituals of healing for ukugula, they were responding to the negative effects of those statutes and legislation.

St. John's cosmology also included the categories "clean" and "unclean," which were drawn from Hebrew Bible texts (e.g., Leviticus) and from an African religious worldview in which the universe had to be kept in balance through the acknowledgment of unseen spiritual forces and the ancestors.[40] Church leaders and designated laypeople bathed and sprinkled sick persons with purified blessed water because pollution and cleansing stood at the center of the church's cosmology.[41]

In addition to sprinkling and bathing, the prescription for many illnesses included induced vomiting and the administration of enemas using holy water. Moreover, once a month, purification rites required members to travel to the coast and be fully immersed seven times in the ocean. Differing from baptism,[42] these practices contributed to building a trusted community of people who shared many things in common.

The political economy of apartheid and the utter destitution that it effected wove a unity based on the desire to be healed, marginal economic status, the experience of being unskilled laborers (the majority of the women were domestics or "tea girls"; one man cleaned a hotel in Sea Point, and two men were unemployed), a low educational level, and the experience of migrating from the Eastern Cape.[43] Perhaps the salient social circumstance that bound them together was that they resided in the Western Cape during the years that apartheid was enforced through influx control.

Each of the persons I interviewed was convinced that healing rituals made a difference in the quality of their lives. For some, their way of being was improved because they believed that they were cured of ukugula and protected from pollution.

For instance, migrating from the Eastern Cape to St. John's Church in the Western Cape, twenty-three-year-old Nyawuza explained why he arrived for healing in 1991.

> I came because I was sick. I have pains on my back, and all the time I have terrible headaches. All the time in my ears there is a voice. It is like somebody is talking in my ears. These voices talk in the middle of the night. I cannot even say what they say. I can only say that they talk, but I do not know what they mean or what they say. I went to the clinic [which practiced Western medicine] and received some pills from the doctor. The pills seemed to make no difference. I did not get better.

Similarly, Mama Ntiliti, who moved to Cape Town in 1942, explained her reasons for joining St. John's:

> I came to St. John's because I was sick and I could not get well. Medicine didn't help. I heard that I could get help from the St. John's people because they prayed. So I went there to the church. Well, I got well and I decided to stay.

She also elaborated on the rationale for other seekers who journeyed to the church.

> You can even go to St. John's when you have problems at your house. One lady at church said that her husband loves to quarrel for no reason at all. Ever since she came to St. John's Church and asked for prayer for her husband, he has stopped everything. They live like a perfect family. So, some people at St. John's are sick, some are not sick. Some come to church because they are unable to have children. They ask for prayer. They say, "We don't have children," and the minister or bishop prays for them. Afterwards, God gives them children.

Mama Mazibula, whose testimony about apartheid was presented earlier, adds further texture to this notion of sickness, travel, and "miraculous" healing.

One day after coming from church, I got sick at home. My family took me to the hospital. I came home from the hospital because I was not serious like before. I was just a little bit better and then I had a vision. I saw St. John's Church in my vision. It didn't take long for me to heal after I went to St. John's.

Thozama, a domestic, opted for both a medical doctor and the healing rituals of St. John's. However, operating beyond a narrow conception of sickness, the church understood the broader implications of illness and therefore was able to perceive her additional ailment of unemployment caused by ukugula misfortune.

I came to St. John's in 1988. I came because I was very sick. When I started St. John's, I was always frightened. When I went to the doctor, he said that I had a problem with my nerves. They treated me and explained that my nerves were what made me sick. I also came to St. John's because I did not have a job.

Finally, Thobeka traveled to Cape Town to be with her husband (separated by influx control laws) and because their child was sick. Once in the Western Cape, she sought out St. John's church.

I went to St. John's for two reasons. First, I was married in the church. Second, I had an illness which would make me become a diviner. We call this illness *amafufunyana*.[44] It is an evil spirit because you just become mad and you don't know what's going on in your body. You don't know what's going on with anything. Sometimes you run straight into a car because you want to be killed. You hit people. You don't know what you are doing. I had this illness for two years, from 1977 to 1979. The first St. John's Church I attended was in the Ciskei.

Some church members combined Western-trained medical doctors with indigenous healing rites. Yet the most consistent thread in the testimonies was that each person actively pursued healing at St. John's because on some level they believed that there was a possibility of being understood, valued, and restored. Those who went to St. John's for assistance knew that others had received positive results from treatments. For those persons, such evidence proved conclusive. St. John's made a difference in poor people's lives, and it had the power to heal.

Restated, healing rituals constituted a cultural system that improved the quality of life for people subordinated by macro- and microsystems controlling a significant part of their lives. Rituals of healing were a way for individuals to use their agency in a world in which they were burdened and plagued by the production needs of the state.

Along with the purification of blessed water and multiple prayer times each day, St. John's cosmology for healing also incorporated the ancestors, a critically important part of precolonial African religion. Born in the Northern Cape, twenty-five-year-old Tshawe talked about rituals conducted to appease the ancestors:

> The ancestors speak to God for us because they are nearer to God than we are. When the ancestors are unhappy, we do a sacrifice. We have to spill the blood of two chickens or a goat. Sometimes we put out sour porridge for the ancestors. Whatever we do for them must be holy and done in a holy place such as the church. If it is a beast that we slaughter, we burn the inside of the beast. We cannot eat the kidney, because that is the meat for the ancestors. The smoke that rises from the cooking of the meat is for the ancestors.

Mama Joxo talked about getting messages from the ancestors in dreams and the consequences one might suffer for not responding:

> When following these rituals, many people dream clearly, and see everything. A person may get messages through their dreams. If the messages are not followed, then it's bad luck for you. Sometimes you dream about your ancestors and they tell you what you must do. Then sometimes you dream of something that happened in the church. Sometimes your ancestors, your grandfather or your mother, the ones who have passed away a long time ago, appear. You dream of them talking to you and they say, "I'm thirsty." Then you have to make Xhosa beer so that everybody can come and drink it.

She continued:

> The only thing that I know is that the ancestors help you. They always keep you safe. The ancestors are related to the living because we come from them. Sometimes I slip into a trouble and

feel an evil spirit, but at the same time I feel that there is something safe that surrounds me. I can feel that there is a heavy thing that is around me. Then I become safe because the ancestors are living. They help me. God is also there. I make Xhosa beer and even slaughter something for my ancestors to show my respect and thankfulness for their protection. The Bible tells about the ancestors. Sometimes you see your ancestors, and sometimes they come straight to you. They say, "Don't go that way." Then if you force yourself to go that way, you have problems. I believe that we are together with the ancestors.

Thobeka, who had an experience with amafufunyana, explained who the ancestors were and the important tie between following their instructions and health.

The ancestors are the people who have died. They can talk to us. Sometimes they talk when you have a dream and sometimes they talk while you are awake. You have to respect the ancestors. You have to do everything they ask of you. One time the ancestors asked me for Xhosa beer. When the ancestors ask something of me and I do it, then I become healthy.

Ndsilibe, a thirty-year-old man who was unemployed and had never attended school, talked about the ways that the ancestors helped God.

We believe in the ancestors at St. John's and I will tell you about what we believe. First of all, the ancestors are ruling. When a child is small, he does not know God, so the ancestors rule the child. When a person becomes an adult and does something for God, he is also taking care of the ancestors. When a person becomes a Christian the ancestors show their actions. They need their work to be done. When a person does the work of the ancestors, he is doing the work of God. The Bible has a chapter that says to respect your mother and father. That's why we respect the ancestors because they talk and give you something. That is why we say the ancestors are working together with God.

The ancestors are a central part of St. John's healing cosmology, and those who migrated from rural areas to the Western Cape brought the ancestors with them.[45] Because church members believed that ancestors could cause or prevent affliction (ukugula), healing rituals incorporated practices that demonstrated appreciation and respect for these living but unseen forces. In short, all of my informants had faith in and venerated the ancestors and performed rituals to acknowledge their beliefs. For instance, some slaughtered animals or offered beer to appease ancestors, and others called on them in prayers. The profound location of ancestors in St. John's cosmology and healing rites enabled members to feel protected from pollution and comforted during times of stress.[46]

CONCLUSION

I have argued that healing rituals performed at St. John's—Guguletu were a proactive communal theo-political support system designed to oppose life-threatening social conditions that resulted from the rigid enforcement of influx control, Cape Coloured Preference Policies, and apartheid laws in the Western Cape. These statutes and policies existed due to the crucial support of globalized finance capital. Because St. John's members defined ukugula as sickness, pollution, stress, and strain, and because the effects of influx control laws and Cape Coloured Preference Policies fit within this definition, therefore the extra oppression on black Capetonians caused by this law and this policy was a form of ukugula. In response, St. John's members sought relief by performing healing rituals.

These rites of spiritual resilience and communal redefinition created an opportunity for people to gather four times daily in sacred space to craft religious routines that integrated significant symbol systems. For instance, members spoke to God about their experience of ukugula, acknowledged their ancestors, periodically slaughtered animals, sang songs, danced, and drank blessed water. These practices demonstrated that people proactively created communal events that brought together individuals who shared analogous life experiences, beliefs, and values. These activities also incorporated people who were similarly disempowered by macro- and micro-structural systems.

Moreover, these rituals were a theo-political device in that people's belief in supernatural powers created a theology of power that emerged from their life experiences. Theology, in this case, refers to

ritualization crafted in response to conscious and unconscious beliefs embedded in a community that performed practices that ex-
hibited their belief in supernatural phenomena. Hence a theology
of power helped the St. John's community reflect on their concrete
social situation as it related to their cosmology. This ritualized cosmology sustained members in changing social environments and en-
sured the continuity of the cosmology for future generations.

More significantly, healing rituals were artfully designed theo-
political strategies in the sense that people used their autonomy to
construct practices that enhanced their lives in a social environment where normal life patterns were actively disrupted and dis-
ordered. When church members came together to perform rituals,
they enacted self-empowerment and opposition because so many
black people lived in Cape Town illegally. While these rituals were
not actions that flew in the face of South African authorities, they
were events that empowered people to persevere in a hostile environment.

Finally, these healing rituals improved the quality of life for poor
black Christians who lived under extraordinary oppression. If one
agrees that people experience insecurity because they are uncared
for,[47] then we can also agree that rituals of healing above all other
factors provided a location and a set of experiences where individuals in the context of community were cared for in a deep sense. As
West so appropriately expresses it, AICs "attempt to create for their
members a more satisfactory quality of life than they might experience in some mission churches, and, a fortiori, in the secular world
outside."[48] There are many reasons for the ascendancy of AICs in
South Africa, and more study needs to be done on their presence in
the Western Cape in relation to Cape Coloured Preference Policies
and the special oppression of Africans. Such study would further expand our knowledge about the experience of discrimination against
black Capetonians and their strategies for survival, given the apartheid legacy contextualized by globalization.

NOTES

1. The postapartheid era has created opportunities for a new African middle
class. Yet the majority of Africans are workers and live in poverty. In particular,
most Africans still live in rural areas and in townships. In addition, monopoly
capitalism (both from abroad and that in the white Afrikaner and English-

speaking groups) remains intact. Political transfer of power has not at this point meant a transfer of capital ownership to the majority of Africans.

2. AICs are churches and denominations initiated and governed by black Africans. These institutions are also referred to as African Independent Churches. See Bengt Sundkler, *Bantu Prophets in South Africa*, 2d ed. (London: Oxford University Press, 1961); Harold Turner, *African Independent Churches* vols. 1 and 2 (Oxford: Clarendon Press, 1967); Martin West, *Bishops and Prophets in a Black City* (Cape Town: David Phillip, 1975); Itumeleng Mosala, "African Independent Churches: A Study in Socio-theological Protest," in *Resistance and Hope: South African Essays in Honour of Beyers Naude* (Grand Rapids: Wm. B. Eerdmans, 1985), 103–11; Itumeleng Mosala, "Race, Class, and Gender as Hermeneutical Factors in African Independent Churches' Appropriation of the Bible: A Final Report to the Human Sciences Research Council," in *Research Report* (Pretoria: Human Sciences Research Council, 1989); Luke Pato, "An Authentic African Christianity: Some Methodological Considerations," in *Toward an Authentic African Christianity*, ed. Luke Pato (Umtata: University of the Transkei, 1989), 25–36. They are also referred to as Churches of the Spirit (M. L. Daneel, *Fambidzano: Ecumenical Movement of Zimbabwean Independent Churches* [Gweru, Zimbabwe: Mambo Press, 1989]), African Initiated Churches, and African Indigenous Churches. See Glenda Kruss, "Religion, Class, and Culture—Indigenous Churches in South Africa, with Special Reference to Zionist-Apostolics" (M.A. thesis, Department of Religious Studies, University of Cape Town, 1985); G. C. Oosthuizen, *Empirical Studies of African Independent/Indigenous Churches* (Lewiston: Edwin Mellen Press, 1992). The term "indigenous" will be used in this essay because it clearly communicates the presence of African cultural artifacts, which are a central part of the rituals of these churches. The use of African cultural forms is a distinctive feature of indigenous churches. The term "independent," on the other hand, defines these churches in relation to various white mission denominations from which many of the indigenous churches separated.

3. Personal communication with Professor David Daniels of McCormick Theological Seminary in Chicago, Ill., 5 March 1996. Daniels reports that AICs are located in New York and Chicago. These churches are situated in U.S.-based urban settings where large numbers of African immigrants reside.

4. See Glenda Kruss's thesis for an extensive survey of the literature on AICs in South Africa before 1985. For publications about AICs in South Africa since 1985 see Jean Comaroff, *Body of Power: The Spirit of Black Resistance* (Chicago: University of Chicago Press, 1985); Mosala, *Resistance and Hope*; Mosala, "Race, Class, and Gender"; Harriet Ngubane, "Theological Roots of the African Independent Churches and Their Challenge to Black Theology," in *The Unquestionable Right to be Free*, ed. I. Mosala and B. Thlagale (Maryknoll: Orbis Books, 1986); Absolom Vilakazi, *Shembe, the Revitalization of African Society* (Johannesburg: Skotaville, 1986); G. C. Oosthuizen, *The Birth*

of Christian Zionism in South Africa (KwaDlangezwa: University of Zululand, 1987); Oosthuizen, "The A.I.C. and the Modernization Process," *Africana Marburgensia* 20, no. 2 (1987); Oosthuizen, *The Healer-Prophet in Afro-Christian Churches* (Leiden: E. J. Bril, 1992); G. C. Oosthuizen and Irwing Hexham, eds., *Afro-Christian Religion at the Grassroots in Southern Africa* (Lewiston: Edwin Mellen Press, 1991); Oosthuizen and Hexham, *Empirical Studies*; J. Kiernan, "The Other Side of the Coin: The Conversion of Money to Religious Purposes in Zulu Zionist Churches," *Man* 23, no. 1 (1988); J. Kiernan, *The Production and Management of Therapeutic Power in Zionist Churches within a Zulu City* (Lewiston: Edwin Mellen Press, 1990); Paul Makhubu, *Who Are Independent Churches?* (Johannesburg: Skotaville, 1988); M. Schoffeleers, "Black and African Theology in South Africa: A Controversy Re-examined," *Journal of Religion in Africa* 18, no. 2 (1988); Schoffeleers, "The Zion Christian Church and the Apartheid Regime," *Leidschrift* 3 (1988): 43–57; Schoffeleers, "Ritual Healing and Political Acquiescence: The Case of the Zionist Churches in Southern Africa," *Africa* 61, no. 1 (1991); David Chidester, "Worldview Analysis of African Indigenous Churches," *Journal for the Study of Religion* 1, no. 2 (1989): 15–29; Luke Pato, "The African Independent Churches: A Social-Cultural Approach," *Journal of Theology for Southern Africa* 72, 1990; Jean Comaroff and John Comaroff, "Christianity and Colonialism in South Africa," *American Ethnologist* 13 (1991): 1–22; S. W. Dube, "Hierophanies: A Hermeneutic Paradigm for Understanding Zionist Ritual," paper presented at NERMIC conference, University of Witwaterland, Johannesburg, 1991; Anderson, Allan H., "African Pentecostalism in a South African Urban Environment: A Missional Evaluation." (Ph.D. diss., University of South Africa, 1992); Khosto Kekana, "The ZCC: 82 Years of Mistery and Secrecy," *Challenge* 7 (June–July 1992); E. K. Lukhaimane, "In Defense of the African Separatist and Independent Movements in South Africa," paper delivered at Conference on People, Power, and Culture: The History of Christianity in SA, 1792–1992, University of the Western Cape, 12–15 August 1992; Linda Thomas, "The Cultural History of Apartheid and the Politics of Healing in a South African Indigenous Church," (Ph.D. diss., American University, 1993); Linda Thomas, "African Indigenous Churches as a Source of Socio-political Transformation in South Africa," *Africa Today* 41, no. 1 (1994): 39–56; Philippe Denis, "Making of an Indigenous Clergy in Southern Africa," International Conference, University of Natal, Pietermaritzburg, 25–27 October 1994; B. Keller, "A Surprising Silent Majority in South Africa," *New York Time Magazine*, 17 April 1994; Allen, Jonathan, "The Political Role of the 'Independent Churches' in South Africa: 1880–1992," paper presented at the Canadian Research Consortium on South Africa. Queen's University Kingston, Research Seminar Series: 4-94/95); Robin Petersen, "Time, Resistance, and Reconstruction: Rethinking Kairos Theology" (Ph.D. diss., Divinity School, University of Chicago, 1995).

5. Sundlker, *Bantu Prophets in South Africa*, 295; Trevor Verryn, *A History of*

the *Order of Ethiopia* (Cleveland: Central Mission Press, 1972); Jean Comaroff, *Body of Power, Spirit of Resistance* (Chicago: University of Chicago Press, 1985); and Linda Thomas, "Cultural History."

6. G. C. Oosthuizen, "The Place of Traditional Religion in Contemporary Southern Africa," in *Afro-Christian Religion at the Grassroots in Southern Africa*, ed. G. C. Oosthuizen and Irvin Hexham (Lewiston, N.Y.: Edwin Mellen Press, 1991); Martin West, "The Shades Come to Town: Ancestors and Urban Independent Churches," in *Religion and Social Change in South Africa*, ed. M. G. Whisson and M. West (Cape Town: David Phillip, 1975), 185–206.

7. Mqotsi, L. and N. Mkele, "A Separatist Church—Ibandla Lika Krestu," *African Studies* 5, no. 2, 1946: 106–25; and Martin West, "The Shades."

8. *Speaking for Ourselves* 1985; and Paul Makhubu, *Who Are the Independent Churches?* (Johannesburg: Skotaville, 1988).

9. Donald R. Aeschliman's Ph.D. thesis, "The Independent Churches of the Coloured People of the Cape Flats" (UCT, 1983), examines the variety and nomenclature of Independent Churches among Coloured people living in the Cape Flats. Aeschliman's focus on Coloureds indicates the significance placed on racial and cultural differences as it relates, in this case, to Coloured and Xhosa-speaking people in the Western Cape. To my knowledge, there are no scholarly publications about Independent Churches among Xhosa-speaking people living in the Western Cape. The Western Cape refers to the western part of South Africa and includes Cape Town and Guguletu, a black township outside of Cape Town. The Eastern Cape includes the rural areas in the eastern part of the country.

10. I am indebted to a personal conversation with Prof. M. E. West on 30 May 1996, who brought this significant issue to my attention and referred me to West, "Influx Control in the Cape Peninsula," *South African Labour and Development Research Unit*, Working Paper no. 50 (Cape Town: Saldru, 1983), 15–36.

11. I agree with Deborah Posel's argument that apartheid was not established as a "single, long-term grand plan," that capitalist interests were central to its functioning, and that the South African state was an active agent in its implementation. I also agree that the "making of apartheid" across the years undoubtedly involved conflicts and compromises among various policy makers and agents. See Posel, "Coloured Labour Preference Policy in the Western Cape during the 1950's in the Context of National Policy on African Urbanization," paper presented at Western Cape Roots and Realities Conference at UCT, 16–19 July 1986. See also Posel, *The Making of Apartheid, 1948–1961* (Oxford: Clarendon Press, 1991). However, I assert that black South Africans in this study who lived with the negative effects of apartheid "spoke" about it as an imposing single construction that was carefully crafted and intentionally executed by those with structural power. This is because although it was a sorted, negotiated, and compromised set of polices, apartheid had a comprehensively negative impact on black people's lives. This essay examines apartheid from the perspective of

those who did not have structural power and presents their understanding of the system's design and effects.

See Bekker and Coetzee, "Black Urban Employment and Coloured Labour Preference," Institute of Social and Economic Research, Working Paper no. 1, Rhodes University, 1980, 1; Tom Lodge, *Black Politics in South Africa since 1945* (Johannesburg: Raven Press, 1983), 212–13; West, "Influx Control," 15; Ian Goldin, "Coloured Preference Policies and the Making of Coloured Political Identity in the Western Cape Region of South Africa, 1948–1984" (DPHIL degree, Oxford University, 1984); Goldin, "The Poverty of Coloured Labour Preference: Economics and Ideology in the Western Cape," South African Labour and Research Unit, Working Paper no. 59 (Cape Town: Saldru, 1984); Goldin, *Making Race: The Politics and Economics of Coloured Identity in South Africa* (Cape Town: Maskew Miller Longman, 1987), 1–3, 71–72; and Posel, "Coloured Labor," 3.

12. During fieldwork, I traveled throughout the country with informants to cultural and church rituals, as well as to religious festivals in urban and rural settings. However, my primary research base and location for data collection on healing rituals was St. John's in Guguletu. Because St. John's members lived in Nyanga, Crossroads, New Cross Roads, and Khayelisha, fieldwork was also conducted in those townships, which are located in the Western Cape. I conducted interviews with eighteen of St. John's forty-eight members. These interviews detail illnesses described by members, their accounts of treatments received at St. John's, and their descriptions of the social situation in which they live. See Thomas, *Under the Canopy: Ritual Process and Spiritual Resilience in South Africa* (Columbia: University of South Carolina Press, 1999); and Thomas, "Cultural History," for details.

13. G. C. Oosthuizen, *Post-Christianity in Africa: A Theological and Anthropological Study* (London: C. Hurst, 1968); H. L. Pretorius, "Historical Trends in Transkeian Zionism," *Missionalia* 11, no. 3, 1983; Comaroff, "Body of Power"; and Kiernan, *Production and Management.*

14. Josette Cole, *Crossroads: The Politics of Reform and Repression, 1976–1986* (Johannesburg: Raven Press, 1987); Francis Wilson and Mamphela Ramphele, *Uprooting Poverty: The South Africa Challenge* (Cape Town: Oxford University Press, 1989); Yvonne Muthien, "Protest and Resistance in Cape Town, 1939–65," in *Repression and Resistance: Insider Accounts of Apartheid* (London: Hans Zell Publishers, 1991), 52–53; and B. Kinkead-Weekes, "Africans in Cape Town: State Policy and Popular Resistance, 1936–73" (Ph.D. thesis, UCT, 1992).

15. For in-depth treatments of U.S. global financial capital's support of apartheid South Africa, see Wellington Winter Nyangoni, *United States Foreign Policy and South Africa* (New York: New World Research Committee of the Society for Common Insights, 1981); Bernard Makhosezwe Magubane, *The Political Economy of Race and Class in South Africa* (New York: Monthly Review

Press, 1979); William J. Pomeroy, *Apartheid, Imperialism, and African Freedom* (New York: International Publishers, 1986); and Comaroff, *Body of Power, Spirit of Resistance.*

16. West, "Influx Control," 18; Goldin, *Making Race,* 71; and *H.A.D.* Vol. 10, 1986, col. 7660.

17. Goldin, "Coloured Preference," 160–61; *Making Race,* 71.

18. Marilyn Budow, "Urban Squatting in Greater Cape Town, 1939–1948" (B.A. (Hons) thesis, UCT, 1976), 41–42.

19. J. Albertyn, quoted in Goldin, *Making Race,* 86.

20. See W. Eiselen, "The Coloured People and the Natives," *Journal of Racial Affairs* 6, no. 3 (1955). See also Goldin "Coloured Preference," "The Poverty," and *Making Race* for a treatment of Cape Coloured political identity.

21. Goldin, "Coloured Preference," 179; *Making Race,* 86.

22. M. Horrell, *Laws Affecting Race Relations in South Africa, 1948–1976* (Johannesburg: SAIRR, 1978), 185; West, "Influx Control," 17.

23. Horrell, *Survey of Race Relations, 1956–1957* (Johannesburg: SAIRR, 1957), 71; Goldin, "Coloured Preference," 182; and Goldin, *Making Race,* 87.

24. See Muthien, "Protest and Resistance," for more on Coloured resistance in the Western Cape between 1939 and 1965.

25. These agencies included the South African Bureau of Race Affairs (SABRA), the Western Cape Committee for Local Native Administration (WCCLNA), and the Technical Advisory Committee (TAC). Kinkead-Weekes, "Africans in Cape Town," points out that WCCLNA and TAC played a surreptitious and unaccountable role in establishing the Coloured Labour Preference Policy (564).

26. Goldin, "Coloured Preference," 181; *Making Race,* 78; and Kinkead-Weekes, "Africans," 564.

27. Eiselen, cited in West, "Influx Control," 15.

28. W. W. M. Eiselen, "The Coloured People and the Natives," *Journal of Racial Affairs* 3, no. 6 (1955): 18; see also Eiselen as cited in West, "Influx Control," 16.

29. Taken from the House of Assembly Debates (HAD) vol. 87, 1955, col. 200. Deborah Posel, *The Making of Apartheid,* 87, notes that in 1951, Verwoerd indicated that the Department of Native Affairs, over which he had jurisdiction, would exercise supplemental constraints on employment of Africans in the Cape Peninsula.

30. Full demographic information about St. John's members can be found in Thomas, *Under the Canopy.* The following information provides salient data about members interviewed: the average age was 43.5 years, and the average level of formal education was 5.7 years. Seven of the persons interviewed were unemployed, five were employed, four were retired, and one was disabled and not able to work. The average monthly income of those interviewed in 1991 and 1992 was R394 ($141) for a family of 5.6. The average national monthly cost of living for an African household of five was R1,217 ($435). See Thomas,

"Cultural History," 171; *The South African Township Annual* (1992), 30. As interviews were conducted in members' homes, I observed that all lived in extremely limited space with several other people. Most dwellings were single-room shacks.

31. Pseudonyms are used throughout.

32. Myira Zotwana was in the original sample; however, this interview about her arrest was conducted on 19 September 1996.

33. West, "Influx Control," 17.

34. Interviews were conducted in Xhosa and translated into English by a research assistant.

35. I present direct quotes from structured interviews in order for the voices of informants to speak for themselves. This is out of respect for the request that members of AICs outlined in *Speaking for Ourselves* (1985). In addition, my goal in this essay is to have layers of voices in the text to which readers can respond, rather than only my interpretations. The selected quotations were chosen because they are linked to the argument of this essay. Full quotations can be found in Thomas, *Under the Canopy.*

36. It is important to note that Nozipo says, "There are so many things that do not encourage *us.*" Xhosa speakers often refer to themselves in the context of the community to which they are connected in conversations. For example, in greetings: Kunjani? (How are *you?*) Response: Sikhona, enkosi (*We* are well, thank you).

37. This and the other unattributed quotations that follow are from interviews, field notes, and research diaries of fieldwork conducted in the Republic of South African in 1991 and 1992. See Thomas, *Under the Canopy.*

38. See Budow, "Urban Squatting," 41–43; and D. Hindson, *Pass Controls and the Urban African Proletariat* (Johannesburg: Raven Press, 1987), 97–98.

39. See "Apartheid Lives On," *New York Times,* 29 October 1994, 19.

40. Mary Douglas, *Purity and Danger* (New York: Frederick A. Praeger, 1966); and J. Ngubane, "Some Notions of 'Purity' and 'Impurity' among the Zulu," *Africa* 46 (1976): 274–84. See West, *Bishops;* J. Ngubane, *Body and Mind in Zulu Medicine: An Ethnography of Health and Disease in Nyuswa-Zulu Thought and Practice* (London: Academic Press, 1977), 77; Kiernan, *Production and Management,* 189–93; W. D. Hammond-Tooke, "The Symbolic Structure of Cape Nguni Cosmology," in *Religion and Social Change in Southern Africa,* ed. M. G. Whisson and M. West (Cape Town: David Phillip, 1975), for information about ancestral shades and other spirit forces.

41. Douglas, *Purity;* Kiernan, "Poor and Puritan: An Attempt to View Zionism as a Collective Response to Urban Poverty," *African Studies* 36, no. 1 (1976): 31–41; and Harriet Ngubane, "Some Notions."

42. Sundkler, *Bantu Prophets,* 2d ed.; West, *Bishops,* 95; and Oosthuizen, *The Birth.*

43. See Thomas, *Under the Canopy,* for additional demographic material and

a full textual treatment on informants. Space does not permit the material to be presented in this volume. Pertinent data are supplied in the larger text.

44. See Ngubane, *Body and Mind,* for more about amafufunyana.

45. West, "The Shades."

46. West, "The Shades," 205.

47. Monica Wilson, *Religion and Transformation of Society* (Cambridge: Cambridge University Press, 1971), 66.

48. West, "Poverty and Relative Deprivation in African Independent Churches," in *Affluence, Poverty, and the Word of God,* ed. K. Nurnberger (Durban: Lutheran Publishing House, 1978), 245.

VIJAYA RETTAKUDI NAGARAJAN

(In)Corporating Threshold Art:

Kolam Competitions, Patronage, and Colgate

Every day at sunrise millions of Tamil Hindu women throughout Tamil Nadu perform the ritual practice called the *kolam*
on the thresholds of their homes, temples, and shrines (see
figures 1 and 2). These kolams, ritual drawings made of wet and
dry rice flour, are designed to invite, host, and maintain close relationships with the goddess of wealth, luck, and good fortune,
Lakshmi, and the goddess of soil and earth, Bhūdevi. Figurative, geometric, and abstract images in the kolam scatter as people walk
over these women's ritual creations; blessing and being blessed, they
are ephemeral "painted prayers," signifying auspiciousness and well-
being. In Tamil the word *kolam* means "beauty," "form," and "play."

This essay, primarily ethnographic in nature, aims to link contemporary changes in the women's ritual art of the kolam in southern India with forces of globalization.[1] This argument does not focus
on the kolam practice as such but rather focuses on one of the aspects
of the kolam, specifically, the expansion in the circle of patronage.[2]
What had previously been village- or neighborhood-scale sponsorships, kolam competitions are now increasingly being sponsored by
corporations, both local and global in the Indian context. The urge
to make the best kolam a woman can create within the competitive
context of other women making the kolam, a phenomenon that is
one of the many aspects of the kolam, motivates millions of Tamil
women. Over the past ten years, this notion of *potti,* or competition,
has been channeled into the context of a public arena. First, I set
out the ritual of the kolam in the South Indian context; second, I explore the contours of three kolam competition sites. In the last sec-

Figure 1. A Tamil woman at sunrise finishing a kolam with rice flour and dark red outline on her threshold during Pongal celebration. January 1999. Thanjavur, Tamil Nadu. South India. Photo by author.

tion of the essay, I analyze the possible reasons why a multinational corporation such as Colgate, based in the United States, would be interested in cosponsoring a kolam competition.

THE SETTING

The setting is southern India, where palm trees, banana groves, and village hamlets are scattered throughout a primarily rural landscape. Urban landscapes, however (for example, the cities of Madras and Madurai), are increasingly becoming more and more important to the shifting globalizing aspects of Hinduism. This essay explores the disjunctures and continuities across this continuum. Within these rural hamlets and urban neighborhoods exists one of the most common daily ritual practices in Hinduism—the kolam. This everyday ritual practice involves women emerging at dawn through the front thresholds of their homes to make rice flour drawings on the ground; the kolams can be simple or elaborate, depending on whether it is a festive day for the family. They are made to create a field of auspiciousness around the home, weaving a temporary drawing that provides Lakshmi (the goddess of good luck, health, and fortune) with an ephemeral abode.

This essay traces the location of symbolic action of this em-

Figure 2. A fourteen-year-old girl finishing a giant labyrinth kolam. Beginning with a grid of dots, she takes one and a half hours to complete the continuous lined kolam. Janury 1999. Mayiladuthurai, Tamil Nadu. Photo by author.

bodied ritual practice, the kolam, from a rural village context to an urban site such as Madurai, the second-largest city in Tamil Nadu. I examine these locations of the kolam through the phenomenon of public viewing and judging of these kolams. This Hindu women's ritual is related to the phenomenon of globalization in a most unexpected way. The public viewings of the kolam are now being enlarged from the small-scale, intimate, lane-by-lane viewings in village-sponsored, noncommercial, ritualized, and informal contexts to large mass public viewings in controlled, sporting arena–like areas in museums sponsored by multinationals such as the Colgate corporation. As Appadurai and Breckenridge inform us, "Mass cultural forms seek to co-opt folk idioms. This zone of contestation and mutual cannibalization—in which national, mass, and folk culture provide both mill and grist for one another—is at the heart of public modernity in India."[3] What we witness in southern India through the kolam is an example of this very zone of contestation and mutual cannibalization, producing new forms of modernity, religiosity, and postcolonialism.

TAMIL NOTIONS OF COMPETITION

From village streets to city neighborhoods, a subtle notion of potti (competitiveness) has long been embedded in the kolam practice. The translation of the Tamil word *potti* as "competition, rivalry, and emulation" does not adequately convey the playful aspects of the competition as perceived by the participants. Tamil women use the word *kolappotti* to mean "We are joining in the contest," with a feeling of participation and camaraderie akin to a ritual procession.

Many older women who had spent the early part of their lives in village contexts recalled the excitement of the kolam in childhood. In the morning, while walking in the village street on their way to bathe and swim in the *kulam* (a man-made pond), they would carefully examine and evaluate each of the kolams drawn on the thresholds of the houses. Together they would comment, critique, and wonder aloud at each kolam, deciding who had made the best that day. My mother once described to me the feeling of excitement when she was a young girl in her village:

> After we each had made our kolam, throughout the day when we were wandering up and down the village streets, we would

look at each other's to see if anyone did something different, interesting, or unusual. We would stand around awhile, memorize them in our heads, and try it on ours the next day. We would all try to make a beautiful kolam. But some days you were inspired, and other days you were not.

An elderly woman in her late sixties, Janaki, from the village of Thiruvar in Tanjåvur District, expressed it this way:

We had a lot of happiness in walking along and looking at each kolam. We would share with each other new ideas and how we could do it differently the next morning. If someone had come up with a new idea or new design, we all would immediately use it in our kolam the very next morning. Each morning that was what we talked about, who had done the best kolam for that day.

CONTEMPORARY KOLAM COMPETITIONS

However, the age-old sense of potti has transformed over time and through space as the kolam competition has moved from the threshold of houses to the sporting arena. Ironically, potti serves to maintain and increase the visibility of the kolam at a historical juncture when one might expect the kolam to become one of the dying traditional arts. In the face of modernity, postmodernity, and postcoloniality, the kolam ritual constantly reimagines and reinvents itself. This reimagining is fueled by the complex interactions between diverse interpretative communities and the shifting concepts of beauty that affect the reimagining process.

The kolappotti is gradually moving the kolam from traditional ritual contexts to public cultural spaces such as museums, temples, women's associations, and large festivals. For example, the kolam competition is being integrated into an annual ten-day event celebrating particular deities at various temples. The sporting-ground atmosphere at some of the kolam competitions is characterized by fixed times and places, prizewinners, and judgments of the "best" kolam. To increase their presence in the public cultural arena of contemporary Tamil Nadu, this movement is actively supported and guided by the women who participate.

The evolution of the kolam into the wider social arena via the publicly organized kolappotti raises important questions: (1) how are the changing distinctions between "public" and "private" cultural spaces reflected in kolam competitions, and (2) how do the kolam competitions reflect women's changing presence in the public sphere?

In my field observations of kolam competitions, I witnessed many changes in the traditional ritual and the nature of women's presence in Tamil Nadu as a whole. Not surprisingly, the sense of potti shifts in meaning and content among kolams created in a range of social contexts. Moreover, I suggest that a paradoxical phenomenon seems to be occurring; on the one hand, the kolam is declining in certain contexts, and on the other, it is becoming increasingly popular in different contexts. This paradox is observable in the increasing number of kolam competitions held throughout Tamil Nadu over the past ten years.

In this essay, I describe three very different competition sites to include a range of sponsors, participants, and environments. The first competition was sponsored by a village community in an informal setting in the heart of Tirunelveli District; the second was sponsored by a women's religious association in Madurai city; and the third, also in Madurai, was cosponsored by the Gandhi Museum and the Colgate multinational corporation. The first two sites represent the traditional context, and the third is modern in focus and intent.

A VILLAGE COMPETITION

The first kolam competition I observed was located in the village Krishanapuram, nestled in a crook of the Tambarani River in the heart of Tirunelveli District (for a parallel informal competition, see figures 3 and 4). Here I found the same scene Janaki had painted of her village potti many years before. Gaining a sense of the space the kolam occupied as an integral part of the ritual experience, I walked around the village streets for five days. The making of the kolam generated a wave of excitement among the women throughout the festivities. The feeling of being in potti (rivalry) for the title of "best" kolam maker in the village brought smiles, laughter, and heightened energy to all the participants.

How did these women compete in a village-style kolam competition? They began the day thinking quietly and discussing with the

Figure 3. A group of children standing on a series of kolams in an urban lane. Pongal celebration. January 1999. Thanjavur, Tamil Nadu. South India. Photo by author.

Figure 4. Village style informal kolam competition. Pongal celebration. January 1999. Kumbakonam, Tamil Nadu. South India. Photo by author.

other women in their households what kind of kolam they would draw that year to best "show themselves off." Then they prepared their materials of crushed powders and cleared the space in front of their houses. By nine or ten o'clock at night, after the work of dinner was finished, the women were free to begin drawing for the entire night. Contemplating the threshold space, they began in the near dark to draw their kolams with startling ease and quickness.

With nothing but the faint glow of kerosene lanterns punctuating the darkness between houses, from fifty to one hundred women performed the ritual throughout the village. For three to four hours, their concentration was unabated as the kolams took shape in the darkness. The women's efforts demonstrated that the kolam is more than a visual art form; it has as much to do with the body as the eye. The women created perfect and beautiful kolams, outlining the edge of the front of their thresholds. In the competition for space, the object was to run the kolams as close as possible to neighbors' houses without invading their territory.

When dawn arrived and the sunlight slowly streamed in, an incredible sight stretched from one end of the village to the other. Every street was covered with kolams, climbing the walls of the houses to about three feet, then traveling into and through the houses, as if an ephemeral carpet had been laid down. The effect was also like a delicate layer of lace, intricate in shape and design—a dazzling white, almost moving image of earth decorated and overflowing with rice. This resplendent image of kolams covering the entire village lasted for only a few hours in the early morning light. As the sun rose higher, the kolams slowly disappeared under the footsteps of passersby, and the sheath of intricate white patterns was transformed into rice flour on the bottoms of feet.

Because these were such elaborate and large kolams, it took the entire day for them to disappear completely. This gave the women ample opportunity to walk among the kolams, comment on each of them, and evaluate their unique qualities. Listening carefully to how they critiqued them and decided which was best, I observed their various impressions of the kolam. For example, one woman had maintained the symmetry over a large surface, while another had made elaborate color fillings. The women walked around all day among the kolams, judging them for their balance, clarity of expression, colors, motifs, and other characteristics.

By four o'clock in the afternoon, there emerged slowly from the informal discussions a consensus on whose kolam was the best and why. Every street had its "better" and "best" kolam makers, whose work was noted in communal memory and commented on further. The four or five women selected as the best kolam makers of that street would also be considered the best kolam makers for that year. In this way, all the discussions and informal aspects of competition and rivalry had remarkably clear results that satisfied the entire community. Everyone had done her best, a few were specially recognized, and no one's efforts were discouraged. Accomplished subtly and elegantly, street by street, village by village, without "judges" or public pronouncements, this was the prevalent form of kolappotti until recent times. Now we move to the second kolappotti, where the context shifts from a village to the city of Madurai, from the street to a more formal setting within the festival of the eighth-century female saint Antal.

AN ANTAL FESTIVAL COMPETITION

In 1993 I attended most of the ten-day Antal Festival and participated in the procession around the city of Madurai at dawn. The festival honoring the medieval woman saint takes place on the Madurai Meenakshi temple grounds, in the *Tiruppavai* office, and in the streets. Nearly one hundred women and children walk the four sacred boundaries—the four streets of the city of Madurai—carrying the image of Antal and stopping to receive gifts along the way. For these women, mostly housewives, the celebration of Antal is a way of getting out of the house and spending time with their friends. Antal, too, is out and about, visiting the city of Madurai. During this ten-day period, life revolves around the festivities of Antal, from kolam competitions, to ceremonies and dramas, to daily rounds of chanting sessions of her song-poems (the *Tiruppavai* and the *Tiruvempavai*).

The kolam competition during the Antal Festival in Madurai was organized by a community leader, Visalaksi, who is committed to circulating the songs of Antal.[4] The celebration of Antal is alive and well in Madurai, thanks to Visalaksi's devoted efforts since the early 1950s to propagate the Antal experience. Visalaksi is a big woman with a raspy voice that projects well in large audience settings. At different times a cheerleader, scolder, teacher, and organizer, she has single-handedly attended to the maintenance of the public cultural space dedicated to the memory of Antal. Visalaksi works tire-lessly throughout the year, especially during the month of Markali, when Antal's presence is highlighted. She runs weekly classes on the *Tiruppavai* that are well advertised in the daily newspapers, and she travels to the villages around Madurai to teach people about Antal. Visalaksi believes that following the path of Antal can reorder one's life priorities and help to cope with the loss of belief that comes with modernity. I had heard much about her over the years, and in 1993 I traveled to Madurai to see what I could learn from her about the relationship between Antal and the kolam.

Each year Visalaksi organizes the Antal Festival on her own. To attract more women to Antal, she decided to include a kolam compe-tition as part of the celebration in 1993. This communal event begins and ends with the singing of the Tiruppavai. In the context of the Antal Festival, the kolam competition is recast as a gift—an offering for Krishna through the women's adoration of Antal. "The kolam is very popular," she explained. "Everyone knows the kolam. Not everyone knows Antal. And I am hoping that the kolam competition will bring in new women for Antal. Everyone loves a kolam compe-tition. People will come to a kolam competition who may not think of coming for Antal." To reflect Antal's importance to growing num-bers of women, Visalaksi emphasized the need to include women from all castes.

At four o'clock on a sunny December afternoon, walking toward a handsome house on one of the narrow byways of the old city of Madurai, I heard the shouts of children running in and out, on the edge of the porchlike *tinnai.* The house had the large, open feel simi-lar to the verandas of the older homes in Madurai. The location of this public kolam competition had all the characteristics of a private affair, as if the interior of the household had simply expanded to the community outside. However, men were discouraged from entering the house, as it was intended to be primarily a woman's space.

A young boy, posted at the front door, politely asked everyone who entered, "Were you coming for the kolam competition?" He recog-nized us from an earlier meeting and ushered us inside with a mature sense of graciousness and a big smile. He had a disarming air of try-ing to do something that could not be done: to contain the energy of excited young girls about to begin a contest. As soon as we crossed the threshold, slipped off our sandals, and placed them on top of the growing pile, we heard the feet and voices of approaching girls. They were racing around the house, chasing each other down, and playfully pulling on each other's arms. "I am going to win!" a girl of about twelve or thirteen said to me, her face glowing with excitement. "No, I will win!" another girl piped up, and they rushed off in a wave of giggles. Looking a bit disconcerted and disoriented by all the commotion, a few small children took their place.

The house had been temporarily transformed into a playground, with no mirrors to crash into, no sofas to spoil, and plenty of open space in which to run around. Antal portraits, paintings, and mounted bazaar prints covered the walls. The women appeared to feel at home in this environment, even though they were among women from many different castes. Clearly there had been a lot of preparation and practice for the competition all week. Flocks of middle-aged Tamil women had organized the veranda on the second floor into a vast competitive space of chalked-out four-by-four-foot squares outlining the concrete floor. The girls, ages five to fourteen, were given a separate division of space from the women. A *pandal* (a broad coconut palm–fronded roof held up by bamboo poles) had been erected, the judges had been seated, and the materials had been organized. Everyone gathered around in the front room, where the sunlight was streaming through a central rectangular opening in the roof.

The women talked exuberantly among themselves about the kolams they were going to create. They exchanged design ideas in their kolam notebooks and chapbooks; in addition, they shared rice flour and other materials with those who did not have enough. Before the competition, each participant had been given a number to use in the contest, and now they were ready. After thirty minutes or so, each of the participants lined up behind the numbered square assigned to her at registration. Then there was silence, and a quiet voice said, "We can begin now." For the next two hours, the concentration was intense as each contestant tried to draw her best kolam.

The entire kolam competition lasted from five in the afternoon until ten in the evening. In this competition, I was unexpectedly invited to be one of the three women judges because I was involved in this kolam research. From this perspective, I was able to observe closely the articulation of the other two judges' tastes and expectations. I was surprised to see that the two judges disagreed on the importance of modern versus traditional designs. One judge felt that the very traditional, highly geometric labyrinth kolams were the most challenging, and therefore the most beautiful, and should be rewarded with a first-place prize. The other judge loved the modern kolams with their huge swaths of color-filled figurative designs. Surprisingly, I ended up being the tiebreaker and felt awkward doing so. In the end, it was innovation, variety, difference, and notions of modernity that prevailed in this competition. The aesthetic qualities rewarded were (1) degree of *latcanam* (shining, brilliance, luster); (2) density, such as whether the surface was constructed from layers of powdered colors, flowers, and even lentils; and (3) *putumai* (newness), that is, modern kolams. Here modernity was represented through more cartoonlike figures and complex pictorial scenes.

When it was decided which three kolams were the winners, all the participants eagerly walked around the site themselves to examine each of the kolams and make their own rankings. Because such drawings were regarded as icons of divinity temporarily invested with sacred power, the women would touch the kolams briefly with their hands and examine them closely with their eyes. These former contestants wanted to see what kinds of innovations had been made; for example, how color was used differently, the way the image was drawn, and how realistic it was. The comments made most frequently among the participants were related to the notion of *vèra mathiri irrukku*, "looking different."

There was a pattern in the kolam designs that was distinctly correlated with age. The older women who created the more traditional labyrinth kolams did not win this contest. The younger women in their twenties, many of whom incorporated newer elements into the kolam, such as pictorial representations and portraits, were awarded the prizes. The criterion of newness was clearly valued over the level of difficulty in execution. The older women (above fifty) complained about the selection of winners based on the "category of newness," which was unfamiliar to them. They felt that the level of difficulty and the symmetry of the frame with the design inside should be far more important.

One mature woman competitor who had made a large and elaborate white labyrinthine kolam complained that the whole idea of the kolam was changing to include color. She wondered aloud at the degree of skill involved in drawing a simple *figure* and filling it with beautiful colors. This launched a serious debate. For example, one woman commented: "If you call it a kolam competition, should you even allow the entry of color, this North Indian influence?" An older woman remarked sadly, "Soon these old kolams will not even be drawn anymore. How can we compete with color? If they wanted color kolams, they should have called it a *rangoli* competition! What is happening to the kolam? You cannot even recognize it anymore. These kolams do not have any *balam* [strength] or *satu* [power]. They are indeed pretty, but is that what a kolam really is?"[5] However, another participant observed, "If you do not allow color, no one will come for the competition."

After a brief, reflective silence, another woman articulated loudly, "We are becoming Punjabis. Just like in our clothes, our children are shifting from our Tamil *tavani* [half sari] to *salwar-kamiz* (loose pants with a knee-length shirt) so the kolam is becoming the rangoli. We are not even fighting for our Tamil culture. We are just wanting to be North Indian without even thinking about it." However, their voiced concerns went unheeded by the judges. Eventually the children became restless, and all the women left together, some disappointed and some delighted with their prizes of pots and pans. Furthermore, there was a sadness in the lack of unanimity between the younger and the older women. Now we move to the third competition, one that is strikingly different from the earlier two, partly because it was cosponsored by the Gandhi Museum and the Colgate corporation.

A GANDHI MUSEUM COMPETITION

In January 1994, a huge and popular kolam competition was held at the Gandhi Museum in Madurai. The setting, at the heart of a large public museum complex, featured huge open fields that could be divided with chalk into 150 individual spaces for the kolam makers. This contest had been advertised with a registration deadline in the daily newspapers. Hundreds of applicants were turned down because of space constraints, and a limited number of participants were finally selected by lottery.

The Colgate multinational corporation, the major cosponsor with the Gandhi Museum, had distributed banners advertising its products throughout the site. Some ten to fifteen managers and supervisors from Colgate were in attendance, supporting and documenting the event with their own film crew. The extensive planning and coordination necessary to create such a presence indicated that Colgate was well aware of the significance of kolam competitions and the potential to further the company's economic goals. Colgate's involvement in this type of cultural event was well timed, since India had recently opened economically to foreign competition.

At ten in the morning, the bright sun shimmered over the heat that was rising on the asphalt. In an open green space behind the Gandhi Museum, nearly 140 women and their assistants lined up behind six-by-six-feet chalked squares, which formed a rectangle the size of an athletic field. Hundreds of observers—mainly family and friends—had come to cheer them on. The competition area had been emptied of idle bystanders and cordoned off with a heavy rope. Although the press received permission to take photographs, the audience was not allowed to get too close to the competitors in order to avoid breaking their concentration.

In another field off to the side, a small area had been set up for nearly twenty men, who had been allowed to enter a kolam competition for the first time. Because the men's section was such a novelty, it attracted a great deal of attention and press. Everyone was curious about what the male kolam makers were going to do and how they would place in the competition. From the outset, they were considered to have a handicap because they were not women, and it was understood that the rules would have to be "bent" for them. Mothers, sisters, wives, and daughters helped the male contestants, and some had one or two male assistants.

The excitement was palpable as the starting time approached. Each woman and her assistant had smoothed the surface of their generous square by clearing it of twigs, leaves, and pebbles. In addition, they had carefully unpacked all the materials from small tin cans or plastic bags held together by rubber bands. Sketchbooks had been brought out, along with rough drawings and plans on small ledger pages that would serve as occasional guides. As the women waited expectantly with their sets of colored powders in front of them, they contemplated the square of space on the ground and imagined how they were going to fill it.

When the gun finally went off, the kolam makers sprang forward to their individual squares on the red earth and began drawing with intensity and purpose. The kolappotti had begun, and the contestants had only three hours to show off their skills. In the heat of the noon-day sun, women and men, Muslims and Christians, all competed at drawing their notion of the best—and hopefully winning—kolam. Their imaginations and aesthetic sensibilities would stand before the judges, who would descend on their final creations to determine the first, second, and third prizes. The winner of the citywide competi-tion would get an all-expense-paid trip to Ooty, a hill town resort in the Eastern Ghats. There were smaller prizes, such as sets of pots and pans, for the second- and third-place winners.

Many of the kolams in this competition took the form of portraits or landscapes that resembled posters or photographs, with words written inside the kolam and phrases tucked into the landscape mo-tifs, such as "Secular Harmony for All." Such writings expressed political sentiments in memory of the recent communal riots in Ayodhya, Bombay, and many cities in Northern India. Some echoed specific symbols of religious institutions; for instance, a cross and cathedral spire, an *om-cakti* sign, a *kopuram* (Hindu temple tower), and a mosque tower.

One man, a professional photographer in his early thirties, had entered the competition with a male journalist. Together they had created a landscape kolam depicting the recent Ponkal festival, in which men had competed in a bullfight. The highly dramatic kolam painting in black, white, and splashes of red featured a matador taunting a bull with his bright red cloth. The judges discussed the nature of this creation and firmly concurred, "That is not a kolam. That is a Western-style painting. That does not qualify as a kolam. We are not gathered here to judge Western-style paintings; we are here to judge the kolam."

The three women judges were keenly aware of the impact of their judgments on the everyday practice of kolam making in Tamil Nadu. They felt the responsibility of guiding the future of the kolam, from citywide competitions sponsored by museums and corporations and advertised in newspapers to neighborhood and village contests. Even "street" kolams—those made in the villages and neighborhood streets—were being influenced by kolam competitions, exhibiting posterlike messages for "Secular Harmony" and so forth.

The women judges, all considered experts on the kolam, debated what constituted a kolam. One judge, who had carried out a good deal of her own research, had a strong opinion that in a "real" kolam competition, no color should be used other than the traditional red and white. If there was too much variety in the colors, she argued, it became a Northern Indian rangoli. Consequently, among other issues, there was contestation about when a kolam should be considered a rangoli and therefore ineligible for the event.

Another judge, considered a great kolam maker in her own right, felt a sense of sadness in witnessing the disappearance of the genre of "labyrinth kolams." These kolams were abstract in nature like the "modern" ones but involved a very different set of design principles. They were created by laying down a series of dots and circling them with complicated, snakelike lines to achieve symmetrical shapes resembling a netting or maze. Traditionally done in white rice flour, the only outline of color was the brick red powder encircling it. Such precision required the ability to imagine the lines around the dots very carefully. If even one line should go astray, like a weaving that has a wrong design in it, the mistake would be obvious to everyone. These kolams were more mathematically difficult than the "landscape kolams" but less colorful than the "modern kolams." The judge expressed her regret that this entire genre was no longer represented in competitions because they were not considered interesting enough.

The third judge was a professor of music at a local college and had finished seminal work relating kolams to particular ragas in the South Indian musical system. The key criterion for her evaluation was creativity; that is, did the kolam maker stretch the genre of the kolam in a significant way?

There was a concern among all the judges about the changing nature of the kolam as a whole. Some important questions raised in this competition were: (1) What is the kolam? (2) In what ways can the form incorporate changes? (3) What types of changes should be encouraged or discouraged? For example, they did not approve of the trend toward secularization or the use of the kolam as a medium for textual messages. No matter how spectacular, the elaborate painting-like kolams and the pictorial-postcard style kolams were immediately rejected and excluded from the definition of the kolam. In the final analysis, the winning entries were those that most closely met the judges' definition of a great kolam: symmetry and balance, geometric complexity, and innovation (for a similar competition, see figure 5).

Today the kolam has come into its own in thoroughly "modern" public spaces, enabling women to carve out a new presence in contemporary Tamil Nadu. This transformation can be observed by women's active participation in hundreds of kolam competitions sponsored by informal village associations, women's groups, festivals, textile mills, museums, and even multinational corporations. Contests for the best-made kolam are even held by women's magazines. The women who participate in these competitions tend to be those who have free time and want to win prizes or make a name for themselves. Thus the kolam contests also provide multiple sites for observing the ways in which women are constructing a secular modern identity.

Yet the context in which women attempt to build a more public presence is layered, complex, and contested. It is important to distinguish the notion of "public culture" in the large-scale, institutionally sponsored kolam competition at the Gandhi Museum from the "public culture" of the rituals conducted by women in villages or city streets.[6] The experience of being selected as an excellent kolam maker in a huge sporting arena with hundreds of spectators is quite different from the semiprivate, semipublic context of the village. In the latter, kolam creations pass before the judgment of a small number of women in neighborhoods or villages, while in the former, aesthetic criteria are evaluated before large audiences in high-profile citywide events. Moreover, these events are covered by the media and thereby enter into the cultural space of a much larger community.

Traditionally, the kolam occupies the threshold space, straddling and linking public and private worlds, a liminal space where women outline the boundaries of their sense of place. The kolams of individual households communicate what is going on inside the house to the outer community. But today the threshold is increasingly becoming a guarded place—boarded, locked, and even screened—as the popular tinnai, or porchlike space, folds into the security of the interior space. The threshold of the physical house is shrinking to the point where street meets doorway, and locked gateways greet the

Figure 5. A Rotary Club-sponsored public kolam competition where each contestant and assistant is given one hour to complete their kolam. January 1999. Tanjavur, Tamil Nadu, South India. Photo by author.

passing visitors. As the outer edge of the house moves farther into the street, the threshold that the kolam occupies is gradually disappearing. This decrease of the porous flow of people provided by the tinnai is a loss for the engendering of community life. Yet with the progressive receding of the threshold, ironically, women's appearance in the public sphere has become more prevalent.

I interviewed several Colgate officials who had attended the third kolam competition that I discuss earlier in this essay. The corporate officials had traveled far and wide, from Calcutta, more than a thousand miles away, and other metropolitan cities throughout India. They were all male. Of what possible interest could the kolam be to Colgate? Why would they invest a significant amount of resources to host this ritual event in a secular context? Let us explore some of the possible reasons why.

At first, I was puzzled that Colgate would be interested in the kolam at all. In the climate of increasing globalization of multinational corporations, it is increasingly clear that Colgate, like Coca-Cola and other global corporations, is attempting to garner some economic entrance to the strong consumer base of nearly 200 million middle-class people in India.

Traditionally, in India "toothpaste" consisted of tooth powders, and these were placed on the hand and used for brushing one's teeth. As late as the early seventies, when I was living in New Delhi, I remember how we used a traditional black powder that was herbally based and locally produced. Other options for dental hygiene included brushing one's teeth with a neem stick, traditionally believed to be cleansing for the teeth. These neem sticks were freely and commonly available. At dawn throughout the Indian subcontinent, one would see men and women brushing their teeth with neem sticks. Neem comes from a plant, a local and indigenously abundant variety, and is available in the noncommercial realm. It is not yet commodified. Here is a daily product that produces traditional notions of "cleanliness" and "purity" that are outside the global market.

Through its local sponsorship of the kolam competition in Madurai, the Colgate corporation seemed to be employing the kolam event as a means of globalization. And yet why would Colgate choose the kolam as a point of intervention in the public sphere? First, household goods, especially those in the category of cleaning supplies, are usually purchased by women. Colgate, for the local Tamil woman, epitomizes the entry into the "modern" and the "global" economy and thereby conveys a cleanliness, a "purity" of result, a set of "white and glistening" teeth. The kolam too, in the traditional context, represents a cleansing of sort, a sign of ordering of the traditional cosmos, a creation of purity on the threshold, however temporary it may be. Although all the Colgate corporate officials I interviewed explicitly articulated their main reasons for involving themselves with the kolam competition as "the corporation's need to get closer to their consumers," "to express interest in women's arts," "to get to know their consumer base," and, in general, "to improve public relations," it is possible to chart some implicitly imaginary and yet blatantly metaphorical correlations linking Colgate with the kolam. We can see that the imaginary of Colgate ties together with the kolam in ways that at first are not so obvious. It is relevant here to quote Appadurai's theorizing of the cultural imagination, which readily applies to the kolam.

> The image, the imagined, the imaginary—these are all terms which direct us to something critical and new in global cultural processes: the imagination as a social practice . . . the imagination has become an organized field of social practices, a form of work (both in the sense of labor and of culturally organized practice) and a form of negotiation between sites of agency ("individuals") and globally defined fields of possibility. . . . The imagination is now central to all forms of agency, is itself a social fact, and is the key component of the new global order.[7]

It is clear that the Colgate corporation, whatever its explicit reasons may be, is only employing one form of public relations that drives its motivation to sponsor local kolam competitions in Madurai. This process is set on a course to legitimize itself within the local context by becoming embedded in a previously local indigenous and cultural and religious practice and by situating itself within the purview of hundreds of women. There were even many kolams that had written within their enclosed space, "Thanks, Colgate." One can wonder, then, whether the "whiteness" and "cleanliness" promised by Colgate ads are being reified in the public imagination through these local cosponsorships of the kolam.

Yet here it is important to note yet another layer of social complexity. The Tamil women who eagerly participate in these globalized contexts also seemed to impart a certain kind of agency, expressing and acting out of a desire to become part of the local public sphere through this transforming of a "domestic" ritual art tradition. Furthermore, the use of the kolam as a base to express political sentiments of religious harmony and encouraging the cleanup of rivers appeared to create an entirely new arena of public voicings of women's concerns, even in a globalizing context.

CONCLUSION

This essay has traced the physical, cultural, and metaphorical transformations of kolam competitions through three very different settings in contemporary Tamil Nadu. Out of the millions of women who make the kolam, only a few thousand participate in the citywide and publicly organized kolappottis. Yet all the kolappottis, from village to urban contexts, can be viewed as "exhibitions" in which ritual has become an aesthetic value. The women have a sense of displaying themselves and their skills in the public context. "We come to show off," many women say to each other while laughing.[8] As we have seen, competition among the women, whether in a village, town, or city, is intense and focused. The qualities of exhibition, critical examination, and aesthetic evaluation are consistent from the ritual context of the village competition to the Antal Festival contests to the Gandhi Museum event. Such adaptability is possible because exhibition is not alien to the traditional ritual practice of the kolam.

Many historians and anthropologists have studied the presentation of "traditional" rituals in public cultural spaces throughout South Asia. For example, Sandra Freitag has examined "the realm in which community has been expressed and redefined through collective activities in public spaces." According to Freitag, this context is

a coherent, consistent one of symbolic behavior—a realm of "public arenas." Such a realm impinged simultaneously on two worlds—that encompassing activity by locally constituted groups, and that structured by state institutions. Originally just the realm in which collective activities were staged, it became an alternative world to that structured by the imperial regime, providing legitimacy and recognition to a range of actors and values denied place in the imperial order.[9]

Although Freitag focuses on the particularities of colonial India, her description of "public arenas" in which symbolic behavior serves to recognize and legitimize a range of local groups and values is useful in understanding the concept of "public culture."

In the Gandhi Museum context, in contrast to the other more traditional kolam competitions I witnessed, there was a widespread inclusion and acceptance of all participants. The "range of actors," or competitors, was expanded to include men, Muslims, and Christians. The theme echoed by participants and spectators alike was "The kolam is not a Hindu ritual; it is really a Tamil cultural activity. Any Tamil can participate, male or female, Hindu, Muslim, or Christian, or from any other religion." In the days following this most publicly displayed kolam contest, I visited some of the Muslim and Christian houses to interview the kolam competitors, their mothers, and even their grandmothers. The grandmothers, as one might expect, were not happy about their Muslim teenage grandsons participating in a kolam competition, and I was discouraged from speaking to them about it. The fathers were also not supportive of their sons participating in a Hindu women's ritual competition. The mothers, however, encouraged the new trend, saying, "It is a talent that should be encouraged and supported and nurtured. The boys are developing their sense of art."

This process of secularization of a traditional customary ritual art form parallels James Clifford's understanding of the creation of the "cultural" or "aesthetic." He argues that "the categories of art and culture . . . are strongly secular. 'Religious' objects can be valued as great art (an altarpiece by Giotto), as folk art (the decorations on a Latin American popular saint's shrine), or as cultural artifact (an Indian rattle). . . . What 'value', however, is stripped from an altarpiece when it is moved out of a functioning church . . . ? Its specific power or sacredness is relocated to a general aesthetic realm."[10]

Lavine and Karp's discussion of museum exhibition sheds a different light on the significance of the Gandhi Museum competition:

> What is at stake in struggles for control over objects and the modes of exhibiting them, finally, is articulation of identity.

Exhibitions represent identity, either directly, through assertion, or indirectly, by implication. When cultural "others" are implicated, exhibitions tell us who we are, and perhaps most significant, who we are not. Exhibitions are privileged arenas for presenting images of self and "other."[11]

I suggest that the sense of exhibition in the kolam competition at the Gandhi Museum engenders a "ritual of belonging." Even in the motifs of the kolams, the articulation of a plurality of identities reveals a commitment to accommodating the presence of the "other" —the Muslim, the Christian, among other themes—in women's public culture in Tamil Nadu. The widening of a competitive arena that had previously been open only to women reveals a confidence and verve for the new directions in which the kolam is moving. Yet I wonder if the "ritual of belonging" that this kolam competition engenders is an entry point into a global identity rather than a Tamil cultural identity.

Today the kolam is transforming dramatically. In the public spaces of the kolam competitions, the artistic form has become the primary focus, secularizing its religious beginnings. The new aesthetics of color range from red and white to vivid purple and green; the geometry ranges from the traditional labyrinth to the elaborate figure, portrait, and landscape drawings. As we have seen, some of the new genres of kolams are posterlike representations carrying messages for mass readership. The penetration of corporate sponsorship into kolam events is increasingly visible, even influencing the drawings themselves. For example, words such as "clean," "white," and "fresh" are increasingly found within the kolam, and some have a bright, advertisement-like quality.

At times it can seem as if modernization and development are slowly turning the kolam into an aesthetic object, stripped of many of its ritual and resonant meanings. Yet paradoxically, while it is widely considered a symbol of "tradition" and culture, the kolam can accommodate remarkable changes in form, substance, and style depending on the context. Meanwhile women are attempting to discourage the changing kolams from becoming a purely aesthetic object, akin to Western-style paintings, by refusing to award them prizes. Henry Glassie observes that "cultures and traditions are created, invented . . . willfully compiled by knowledgeable individuals . . . out of experience."[12] Thus indigenous religious kolam competitions can be analyzed as sites of significant cultural activity that reflect complex, shifting values and preferences within the broader Tamil society now impacted by global realities.

NOTES

1. I would especially like to thank Lois Lorentzen, who first asked me to revise this essay for this book, and Eduardo Mendieta for his clear, perceptive, and incisive comments. The material in this essay is largely an extended and altered version of essay 6 in my doctoral dissertation at the University of California–Berkeley, submitted in 1998. This essay was first written in 1994 for the Western Regional Conference of the American Academy of Religion in Claremont, California. I would especially like to thank Paula Richman and Linda Hess for their early enthusiasm for the ideas expressed in this essay. Without their interest and support, the essay would not have the shape it has currently taken. And I want to thank K. Krishnamurthy, my research assistant, who tirelessly assisted me in attending, documenting, and recording numerous kolam competitions. I am grateful for the University of San Francisco Research Award that enabled me to do follow-up fieldwork on the kolam during the winter of 1998–1999. I am also thankful for the Fulbright-Hays Doctoral Dissertation Research Fellowship (1992–1994) and the Institute for the Study of Natural and Cultural Resources for financial support during my many years of sustained research and fieldwork on the kolam (1987–1992).

2. For an introduction to the subject, see J. Layard, "Labyrinth Ritual in South India: Threshold and Tattoo Design," *Folklore* 48 (1937): 115–182; and Vijaya Rettakudi Nagarajan, "Hosting the Divine: The Kolam in Tamil Nadu," in *Mud, Mirror, and Thread: Folk Traditions of Rural India*, ed. N. Fisher (Albuquerque: Museum of New Mexico Press, 1993). For a detailed and more thorough examination of the kolam in its religious and cultural context, see Nagarajan, "Hosting the Divine: The Kolam as Ritual, Art, and Ecology in Tamul Nadu, India," submitted for doctoral dissertation (University of California–Berkeley, 1998). For a critical and ecological interpretation, see Nagarajan, "The Earth as Goddess Bhu Devil: Toward a Theory of 'Embedded Ecologies' in Folk Hinduism," in *Purifying the Earthly Body of God*, ed. L. Nelson (Albany: State University Press of New York, 1998). For scholarship on the kolam in Tamil, see V. Saroja, *Mannin Manam* (Madurai: Vanjiko Pathipahm, 1992); and R. Saraswathi and L. Vijayalakshmi, *Kotaiyar Itum Kolankal*, 2 vols. (Madras: Illakumi Nilayam, 1993).

3. Arjun Appadurai and Carol Breckenridge, "Public Modernity in India," in *Consuming Modernity: Public Culture in a South Asian World*, ed. Carol A. Breckenridge (Minneapolis: University of Minnesota Press, 1995), 5.

4. I wish to thank Visalaksi and the wonderful group of women and chil-

dren who helped explain to me what Antal and the kolam mean to them. For an elaborate exposition of the saint Antal, see the excellent introduction and translations by Vidya Dehejia, *Slaves of the Lord: The Path of the Tamil Saints* (New Delhi: Munshiram Manoharlal, 1988); and Dehejia, *Antal and Her Path of Love: Poems of a Woman Saint from South India* (Albany: State University Press of New York, 1990), among others.

5. One of women's expressive traditions in Northern India, the rangoli is a ritual art parallel to the kolam. The word *rang* means color in Hindi and refers to the most significant aspect of these designs, which is their bright colorfulness.

6. Breckenridge, *Consuming Modernity*.

7. Arjun Appadurai, "Disjuncture and Difference in the Global Cultural Economy," in *Colonial Discourse and Post-colonial Theory: A Reader*, ed. Patrick Williams and Laura Chrisman (New York: Columbia University Press, 1994), 327.

8. It has become a trend in recent competitions to write down the names of the makers alongside the kolams to identify the competitors.

9. Sandra Freitag, *Collective Action and Community: Public Arenas and the Emergence of Communalism in North India* (Berkeley: University of California Press, 1989).

10. James Clifford, "On Collecting Art and Culture," in *The Cultural Studies Reader*, ed. Simon During (New York: Routledge, 1993), 59.

11. Steven Lavine and Ivan Karp, "Introductory Essay," in *Exhibiting Cultures: The Poetics and Politics of Museum Display* (Washington, D.C.: Smithsonian Press, 1991), 15.

12. Henry Glassie, "Tradition," *Journal of American Folklore* 108, no. 430 (1995): 398.

KATHRYN POETHIG

Visa Trouble: Cambodian American

Christians and Their Defense of

Multiple Citizenships

Rev. Phal was pastor of a small congregation in the United States in the mid-1980s when he "received a message from the Lord" to return to Cambodia.[1] In Phnom Penh a decade later, he reaches for a Bible and reads Genesis 46:3. "Do not be afraid to go to Egypt and stay there and I will make a nation out of you. I will go to Egypt with you . . . and then I will help to bring you back." His fingers linger on the page as he recounts, "The Lord seemed to be speaking to me: 'Go back home . . . I will go with you.' I was so fearful to go back to Cambodia."

Cambodia in the 1980s was still under Vietnamese occupation and subjected to international isolation. Emboldened by the Lord but concerned nonetheless about the political stability in this particular "Egypt," Phal and his wife visited Cambodia several times after the United Nations–brokered peace plan that was signed by the four Cambodian factions in 1991.[2] By their third visit, they were determined to "reach and preach and nurture [Cambodians] in the fear of the Lord," and they returned as missionaries to the homeland they had fled as Buddhists.

Rev. Phal and his wife joined an influx of jubilant former refugees eager to return after nearly twenty years of exile. Sporting new accents and fresh passports from the United States, Australia, Canada, Germany, Switzerland, and France, most saw their mission as the democratization of the impoverished, strife-torn nation. Cambodian American Christians arrived in Phnom Penh for another sort of mission—the conversion of Cambodia to a Christian nation. Although returning Cambodians had been recruited aggressively by international development organizations that poured into Cambodia on the heels of the UN peacekeeping forces, they were received more coolly by officials of the former regime and Cambodians who had remained behind. Their arrival inaugurated vigorous debates on the meaning of Khmer citizenship in the postsocialist Cambodia.[3]

I did not go to Phnom Penh in search of Christians. I had accompanied returning Cambodian Americans to investigate the range of moral discourse employed by dual citizens while they trained their compatriots in democratic citizenship. It was several months before I became aware of the Christians among the Cambodian Americans I had been interviewing. As members of this influx, Cambodian American Christians claimed legitimacy as dual "kingdom workers" —citizens both of the revived constitutional monarchy and the kingdom of heaven. Their multiple and multileveled allegiances to the United States, Cambodia, and Christ brought an unusual twist to transnational belonging. As dual citizens of both the United States and Cambodia, these Cambodian Americans reimagined a Khmer identity that was transnational and non-Buddhist. This was partly a response to the local reference to overseas Cambodians as *anika-chun* (immigrant), implying less-authentic Khmerness. It was also an attempt to disengage Cambodia's elision of nationality (*sah*) and religion (*sahsana*) that associated Khmerness with Buddhism. As missionaries who were also former refugees, Cambodian Americans balanced their goal of a Christian nation with their ambivalence toward any single national affiliation, constructing instead an eschatological membership in heaven. This essay reconstructs various angles of this legitimizing discourse for Cambodian American membership in Cambodia as both dual citizens and Christians.

DIASPORA POLITICS AND NATIONAL IDENTITY

The Cambodian American quest for national belonging must be set within twenty-five years of proxy politics, a protracted civil war, and a highly visible exile resistance. Cambodia's national identity has been splintered by a sequence of regimes initiated by General Lon Nol's coup in 1970, which replaced Prince Sihanouk's anti-American government with one that aided U.S. hostilities in neighboring Vietnam, culminating in massive bombing campaigns along the Cambodian border, intending to flush out the Viet Cong. This U.S.-Cambodian collaboration was brought to a catastrophic end when in 1975 the Khmer Rouge marched into Phnom Penh and inaugurated four years of a radical nationalist communism that promoted genocidal policies and the destruction of political and cultural institutions in Cambodia. All religious institutions were suppressed, particularly Theravada Buddhism, the state religion that claimed more than 90 percent of the population as adherents. The Khmer Rouge's Chinese-supported "Democratic Kampuchea" was felled by a Vietnamese incursion in 1979. This transition precipitated a massive refugee flight over the border into Thailand. The Vietnamese, backed by the Soviet Union, remained for a decade to reconstruct Cambodia as a socialist state, finally withdrawing as a result of international pressure in 1989. Their withdrawal had been a primary stipulation of the peace plan that brought Cambodia's long isolation to an end.

Resettled in affluent nations in Europe, the Pacific, and North America, Cambodians set up a transnational matrix of lobbyists who helped to engineer Cambodia's transformation from a socialist regime to a fragile constitutional monarchy in 1993. When the UN-monitored elections were set in place, the exiled royalist party FUNCINPEC won the largest number of seats in the new government. Though FUNCINPEC unseated the reigning communist Cambodian People's Party, the latter refused to concede defeat and forcibly extracted joint leadership in the government. The Khmer Rouge, who had withdrawn from the compact, continued to conduct military campaigns throughout the country.

Given the devastation of culture, a reinvigorated nationalism at the departure of the Vietnamese, and the significant presence of returning refugees both from the refugee camps in Thailand and from the affluent West, the question of cultural identity was an important issue to resolve in the first years of new democracy.[4] An ethnic definition of citizenship in which Khmerness was the signifier of true citizenship became the epicenter of this debate, appearing in the revised constitution and redrafted immigration and nationality laws. In both of these sets of documents, definition of Cambodian citizenship as an ethnic category was intended to disqualify Vietnamese settlers from Cambodian nationality. It also, however, offered overseas Cambodians who arrived on second passports an opportunity to resume Cambodian citizenship. This resulted in a large number of dual citizens holding high government posts. Overseas Cambodians' legitimization of Khmer identity began as the legal recognition of citizenship. For dual citizens, and for Christians in particular, this battle was an important one.

THE DECADE OF RETURN

The exodus of overseas Cambodians from their comfortable sites of resettlement to their volatile homeland represented a new form of transnational politics in the 1990s, heralded as the refugee "decade of return."[5] Arjun Appadurai's dissection of transnational cultural flows into "scapes"—ethnoscapes, financescapes, mediascapes—has become a handy heuristic tool for mapping this global phenomenon.[6] These returning refugees occupy an "ethnoscape" that populates a broad semantic domain: immigrants, expatriates, guest workers, exiles, overseas and ethnic communities, and diaspora cultures.[7] Anthropologists claim[8] that these deterritorialized peoples upset the assumption that one's identity is fixed to a place or a national culture,[9] indicating instead that transnational cultures are formed through multistranded social relations between homelands and settlement.[10] The identities of those who shuttle across borders are thus hybrid, their allegiances multiple.

Citizenship is a critical form of political identity for those who travel between nation-states. It has both legal and cultural expressions. As a legal status, the dual possession of citizenship occurs because there is no uniform guidance under international law for the acquisition of citizenship.[11] The Cambodian Americans who returned to Cambodia acquired dual citizenship through naturalization and chose to retain their original citizenship when they learned that recent U.S. rulings were amenable to dual citizenship. One could possess two passports as long as the dual citizen produced the U.S. passport when entering U.S. territories. Though there was considerable confusion around the parameters of Cambodian citizenship, it was generally understood that returning Cambodian nationals could regain citizenship status if they requested new passports and used them in Cambodia. Most dual citizens, however, used their U.S., Australian, or French passport to enter Cambodia and were thus treated as aliens requiring residency visas.

If the legal status of dual citizens was murky, their cultural expression of citizenship proved even more complicated. Aiwha Ong[12] argues that cultural citizenship is an identity that newcomers negotiate vis-à-vis U.S. state bureaucracies and other service institutions (mutual assistance associations, clinics, schools) that assimilate potential citizens into the social body. Some of the largest and most active contributors to this resettlement process were Roman Catholic, Protestant, and Mormon refugee programs. A plethora of American-financed religious nongovernmental organizations (NGOs) provided assistance in the refugee camps along the Thai border as well as a wide range of resettlement services in the United States. Many of the preliminary conversions of Cambodians occurred in these refugee camps and in response to church sponsorships, although this group is a small minority of the diaspora community. For those sensitive to the bond between nationalism, ethnicity, and religion, "authentic" American identity was Caucasian and Christian. Cultural citizenship would thus be more easily achieved by conversion. Cambodians who became Christian took on a more permeable social membership in the United States because their ethnicity and religion were no longer linked, a point I will return to later.

The American ideology of civic citizenship and its implicit racism, however, sent a mixed message to Cambodian newcomers, encouraging national belonging without requiring a dissociation from one's ethnic community while attributing to the hyphenated citizen a secondary citizenship. For one Cambodian American Christian, resettlement in the United States had rewarded him with "God's gift" of "two cultures, West and Cambodian." This gift, however, was unsettled by its racial contradiction. "In the States I say, 'I am American.' But I am not. My skin is Cambodian." Former refugees were thus encumbered by a hyphenated American cultural citizenship as they encountered Cambodia's own criteria for belonging.

If cultural citizenship in the United States presumed a civic citizenship that was riven with contradiction, Cambodia's cultural citizenship was informed by its strong sense of ethnic nationalism founded on a contested notion of purity. Like much of Southeast Asia, Cambodia's link between ethnicity and nationality is invested with political interests.[13] A majority of Cambodians are ethnic Khmer and Theravada Buddhists. This fusion between religious and national identity, as I mentioned earlier, is evident in the derivation of the Khmer word *sah,* translated as ethnicity or nationality, from *sahsana,* which means religion (literally, to pray).[14] For Khmer, this ethnic self-definition is linked to a sense of historical continuity and culture comprising folk and classical dance, architecture, and religion. Its primordial beginnings are traced back to the vaunted Angkorian empire that once spanned Burma, Thailand, Laos, and Vietnam, a history ironically reinvested with significance by the French colonial "discovery" and restoration of Angkor Wat.[15]

The register of authentic Khmerness (language, customs, heritage) has historically been employed to determine eligibility for citizenship to discourage Vietnamese settlers from gaining Cambodian nationality.[16] But it became useful again as overseas Cambodians returned from the West. Local Cambodians quickly began to separate themselves as "Khmer Angkor" (loosely translated as "true Khmer") from those returning, whom they called *anikachun*. While Cambodian Americans translated anikachun variously as immigrant, foreigner, minority, or ethnic Khmer, its association with unassimilable Vietnamese settlers was particularly troubling to overseas Cambodians. Furthermore, Cambodia has had a historic enmity toward Vietnam owing to a history of Vietnamese occupation and cultural imperialism. If anikachun were no longer Khmer Angkor, this was because they had been corrupted by their new cultural citizenship. Cambodian Americans were often told that they no longer walked, talked, and acted Khmer.

Given the Khmer affiliation with Theravada Buddhism, anikachun Christians were further alienated from true Khmerness. Indeed, Christianity has had a strained or neutral reception in Cambodia,[17] a relationship similar to most Theravada Buddhist countries.[18] Protestantism arrived with the Christian Missionary Alliance in the 1920s. In the 1960s, Phal Sareth recalls, anticolonial sentiment against Christians was reflected in accusations against them as "nation sellers" (*luk chheat, luk sasnaa*). The Khmer Rouge and the subsequent decade of Vietnamese socialism suppressed Christianity as a colonial remnant. All foreign missionaries were ejected after 1975, churches were destroyed, and most Christians were killed. After 1979, house churches began to spring up in secret, initiated by a remnant of Khmer Christians. As the outgoing socialist government in Phnom Penh opened doors to the Christian Church in 1990, a range of transnational mission groups descended on Cambodia. In four years, the Christian church grew from 4,000 to 21,000, a vitality that concerned both government officials and the Buddhist *sangha* (clergy).[19]

Christian anikachun then represented a betrayal of both the nation and the dharma. At its root, noted Phal, was the accusation that he didn't "love the country enough. . . . They say, 'You are going through the blood, but you are beside the blood, don't want to soak yourself in the blood with us.' " While Christians were "washed in the blood" of Jesus, it was Khmer blood that had been expended through suffering, the suffering that continued through the long, harsh era that refugees had escaped. Returning Cambodians had to legitimate their Khmerness while professing a Christianity gained at the site of resettlement. This was a delicate, difficult task.

VISA TROUBLE IN "EGYPT"

For Phal, this struggle over legitimization as an American and Khmer was waged between two communities of membership in Phnom Penh. Like many, he used his U.S. passport to enter Cambodia and faced the expenses of visa extensions for his entire family. More-privileged overseas Cambodians in business and government received "free visas." "Why do I have to pay?" he asked heatedly, when the issue was raised in our conversation. "Why do American citizens working for the government prejudice against its own American citizen as far as extension visas is concerned? What's the value in America? Why didn't they apply [that] kind of value here in Cambodia?" This American "value" is nondiscrimination. Either waive all visa extensions to Cambodian Americans or expect all to pay equally. Preferential treatment is un-American and should not be awarded with the privilege of serving in the Cambodian government. For Phal, as a U.S. citizen in Cambodia, American principles should set the official Cambodian guidelines for visa extensions to dual citizens.

However, when Phal confronts local Cambodians who pressure him about visa extensions, he shifts his primary value to Khmer. The immigration issue is "very sensitive," he says, asking me to turn off the tape recorder. He was willing to recount his experiences if his comments were published only in the United States. Because of problems with visa extensions, Phal has had several encounters with the local military and the chief of the village. Visiting his house in his absence, they notified his neighbor and house sitter that his visa had expired a month earlier. Had he left the country yet? When he returned, he called on the chief of the village, who claimed that they were merely paying him a social visit. "I said, 'OK, that's how good you are.' But I know behind their back, it's not that they want to visit me. They consider me to be a foreigner."

Phal then engages them in an exchange that presses them on separations of local and overseas Khmer. "How do you define foreigner?" he asks blandly. "Those who have abandoned their Khmer nationality," they respond. "How do you define abandoned?" he presses. "They don't have a passport," they reply, following his intended line of logic. He then attacks, "The people out there in the rural area don't have a passport; are they foreigners?"

> And then they said, "You abandoned Khmer nationality." But I said, "I abandoned Khmer nationality on paper, but my blood is Khmer. Don't you know that? My blood is Khmer, my language is Khmer. Is there any Khmer flaw in my speaking right now to you?"
>
> "No."
>
> "Then, I'm Khmer. Unless there is a law that says I'm not Khmer, I'm Khmer. Up to this point, you don't have any law in your country, so I'm Khmer."

As a dual citizen defending his Khmerness, Phal follows the logic of equal application that he has applied to Cambodia's dual officials. In light of the Cambodian government's undetermined policy on aliens and dual citizenship, its earlier determination of citizenship of jus sanguinis—citizenship by descent—determines the Khmer citizen, and he is thus a Khmer citizen. He can be both a U.S. citizen and Khmer citizen because their requirements for citizenship differ and do not (yet) require him to declare allegiance. He invokes the capital of Angkor Khmerness—blood, tongue, and skin—to argue against the more recent expressions of Khmerness through the production of passports. It's true, he admits, that he has another "paper" nationality, but this cannot equate with an embodied proof of his Khmerness. And if they argue that the absence of a paper nationality (his passport) trumps Khmerness, then the true representatives of Angkor Khmerness—rural folk who have no passport—are also foreigners, as they lack proper documentation of their national identity. Furthermore, if Khmer Angkor are truly Khmer because of the significations of Khmerness (e.g., speaking the language flawlessly, looking Khmer, and having the right descent), then how can authorities argue that he is not Khmer? He wins his match: skin, blood, and tongue trump paper.

But the relief from the battle for recognition as both American and Khmer is only temporary, notes Phal Sareth.

> They don't have Nationality Law here, so when people dislike us, they say, "You are American." When people say, "Oh, you are beneficial to us," you are dual, a Khmer American. It's up to the people. You are needed, you are Khmer American, you are not needed, you are American.

Thus the legal status of dual citizenship required constant management. Cambodian American Christian missionaries made up for their lesser privileges in Phnom Penh with cultural stealth. As Phal Sareth so eloquently indicates, anikachun could argue for the waiver of visa fees on two fronts: as an American assuming the shared civic virtue of nondiscrimination and as an ethnic Khmer for whom "paper" nationality was negligible.

Additionally, as dual-cultural citizens, Christians and their transnational compatriots stressed the cultural constructedness of Khmer ethnicity. Although returning Khmer could claim blood and skin, local Cambodians criticized their performance of Khmerness—language, customs, demeanor. Mortified at what one returning Cambodian described as Cambodia's "poverty of culture," they were impatient with local Cambodian claims to an Angkor Khmerness denied them. "Nobody can claim cultural purity," one overseas Cambodian argued. The cultural devastation of Pol Pot had left a vacuum filled by the decade of Vietnamese occupation. In the new age of capitalism, Thai media and products dominate the market.

> Cambodian identity, we are now no longer pure, we are mixed. It should apply to citizenship law. You mix Chinese, you mix Vietnamese, you mix American. We're all mixed, we come from everywhere, coming back. Now we are a mixed culture; it's a new Cambodia.

Returning Cambodians as anikachun thus posed a challenge to their local compatriots: Khmerness was never static, and the criteria for authority expanded. Overseas Cambodians also called for a "multi-cultural" civic citizenship that would dismiss ethnic, national, or religious purity as the basis for national identity. One argued that the tie between ethnicity and religion was not always secure. There were, for example, not only Chinese Confucians but also Chinese Christians. Not all Americans were Christian; indeed, some were Buddhist. Why not Khmer Christians? Finally, overseas Cambodians argued that the new government should encourage the return of diaspora Cambodians, not unlike the examples of Haiti and Israel.[20] For Christian anikachun, such a transnational multicultural space would not be realized without the separation of Khmer ethnicity from Buddhism. This separation, they argued, could be managed without forfeiting the symbols that gave Cambodia's ethnic nationalism its emotional power.

THE CAMBODIAN NATION AS ANGKOR CHRISTIAN?

Returning Cambodian American Christians had to defend themselves not only against the criticism that they were traitors to Khmerness but also against the claim that they were traitors to Buddhism. Most articulate on this issue was Khun, a Christian and Cambodian American businessman. His decoupling of Buddhism from Khmerness did not dismiss ethnic nationalism as the ground of Cambodian identity.

> To be a Cambodian, you have to be a Buddhist, to be born here. I want to argue, no you don't have to be a Buddhist to be a Cambodian. . . . To be a Cambodian, one has to be able to answer this question: did your ancestors build Angkor Wat?

For Khun, authentic Cambodian identity is intimately bound to a genealogy tracing its ancestry back to the early centuries of the Angkor empire. Ignoring the possibility that these "ancestors" might as easily have been the slaves that the Angkorian rulers suppressed, Khun argues that it is not Buddhism that makes one Khmer but this lineage anchored in Cambodia's primordial identity. Thus, he reasons, one can be Khmer Angkor and Christian. Generations of Angkor Khmerness replace Buddhism as the primary ethnic marker.

If Christians could be Khmer Angkor, the nation could be Angkor Christian. This claim demanded a refutation of the political legitimization of Theravada Buddhism as the state religion. For Khun, the tragedy of Cambodian history was due to its adherence to a "self-centered" religion. "Buddhism is an introverted religion. Christianity is extroverted. The most corrupted officials are very religious." Christianity, on the other hand, is more "transparent" and altruistic. "When you're taught that the Lord is looking out for you all the time, you can start taking care of other people."

If Khmer Christians had a stake in Cambodia's past, Khun reasoned, Christians could also claim a stake in Cambodia's democratic future. Christianity embodied modernity and democracy, stressing the civic virtues necessary for transforming Cambodia's political institutions after decades of civil war, patronage, and corruption. A Christian ethic could purge the Cambodian body politic of its backdoor dealings. For Chantal, the wife of the founder of a thriving evangelical mission in Phnom Penh, the Christian basis of American democracy offered "justice, I like justice," and legal aid for the indigent, unlike Cambodia's judicial system, in which "the ones with more money are the ones that can win." These Christians resisted the call to engage directly in Cambodian politics. They chose instead to "share Christ" with government officials. Chantal often prayed that government officials might have "wisdom from God to lead the country," and better still, salvation. If Cambodia was to be a Christian nation, she and her husband asserted, God would surely bless it. A Christian nation would make a strong state.

Though the Cambodian American vision of a Christian nation did not differ significantly from that of Khmer Christians who had remained in Cambodia during the long ordeal, their authority in promoting its ideal was derived from their diaspora status. Cambodian American Christians had lived in a democracy with a Christian majority and were pragmatic about its pitfalls. A few referred to America as a Christian nation while separating those traits that were Christian (honesty, faithfulness) from those that were not (decadence, materialism). Nonetheless Cambodia's modernization required both democracy building and the Christian conversions of state officials, and they were ardent advocates of this merger.

BETTER A HEAVENLY CITIZENSHIP

On a rainy afternoon, I sat with Chantal on the porch of the mission compound that she and her husband had established with support from a U.S. evangelical organization. She held an unusual legacy of two generations of Cambodian Christians, and like the other Cambodian Americans I had met, she believed fervently that God had secured her escape from the Khmer Rouge for a higher purpose.

> Sometime I pray to God. "You keep me alive, because this is my second life." My first life [was] supposed to die under the communists. . . . That is why when I arrived in the States, I start to serve God right away. I have faith that God kept me alive because He's not finished with me yet. He gave a vision to me. He is faithful. . . . I pray. "You give life to me and freedom to go back. Please give Cambodia to me. If you do not give Cambodia to me, why you let me come and make me suffer again!" It's not easy. Fifteen years in the United States to settle everything. It's not easy to come back, with mosquito bites and everything . . . it's up to God. God wants to build His kingdom, and I'm His servant, his slave.

Chantal's passion that God "give Cambodia" to her was set within a longer narrative of survival and service to luckless Cambodians assaulted by American decadence, Thai callousness and Cambodian brutality. She recalled her despair when she returned to work in the refugee camps in Thailand in the late 1980s. Cruelty had no reprieve; Thai treated Cambodians as pariahs, and the Thai military exploited the refugees; but Cambodian leaders were no better, manipulating their people for their own ends. "Cambodia," she mused, "is a small country on the map that suffers more than other countries in the world." When I asked her to identify her citizenship, she hesitated. First Cambodian, then American, then Cambodian revived, she finally folded her multiple relocations into the enduring theme of Christian exile. Membership in this body of suffering was sometimes too unbearable, and her hope was grounded in the belief that "I'm not a Cambodian citizen for long. One day, I have a new citizenship, a citizenship in heaven."

Chantal's words conveyed a longing expressed by others weary of managing so many loyalties. Beyond the contentious earthly kingdoms, and the hierarchical pluralism in both her countries of membership, was the heavenly kingdom, a kingdom that did not betray and brooked no competing loyalties. Chantal's soliloquy echoed the classic theology of the fourth-century North African bishop Augustine, who depicted the earthly city as the terrain that Christians travel on their way to the heavenly city, a site both present in the church and eschatological. "One day," she mused at the end of our visit, "I will be in one world and have no tears. I have faith that this world is not my home, I am just passing through. I belong in one kingdom that is forever."

For Cambodian Americans whose conversion occurred in the refugee camps or in the United States, Christian discipleship had perplexing affiliations. American political identity was fused with Christian evangelism, but as Chantal illustrates, a theology of exile expressing an ambivalence to national identity guided their deeper ruminations. Nicole Rodriguez Toulis's study of immigrant Pentecostal communities in Britain suggests that Christian identity usurps political and ethnic affiliations.[21] Similarly, while dual citizens attributed democratic principles to Christianity, they also maintained a theological rationale for extracting Christianity from national identification altogether. This argument was made by those in transit between two "earthly cities" who knew both the necessity of citizenship's legal status and the contrivances of cultural identity it assumed. Multiple membership was fickle. One site required a particular form of membership; the second site, another. Furthermore, what did it mean to be a Christian nation? What was Christian political culture? For transnational Christians, it was ultimately their affirmation of a citizenship that was hybrid and shifting that inspired their trend toward transcendence.

CONCLUSION

If transnational political and cultural identity has been a growing source of theorizing, what of transnational religious identity? How do they intersect? What implications can we draw from Christian dual citizens' multistranded struggles for belonging? As citizens of both the United States and Cambodia, Cambodian Americans in Phnom Penh resented the unequal distribution of visa privileges within their own community of dual citizens. To circumvent the status of anikachun, they asserted a hybrid national identity in a period of national reconstruction that challenged the stress on purity. No one was purely Khmer, neither those left behind nor those returning. If cultural citizenship was constructed, it could be reinvented. As Khmer Christians, they reimagined a Khmer identity that was both transnational and non-Buddhist. As Christian democrats, they could forge a Christian state while remaining dual citizens.

The discourse of refugees returning as dual citizens raises the problem of multiple memberships and, as Lisa Malkki suggests in her work on Hutu refugees, denaturalizes the narrative of national belonging.[22] For Malkki, refugees isolated in their exile produced their own mythologized historical narrative. In the case of Christian dual citizens, multiple national affiliations produced such longing for authentic belonging that it could be satiated only by a heavenly home. Chantal's reconstruction of Augustine's dual citizenship offers some insight into a Christian exile and transnational theology emerging from refugee flight and return. Many Christians holding multiple citizenships in two earthly and one heavenly nation assert a primary membership in heaven. If Christians are transnational in this sense—crossing the borders of heaven and earth—to Chantal and her fellows, it is as refugee pilgrims who traverse finite space and eternal time. Juggling actual dual citizenships, but ultimately unbound by them, they claim an eschatological rootedness—eternal citizenship in a future kingdom. There is much to recommend further reflection on such mobile citizens.

NOTES

1. All names have been changed.

2. The four Cambodian factions that signed included two anticommunist resistance groups (Sihanouk's royalist FUNCINPEC and former prime minister Son Sann's Khmer People's National Liberation Front [KPNLF]), the Khmer Rouge, and the current Vietnamese-backed government, the People's Republic of Kampuchea (PRK), which changed its name to the State of Cambodia (SOC) in 1989 when the Vietnamese were forced to withdraw from Cambodia after a decade of occupation.

3. "Khmer" and "Cambodian" are often interchanged by Cambodians themselves. I will use "Khmer" to refer to ethnicity and "Cambodian" as national identity.

4. May Ebihara, Carol Mortland, and Judy Ledgerwood, eds., "Cambodian Culture since 1975," in *Homeland and Exile* (Ithaca: Cornell University Press, 1994).

5. UNHCR, *Newsletter of Public Information Service of UNHCR* (Geneva: UNHCR, 1991). In the United States, the lobby and return of recently naturalized Filipinos, South Koreans, Haitians, and Eastern Europeans to former homelands is illustrative of this phenomenon. See Yossi Shain, "Marketing the

Democratic Creed Abroad: U.S. Diasporic Politics in the Era of Multicultural-ism," *Diaspora* 3, no. 1 (1994): 85–111.

6. Arjun Appadurai, "Disjuncture and Difference in Global Cultural Econ-omy," *Public Culture* 2, no. 2 (1990): 1–24.

7. James Clifford, "Diasporas," *Cultural Anthropology* 9 (1994): 302–38; and Khachig Tölölyan, "The Nation State and Its Others: In Lieu of a Preference," *Diaspora* 1 (1991): 3–7.

8. Akhil Gupta and James Ferguson, "Beyond 'Culture': Space, Identity, and the Politics of Difference," *Cultural Anthropology* 7 (1992): 6–23; Lisa Malkki, "National Geographic: Rooting People and the Territorialization of National Identity among Scholars and Refugees," *Cultural Anthropology* 7, no. 1 (1992): 24–44; Roger Rouse, "Questions of Identity: Personhood and Collectivity in Transnational Migration to the United States," *Critique of Anthropology* (1995); and Eric Robert Wolf, *Europe and the People without History* (Berkeley: University of California Press, 1982).

9. Gupta and Ferguson, "Beyond 'Culture' "; Malkki, "National Geographic"; Rouse, "Questions of Identity"; and Wolf, *Europe and the People without History.*

10. Nina Glick Schiller, Linda Basch, and Cristina Szanton Blanc, "From Im-migrant to Transimmigrant: Theorizing Transnational Migration," *Anthropo-logical Quaterly* 68 (1995): 48–63.

11. See P. Weis, *Nationality and Statelessness in International Law,* 2d rev. ed. (Alphen Canden Rijn: Sitjthoff and Noordhoof, 1979), 161–203; and Nissim Bar-Yakov, *Dual Nationality* (New York: Praeger, 1961). Dual citizenship may also be acquired by the birth of an illegitimate child in one country after which the foreign-born father is identified, naturalization in a second state, serving in the military of a second state without loss of earlier citizenship, acquiring citizenship by a child through the naturalization of their parents, acquisition through marriage, and return to the country of origin and reactivating former citizenship. See Therese Keelaghan-Silvestre, "Dual Nationality and the Prob-lem of Expatriation," *University of San Francisco Law Review* 16, no. 2 (1982): 294–95.

12. Aihwa Ong, "Cultural Citizenship as Subject-Making," *Current Anthro-pology* 37, no. 5 (1996).

13. Charles Keyes, "Why the Thai Are Not Christian," in *Conversion to Christianity: Historical and Anthropological Perspectives on a Great Transfor-mation,* ed. Robert W. Hefner (Berkeley: University of California Press, 1979); Michael Moermann, "Ethnic Identity in a Complex Civilization: Who Are the Lue?" *American Anthropologist* 67 (1965): 1215–30; and Ananda Rajah, "Eth-nicity, Nationalism, and the Nation-State: The Karen in Burma and Thailand," in *Ethnic Groups across National Boundaries in Mainland Southeast Asia,* ed. G. Wijeyewardene (Singapore: Institute of Southeast Asia, 1990).

14. This conjunction between nationality and religion has survived the shift-

ing linguistic references to Khmer identity and citizenship of the last three political regimes. See Steve Heder and Judy Ledgerwood, "Politics of Violence: An Introduction," in *Propaganda, Politics, and Violence in Cambodia: Democratic Transition under United Nations Peace-Keeping* (Armonk: M. E. Sharpe, 1996).

15. Clifford Geertz, *Interpretation of Cultures* (New York: Basic Books, 1973), 259.

16. William Wilmott, *The Chinese in Cambodia* (Vancouver: University of British Columbia Publications Center, 1968).

17. See Mary Ebihara, *"Savy, a Khmer Village in Cambodia"* (Ph.D. diss., Columbia University, New York, 1971); and Francois Ponchaud, *The Cathedral and the Rice Paddy: 450 Years of History of the Church in Cambodia* (Paris: Fayard, 1990). Roman Catholicism has a longer history in Indochina owing to one hundred years of French colonization, but Khmer associate Catholicism with the Vietnamese. This is because most Catholics in Cambodia have been ethnic Vietnamese settlers, a deterrent to Khmer conversions.

18. Keyes, "Why the Thai Are Not Christian."

19. These figures are estimates of the Cambodian government's Ministry of Religion and Cults and include "cults" such as Mormons, Seventh-Day Adventists, and the Apostolic Church, which is growing rapidly in the provinces. The primary Christian denominational groups are the Christian Missionary Alliance, Assemblies of God, Methodist, Campus Crusade for Christ, Baptist, Nazarene, Church of Christ, New Apostolic, Seventh-Day Adventist, Independent Khmer Churches, and Roman Catholicism.

20. In their discussions of state support of dual citizenship, many Cambodian Americans referred to Israel's law of return for the conferring of citizenship on returning Jews. For a comparison between Israel and Thailand on ethnicity, nationality, and citizenship, see Erik Cohen, "Citizenship, Nationality, and Religion in Israel and Thailand," in *The Israeli State and Society: Boundaries and Frontiers*, ed. Baruch Kimmerling (Albany, N.Y.: SUNY Press, 1989), 66–92.

21. Nicole Rodriguez Toulis, *Believing Identity: Pentacostalism and the Mediation of Jamaican Identity and Gender in England* (Oxford: Berg Press, 1997).

22. Lisa Malkki, *Purity and Exile: Violence, Memory, and National Cosmology among Hutu Refugees in Tanzania* (Chicago: University of Chicago Press, 1995).

BERIT BRETTHAUER

Televangelism: Local and

Global Dimensions

Malcolm Waters begins with a quote from Theodore Levitt, "Think global. Act local" in his introductory notes to his theories of globalization.[1] He describes globalization and localization as Janus-faced aspects of the same process. Roland Robertson had long before diagnosed a parallel development of processes of globalization and localization. Poignantly, he referred to it as glocalization.[2] Reflecting on the limits of globalization, Alan Scott remarked in a similar way that globalization is held to be a complex interaction of globalizing and localizing tendencies.[3]

How exactly can we describe the relation of globalization and localization? If globalization is defined as a reduction in the geographic constraints on social arrangements, what is its position vis-à-vis an enduring local focus of social life? Does the local itself lose its connectedness to territory? Do even local practices leave geographic constraints behind? Arjun Appadurai argues for such a deterritorialization of the local. He sees locality as relational and contextual, not as scalar and spatial. Locality, then, means a series of links between a sense of social immediacy, technologies of interactivity, and the relativity of contexts.[4] In a similar vein, historians and sociologists propose to redefine community as social space not bound to a particular territory. Indeed, if territorially based interaction is no longer the essence of locality, one might claim that localization is reinforcing globalization, since the latter means the disappearance of territoriality as an organizing principle of social and cultural life.

But what happens if much of local life remains coterminous with a specific territory? Is localization then opposed to globalization?

Or do we merely face a nontraditional renaissance of the local that remains part of the process of globalization, as Ulrich Beck might suggest?[5]

In this essay, I want to demonstrate the interrelatedness of religious globalization and localization, taking televangelism as a prime example for a parallel development of both trends. Televangelists' strategic combination of local community building and mass media evangelism points to the limits of media evangelism and to the inherent limitations of religious globalization. I will develop my argument in four steps: First, I am going to show that televangelists are indeed global actors. Second, I will point to a strategic dilemma of their global media campaigns, the ineffectiveness of evangelism via media. In the third part, I will focus on the strategic solutions chosen by American telechurches, primarily as a combination of global and local activism. Finally, I will return to the relation of globalization, localization, and community building.

In focusing on the globalization of televangelism, one should keep in mind the long-standing evangelical interest in the potentials of modern mass media. Already in the nineteenth century, evangelicals learned to use the printing press and developed techniques of internal communication that would become standard operating procedures of the modern business firm. Thus conservative Protestants fought their enemy (that is, secular newspapers, novels, and political tracts) with the same weapon: the printing press. Evangelicals successfully entered the market of print culture.[6] At the same time, the American Board of Commissioners for Foreign Mission and the Baptist Missionary Society sent thousands of missionaries to the Pacific Islands and to Asia. By the turn of the century, the number of American missionary societies claiming the world for Christ had grown to ninety-four.[7] The development of electronic mass media reinforced the global orientation of evangelicalism. Immediately after the creation of Radio Vatican in 1931, American evangelicals founded their own international religious broadcasting organizations.

The three largest American organizations today are the Far East Broadcasting Company, Heralding Christ Jesus Blessing World Radio, and Trans World Radio. These three transnational broadcasters alone are estimated to produce about 20,000 hours of programming each week in more than 125 languages. They are broadcasting more hours per week in more languages than any other transnational service.[8] Clearly, the three large broadcasting organizations are global actors, even though it remains difficult to say how many people are regularly listening to their programs.

American televangelists are active on a global scale as well. Pat Robertson's Christian Broadcasting Network, for instance, claims to invest almost $20 million a year for international media outreach programs and around $7 million for the worldwide distribution of religious materials. An international edition of CBN's anchor show, *The 700 Club*, is transmitted to more than forty countries. In addition, CBN continues to launch special media campaigns in Asia, North Africa, former socialist countries such as Albania or Kazakstan, and Latin America. It comes as no surprise, then, that leading American televangelists such as Jimmy Swaggart are known throughout Latin and Central America.[9] Their media presence is held to be at least partially responsible for the evangelical resurgence in the region.

Robert Schuller concentrates his media activities in Eastern and Western Europe. His first appearance on Russian TV on 25 December 1989 was also the first religious broadcast from the United States to be shown in the region. A year later, Schuller aired several half-hour shows called "Heart to Heart" on Channel 1 to all of the former Soviet Union. His program *Hour of Power* is one of the few evangelical programs from the United States to have been broadcast on a relatively continuous basis in Europe.[10] When Super Channel dropped all religious programs in 1993, Schuller was able to find another network that agreed to sell airtime to *Hour of Power*. Each Sunday morning he can now be followed on NBC-Europe. While most televangelists retreated from the European market, Schuller still spends more than $1 million per year for airtime and the operation of a small office on the continent. Because his European supporters cannot cover all these expenses, they are compensated for partially by donors from the United States and Canada.

Thus global missionary activities seem crucial for the self-understanding of American televangelists. As Evangelicals and Fundamentalists, they take seriously Christ's command to go to the world and to preach the gospel. Even their financial support depends on the belief that evangelical television can reach and convert non-Christians.

Mostly of conservative Protestant background, their followers do support them because they want to further the goal of mass evangelism.

However, research on religious conversion has emphasized the inherent limitations of media evangelism. Few people are actually converted via media.[11] Successful evangelism has to rely on face-to-face contact. Not more than 5 percent of all conversion experiences can be traced back to mass evangelism. Moreover, according to the Institute for American Church Growth, merely 0.01 percent of 40,000 surveyed church members joined their congregation because of the impact of mass evangelism. Eighty-five percent were recruited by their friends, neighbors, and family members.[12] Religious communities—so it seems—gain most of their members through existing interpersonal bonds. Members recruit their friends, neighbors, or family members. Thus televangelism is hardly an effective way to provoke change in religious identity. Nor do religious media often bring about a radical personal transformation from a born-again experience.

How do American telepreachers confront this situation? How do they face the dilemma to legitimize their sizable expenses in the name of a divine call to evangelism even though missionary efforts via media seem not to be very effective? In the third part of my essay, I want to outline televangelists' strategic solutions: First, during their TV programs, most telepreachers present themselves as actively converting people via media. Second, televangelists combine their media campaigns with the creation of local communities, which facilitate face-to-face evangelism.

Let me illustrate the first solution. If one follows an evangelical TV program in the United States, one will soon learn of televangelists' claims to stimulate conversion experiences via electronic media. Indeed, content studies of religious TV programs have shown that conversion is a prominent and persistent theme of the shows. Letters of newly converted viewers are read, incoming calls are mentioned, guests talk about their conversion experiences brought about by religious television, and conversion stories are reconstructed in short film segments. Pat Robertson's *700 Club* regularly includes such a conversion narrative. A drug dealer, for instance, reports about his miraculous conversion upon waking up in the middle of night when the TV had been turned on through divine intervention. He claims that an airing of *The 700 Club* turned his life around. Similarly, a young woman recounts a born-again experience brought about by *The 700 Club* at a time when she was planing to have an abortion. Film segments such as these are produced to reinforce the myth of televangelism as a powerful means of conversion.

Televangelists' second strategic attempt to confront the dilemma of media evangelism leads us back to the parallel development of religious globalization and localization. American telepreachers complement their worldwide media campaigns with the creation of local networks. These territorially based communities allow them to offer not just media but direct face-to-face evangelism. All funded by American telechurches, three types of organizations have to be distinguished: congregations, purpose groups, and fan clubs. They differ in respect to their capacity to introduce members to a Christian lifestyle. All three vary also to the degree to which they are bound to a specific territory and allow for a rich communal life.

The following detailed case studies of two leading American telechurches will examine the potentials, problems, and limits of televangelists' community-building strategies.[13] The data presented are based on extensive field research during 1995 and 1996 at Robert Schuller's mega- and telechurch in Garden Grove and at CBN Headquarters in Virginia Beach. The research process included more than fifty qualitative interviews with leaders and activists of a megachurch, two special purpose groups, and a fan community. Interviews were complemented with a period of participant observation at the megachurch and a review of all relevant publications of these organizations. Although not representative in a statistical sense, the data do help to outline the various dimensions of community-building strategies typical for American televangelism.

Robert Schuller is one of the stars of religious television in the United States. Born in 1926 to Dutch immigrant farmers, Schuller built his career as pastor of the Reformed Church in America. When he moved to southern California in 1955, he intended to build a new congregation, gathering the unchurched people of Orange County. In the beginning, Schuller preached from the roof of a snack bar in a drive-in theater. His appealing slogan "Come as you are in the family car" attracted new visitors. Supported by radio preacher Norman Vincent Peale, Schuller was soon able to found his own church. Today Robert Schuller is heading the Crystal Cathedral Congregation, a 10,000-member megachurch in Orange County. The famous church building was designed by Philip Johnson. The media reported extensively about the enormous expenses for the Crystal Cathedral. Magazines such as *Time* and *Newsweek*, TV programs such as *60 Minutes* and talk shows with Mike Douglas and Phil Donahue covered the subject. Schuller's congregation gained publicity throughout the country.

However, many Americans had heard about the megachurch in Orange County even before the completion of the Crystal Cathedral. Since 1970 the congregation had televised its church service. *Hour of Power* was paid for by the congregation at the beginning and soon became one of the most popular religious television programs in the United States. Some 1.4 million households watch the program on a regular basis. Thus during recent decades, Robert Schuller managed to successfully combine the growth of a television ministry and a megachurch. Yet he is not the only televangelist who is heading a large congregation in the United States. Rex Humbard made his career as pastor of a megachurch and telepreacher before he resigned. Jimmy Swaggart still has his own TV program and is leading a congregation, though he lost viewers and members after the sex scandals at the end of the 1980s. Jerry Falwell and John Hagees continue to preach to large congregations and to sizable television audiences. In fact, Falwell claims that his media success helped to build the 15,000-member Thomas Road Baptist Church:

> Between that local radio broadcast every day and that weekly telecast. . . . Thomas Road Baptist Church came alive. There's no way to discount the fact that without the media we could not have made an entrance into the lives of that many people so quickly. Granted, some other things went into it, such as knocking on doors. When we knocked on doors and introduced ourselves, the people already knew us. We were welcome. The media became the tool for building the church.[14]

Robert Schuller had similar experiences. He reports that almost 90 percent of the members of his congregation joined the church owing to *Hour of Power*.[15] Even though Schuller probably overstates the impact *Hour of Power* had on the growth of the Crystal Cathedral Congregation,[16] it seems clear that megachurches profit from the use of a television program to gain new members. Large churches benefit in yet another way from a televised church service. Viewers often not only support the production and distribution of the TV programs but extend their financial help to the congregation. To give an example: the $20 million church building in Orange County could not have been built without countless donations from viewers of *Hour of Power*.

Moreover, since 1995 the Crystal Cathedral Congregation has directly benefited from viewer support because it shares a common budget with the television ministry. In terms of personal and financial resources, Schuller's megachurch gains from its media presence. In addition, evangelism via TV can strengthen the normative integration of a large church. Members of the Crystal Cathedral Congregation, for instance, strongly support the missionary zeal of their senior pastor. Schuller places the needs of the unchurched people even before the demands of his own congregation.[17] Mostly from evangelical backgrounds, the members of the Crystal Cathedral Congregation share his emphasis on evangelism. The success of the TV program increases their identification with a community that is as much a mission church as a local ministry. Altogether, the experience of the Crystal Cathedral Congregation shows that megachurches as local ministries profit in various ways from an involvement with religious television.

In the 1980s, however, the increasing media activism of Robert Schuller created problems for his congregation. During this period, staff and finances for the highly professionalized field of program production and distribution expanded, whereas the number of pastors and lay preachers in the congregation stagnated. Schuller concentrated on international media evangelism, but his international popularity led to a neglect of congregational growth in Orange County. Consequently, Schuller's congregation lost members and did not manage to recruit a younger constituency. Whereas the church enrolled 13,207 members in 1983, its membership shrank to approximately 10,000 in 1996. A parallel development was the aging of membership. Today 60 percent of its members are older than 55, and only 15 percent report an age below 34. Moreover, 70 percent of the more than 2,000 volunteers for congregational tasks are older than 45.[18]

In the middle of the 1990s, the leadership of the Crystal Cathedral Congregation made attempts to correct these developments. Schuller's staff again emphasized the growth of the local community. New pastors were employed, and more than a hundred deacons and elders were elected to care specifically for the needs of the congregation. In addition, large numbers of volunteers were trained as lay pastors. They would later build up support groups on their own. With an expanded small-group ministry, the congregation hoped to appeal to its members and to attract a younger membership. Whether these attempts will ultimately succeed remains to be seen.

Although the Crystal Cathedral Congregation profited for a long time from its TV program, the recent history of the megachurch reveals a conflict between its focus on global evangelism and local community building.[19] Congregational leaders faced the problem of assigning limited resources in a balanced way to both fields of action. A tension between the goal of global evangelism and communal belonging was also apparent in the orientation of regular church members. Some activists at the Crystal Cathedral decided to join the congregation primarily because they wanted to support a missionary project with an international media appeal. They became heavily involved in various areas of congregational life and cherished Schuller's church as a vibrant religious community. However, these mission-minded people would leave the congregation if it could no longer support a television ministry. The global impact of media evangelism is more important to these church members, owing to their professional or religious background, than the local community to which they belong.

Thus a similar conflict between local bonds and global missionary efforts can be discerned in the orientation of individual members and in the development of the church at large. It can be reframed as a tension between conflicting goals and divergent types of social interaction. On the one hand, the congregation aims at a rich communal life. On the other hand, as a mission church, the Crystal Cathedral Congregation attempts to present its religious message via media on a national and global level. For the purpose of community building, the congregation furthers intensive and frequent contacts among its members via spontaneous communication and expressive rituals. These types of interactions secure the emotional and normative integration of its members.[20] Thus, despite its enormous size, the Crystal Cathedral Congregation is a lively religious community.

For instance, long-term members concentrate almost all aspects of their social life at the Crystal Cathedral. Their best friends belong to the congregation. They turn here for help in difficult times. Being active in various small groups does not prevent these "old-timers" from attending the Sunday services regularly. More recent members of the congregation often join small groups. In support groups, they find the intimacy that might be missing at larger church gatherings. Besides Bible classes and Sunday schools, the Crystal Cathedral Congregation offers newcomers more than a hundred support groups to make them quickly feel at home in Schuller's congregation.[21]

For the purpose of evangelism, the megachurch employs more than a hundred paid media specialists who produce and distribute *Hour of Power*. Schuller's media activities expanded in the 1980s while the communal life of the congregation was neglected. With the help of active church members, the leadership of the megachurch has set out to correct this development. Schuller and his staff realized that a church can only profit from a television program when the media involvement does not diminish its investments in congregational life. It needs a careful balance between an emphasis on local community building and global missionary efforts to combine them in a productive way.

The Crystal Cathedral Congregation is not the only organization founded by televangelist Robert Schuller. During recent decades, he created several fan clubs to finance the production and distribution of his television program. Because televangelists cannot rely on an income from selling airtime for commercials, they have to find other ways to secure regular financial support. Some telechurches depend on telethons. Several times a year, they reserve days of airtime and ask viewers to call the telechurch and to pledge financial support. Pat Robertson was the first to use telethons. His Christian Broadcasting Network still relies on telethons for a part of its income. However, most telepreachers create specific fan organizations to secure financial support. Jerry Falwell formed the Faith Partners; Oral Roberts built an organization called Prayer Partners. Rex Humbard could rely on donations from his Prayer Key Family. Pat Robertson has a comparatively large fan organization: the 700 Club Partners. Robert Schuller is known as a televangelist who rarely asks for donations during his program. He depends almost exclusively on the support of his fan clubs. The 30,000 members of Schuller's Eagles Club, for instance, each donate $600 per year. Created in 1982, the Eagles Club soon replaced an older fan organization: the Crystal Cathedral

Church of the Air. In 1993 Schuller founded an additional donor organization: the Sparrows Club. Its members pledge only $240 per year. The Sparrows Club grew rapidly. After three years of existence, it could already claim as many members as the Eagles Club. Both fan organizations together provide the annual $45 million budget for the operation of *Hour of Power*.

Fan clubs are of crucial importance for the survival of all television ministries. Not surprisingly, telechurches invest a lot of time and energy to secure the support of their members. Robert Schuller alone employs forty people in his department Donor Services. Their sole responsibility is to ensure an ongoing communication with donors. The telepreacher already has a first chance to "interact" with supporters during his TV program. He can address viewers during the show and thank them for their help. However, this kind of parasocial interaction remains one-sided.[22] Although viewers might have the illusion of "meeting" with Schuller via TV, the telepreacher will not receive direct feedback from his viewers. To get feedback, he relies on additional forms of personalized communication. With the help of his staff at Donor Services, the telepreacher can supplement his TV interaction through contacts via mail, Internet, and phone. Each year, employees at the service department mail the porcelain Eagle to members of the Eagles Club. "Sparrows" obtain a more modest gift to acknowledge their membership. In addition, employees of Donor Services write regularly to Schuller's supporters as soon as they receive the monthly payment for *Hour of Power*. At the end of each year, donors are contacted via phone. The staff at Garden Grove calls each "Eagle" and "Sparrow" to express the gratitude of the telechurch and to secure a continuation of financial support.

Since the summer of 1997, viewers and supporters can also visit the Web site of the Crystal Cathedral to receive the latest news from the mega- and telechurch.[23] In addition, more than ten staff members offer counseling to donors who are searching for help. Counselors reply to phone calls and letters and address the personal problems of Schuller's fans. Each day dozens of letters are sent to members of the Eagles and Sparrows Clubs. For this purpose, counselors select from fifty different letter formats on their hard disk, each one written and signed by Robert Schuller. They merely adjust these standardized letters to the personal data of the respective donor. Eagles who have practical or technical problems can turn to Schuller's Detail Department or the Heart Line. With its diversified services, the telechurch in Garden Grove tries to complement the parasocial interaction started through *Hour of Power*. The service center demonstrates to Schuller's fans that they can expect more than just "meeting" their telepreacher on TV. Donors are encouraged to contact the telechurch in difficult times. Ultimately, the telechurch counts on their help as well. The primary task of all service activity is to ensure the continuous financial support of donors.

Televangelists use the potentials of personalized communication via electronic media quite successfully. Enthusiastic viewers believe that their favorite telepreacher really cares about them. Nineteen percent think of the televangelist as a friend.[24] Almost half of the viewers pray or read the Bible in preparation for the TV service. This kind of viewer involvement with religious television has been characterized as an experience of translocal *communitas*,[25] introducing the audience to the broader evangelical community. Religious television might even help viewers to find solidarity in their distance from American mainstream society.[26] One may wonder whether this media-generated experience of belonging has a local dimension as well. If viewers feel like being part of a religious group that differs from mainstream society, will they ever have a chance to establish their union face-to-face? Successful telepreachers have a large group of supporters. Robert Schuller, for instance, can rely on several hundred donors in each American city. Living in the same area, do his supporters seek to meet each other?

Even secular TV shows can bring their fans together. Some viewers develop close contacts because of their common enthusiasm for a program. A couple of years ago, Henry Jenkins pointed to the lively relations between members of media fandom in a *Star Trek* fan community.[27] Members of this group write books about their favorite TV personalities and produce their own videotapes, rearranging scenes from various *Star Trek* programs. These fans exchange their productions via mail or meet each other at fan conventions. At several conventions a year, members of media fandom can gather for a couple of days and get to know each other. During the meetings, they sing their own folk songs. These songs reflect the group's criticism of a passive consumer culture, their own cultural preferences, and experiences of togetherness. Fans who often participate in conventions can develop a strong sense of belonging to a community of like-minded people. Thus Jenkins's media fandom is a colorful example of media-generated primary ties that promote a rich communal life. With regard to religious television, one has to ask whether American televangelists create similar attachments.

The example of the Eagles Club shows that Schuller's commitment to connecting his supporters has declined over the years. In the eighties, he still organized special development banquets in selected American cities. On these occasions, his supporters could meet their favorite telepreacher face-to-face. However, they also had the chance to socialize with other Schuller fans living in the area. For financial reasons, Schuller's telechurch stopped organizing these meetings. In the 1990s, only major donors received an invitation to dine with Robert Schuller. They contributed at least $500,000 a year for a limited time period.[28] The supporters who donate less to *Hour of Power* will no longer be asked to spend an evening with Schuller. However, there are still a few chances left to meet the telepreacher. Touring the country to promote his newest book, Schuller regularly addresses his fans in major American cities. Members of his fan organizations can assemble on such occasions and meet their favorite telepreacher face-to-face.

Yet the promotional gatherings hardly allow for socializing among his supporters. People who participate are not necessarily members of the Eagles or Sparrows Clubs. In addition, no rituals such as a common meal or drink are initiated that would facilitate contacts among members of Schuller's fan organization. To enjoy an exclusive meeting between the telepreacher and his supporters, one has to visit a conference at the Crystal Cathedral. It is only during these conferences that special meetings are scheduled for Eagles to talk to Schuller and to get to know each other over a cup of coffee. However, most members of Schuller's fan organization will not travel to California just to meet other supporters of the telechurch. If they want to contact Schuller donors in their neighborhood, the telechurch in Garden Grove will be of little help to them. The staff at Donor Services is not allowed to hand out names and addresses of donors. Although the television ministry devotes a lot of time and energy to secure the financial support of its fans, it makes little effort to connect donors with each other. From the point of view of the telechurch, the fan organization has only one purpose: to provide the finances for *Hour of Power*. To fulfill this task, the telechurch does not need to create dense social networks between its fans. The financing of global media evangelism is prior to the establishment of local bounds among Schuller's supporters.

Most members of the Eagles Club do not attempt to build local fan networks, either. These donors have no interest in meeting other Schuller fans within their neighborhood or city, though they have different reasons for their social reserve. Partially, donors practice a privatized religion. They lack interest in belonging to any type of religious community. These religious individualists have left organized religion when they were young. Some, during parts of their adult life, still searched for a congregation that would match their expectations until they finally gave up on their quest for the "right" religious community. Most of these Schuller fans felt overburdened and dissatisfied with the demands of congregational life.

In the end, these Eagles discovered that the benefits of belonging to a congregation were simply not worth the effort. Schuller offers them a comfortable alternative. As religious individualists, they appreciate *Hour of Power* because it provides a church home and does not demand their strong personal involvement. They can "join" his Sunday morning service from their living rooms and do not have to get dressed up for the occasion. Some of them might even sing or pray with the program and feel like participating in the collective ritual at Garden Grove. For these viewers, *Hour of Power* satisfies their religious needs at low personal costs. Because the program enriches their privatized religious life, they are willing to support it financially. That was why they joined the Eagles Club. As religious individualists, they have no interest in meeting other Schuller fans.

Not all members of the Eagles Club practice such a privatized religion. In fact, the majority of donors are active churchgoers. Some belong to Schuller's own megachurch in Orange County. They support the television ministry of the Crystal Cathedral Congregation as a means to reach out to the unchurched people of the United States and to other parts of the world. A few have personally experienced the powerful impact of religious television when they were away from their congregation. As members of the Eagles Club, they want to help Schuller to touch others in a similar way through religious media.

However, being actively involved in the life of the Crystal Cathedral Congregation, they do not pursue contacts with other Eagles who belong to different congregations. This latter group of donors find intimacy and support in their own congregation. Eagles Club members in other parts of the country are not affiliated with Schuller's megachurch. They are part of congregations with different religious orientations and rituals. Some of these churchgoers feel alienated from their own congregation. In this situation, *Hour of Power* became an important supplement to their church life. Schuller's positive message and the high-quality music offered via TV satisfy the religious needs of these viewers. More importantly, *Hour of Power* does not compete directly with their local church. All viewers are being asked for is to support the telechurch financially. Without much emotional strain, these donors divide their loyalty between a congregation and a fan organization. As churchgoers, they have little interest in meeting other Schuller fans or in becoming involved in an additional religious community. What they appreciate about *Hour of Power* is the nondemanding comfort it offers.

There is only one group of donors who would value contacts with other members of the Eagles Club. These donors have been active members of a congregation for a long time. However, because of personal illness, they are now bound to their homes and have had to give up congregational involvement. Being isolated from the larger society, these Eagles learned to rely on religious television. Evangelical programs became one of their few channels to the world. Rejecting secular television for its violent or explicitly sexual content, these viewers value Schuller's positive message that helped them in times of crisis or isolation. *Hour of Power* gradually turned into their church service. They support the program because it has such a central place in their lives and might become important to others as well. In their isolation, these members of the Eagles Club would welcome contacts with other Schuller fans.

Yet the fan organization will hardly satisfy their need for communal bounds. The telechurch and the majority of its supporters have no interest in building up local fan communities. For coordinators of the Eagles Club, the extension of financial resources for global missionary efforts takes priority to local network building. Donors feel that they belong to a translocal value community and agree on basic religious beliefs. However, they make no attempts to turn the imagined collectivity into a community, effectively cooperating on a local level.

Religious fan organizations do not link global media campaigns and local activism, but evangelical special purpose groups establish such connections. Televangelists are actively supporting the rise of purpose-oriented groups. During their programs, telepreachers direct viewers' attention to special purpose groups all over the United States. In addition, telechurches create their own parachurch organizations. Although special purpose groups had a considerable impact on the religious landscape as early as the nineteenth century, the period after 1960 has been characterized by an impressive boom of these organizations. Not only did the number of special purpose groups in the United States double within the last fifty years, but their membership grew enormously during the last decades. In terms of size, the largest special purpose groups are now comparable to denominations that have long been the dominant mode of religious affiliation in the United States.

Nevertheless, special purpose groups differ from denominations, since the former pursue a concrete political or moral agenda and accept members from different religious communities. As an alternative form of religious identification, special purpose groups weaken the significance of denominational belonging.[29] Denominations have not ceased to exist but have to a large extent become diverse federations of special purpose groups rather than monolithic, homogeneous structures. The rise of special purpose groups can thus be characterized as a major restructuring of American religion. Televangelists endorse the spread of such parachurch organizations. Most telepreachers refer their viewers to various special purpose groups.[30] They ask them to become active in prison ministries, healing ministries, Bible study groups, and charismatic or missionary groups. In addition, televangelists create parachurch organizations such as phone counseling centers, humanitarian aid groups, political and juridical organizations, and groups in support of world missionary efforts. With the help of these special purpose groups, American telepreachers mobilize thousands of supporters who voluntarily contribute their time and energy to a common cause. Parachurch organizations also strengthen the local dimension of evangelical broadcasting. The recent history of the Christian Broadcasting Network illustrates how media campaigns and parachurch activities enable telepreachers to influence the local and global religious landscape.

Pat Robertson's Christian Broadcasting Network is one of the most successful media empires in the United States. Founded in 1961 as the first religious TV station, it also produced the first Christian talk show, *The 700 Club*. Ten years after its inception, CBN started using satellites. Soon it belonged to the leading cable networks. In the mid-1970s, CBN was even listed as the third-largest cable network in the United States. More than twenty years later, it is still well positioned in the dynamic market of American cable TV, with an annual budget of more than $200 million. A successful entrepreneur, Robertson did not hesitate to add a commercial network to his religious media empire. The Family Channel belongs to Robertson's International Family Entertainment, with revenues of more than $295 million per year. The channel offers family-oriented programming and can be found in 98 percent of all basic cable packages in the United States.[31] Part of its daily program schedule is *The 700 Club*, Robertson's anchor show. As one of the longest-running programs in broadcast history, *The 700 Club* combines news, commentary, interviews, feature stories, and evangelical ministry. Nonetheless Robertson's media empire reaches beyond the American market. Increasingly, the networks' missionary efforts rely on a combination of local community building and context-sensitive programming in various parts of the world.

Parachurch organizations are of strategic importance to CBN's local work. During the last decades, the network created a wide range of such special purpose groups. Robertson founded the American Center for Law and Justice, a legal advocacy firm, which champions the rights of religious conservatives in the United States. After his defeat during the presidential campaign in 1988, he gathered his supporters in a newly established political organization, the Christian Coalition. Today this conservative grassroots organization claims to have 1.7 million members. Even though realistic estimations point to a membership of half a million, the Christian Coalition is considered to be a powerful political group.[32] Apart from political organizations, Robertson heads several religious special purpose groups, which are primarily dedicated to the goal of evangelism. One of these organizations is CBN's phone counseling center. Founded in 1974, the National Counseling Center provides twenty-four-hour prayer and spiritual advice to viewers of *The 700 Club*. In addition, prayer requests from viewers are collected. During its daily devotions, the staff at the CBN Headquarters includes those requests in collective prayers. If a person calls the center in search of religious salvation, counselors will pray with the caller for a born-again experience. In fact, the center claims to provide the ground for thousands of conversions a year. Apart from helping viewers of *The 700 Club*, the National Counseling Center aims to extend the donor basis of the Christian Broadcasting Network. For this purpose, each caller is asked for his or her name, address, age, and religious affiliation. CBN will later contact them via direct mail and ask for financial support. Thus CBN's counseling center has a dual function: it is a crucial means of evangelism, and it helps to extend the financial resources of the network.

In the past, these goals mobilized thousands of Americans to volunteer their time and energy as CBN counselors.[33] The 1980s were characterized by a remarkable expansion of counseling activity. During this period, CBN opened ninety local counseling centers in major American cities. Mostly volunteer counselors from evangelical backgrounds operated the phones. In smaller cities, not even the director of the center held a paid position. The system of local counseling centers was a unique accomplishment. No other telechurch has ever reached the same degree of widespread local participation in the United States. Viewers of *The 700 Club* could call the phone centers or visit the local projects to meet with counselors. Media evangelism went hand in hand with direct human encounters.

Moreover, the phone centers developed a rich communal life. Counselors often felt closer to other volunteers at the center than to members of their own congregation, since they were all motivated by a religious call to evangelism. Sharing basic beliefs and establishing a common horizon of meaning was facilitated by frequent interpersonal contacts at the center. Thus in the eighties CBN was as much a media empire as a web of local communities—both aiming to reinforce its missionary outreach.

This situation changed rapidly by the end of the decade. Owing to the scandals concerning other televangelists and Robertson's own absence from *The 700 Club* during his electoral campaign, CBN lost viewers and supporters. Between 1986 and 1989, Robertson lost 30 percent of his viewers. Moreover, the revenue from donations declined every year by $10 million. As a result, the network had to cut its spending. At the same time, the number of calls to the phone centers continued to expand. With low operating budgets and mostly volunteer staff, the local centers could not handle all incoming calls. In this situation of financial strain and a growing demand for counseling, the network decided to close the local centers to organize its counseling activity more efficiently. By 1990 all phone services were concentrated at the CBN Headquarters in Virginia Beach. The National Counseling Center expanded and stopped recruiting volunteers. Instead it hired paid counselors at a minimum wage. The new director of the counseling center employed paid staff, since they were more disciplined than volunteers and could be asked to come in on a regular basis. Consequently, in 1996 the National Counseling Center had only a few volunteer counselors left. The majority of its staff received a salary and worked on a part-time basis.[34] The system of local phone centers had been dissolved.

Similar to the developments at Robert Schuller's megachurch in Orange County, the recent history of CBN's phone counseling projects reflects a conflict between different goals. Like the megachurch, Robertson's counseling centers support the missionary outreach of the telechurch. At the same time, the phone centers aim at a rich communal life. In a situation of scarce resources, CBN was willing to sacrifice its network of local communities and build a more efficient, professionalized counseling center in Virginia Beach. The purpose of mass evangelism had once helped the network to establish local phone centers; it was now used as a reason to close the local projects down.

Yet not all local centers discontinued their services. Some remained open even after their separation from CBN. The New York–based Christian Hope Network (CHN), for instance, continued. Founded in the late seventies as a CBN affiliate for the New York area, CHN had the same tasks as the National Counseling Center while limiting its services to the local domain. When CBN stopped cooperating with the local centers in 1990, seven of CHN's formerly paid counselors decided to continue to work for the center on a volunteer basis. All of them are still active without any salary. Most volunteers stayed as well. Until the mid-nineties, CHN managed to build an independent financial base. The center is now supported by a network of cooperating churches and individual donors. Most of its counselors are still working on a volunteer basis. They operate the phones and offer a twenty-four-hour counseling service. In addition, CHN established its own prayer chain on the Internet with almost

2,500 participants. Some of CHN's two hundred volunteers are active in a prison ministry as well. The development of the Christian Hope Network illustrates the capacity of religious TV to create lively communities on a local level. Such groups have the strength to survive even after their forced separation from the media empire.

Although the Christian Broadcasting Network dissolved its system of local centers within the United States, it recently launched another project to combine media campaigns and local community building. With the founding of CBN WorldReach Centers, the network adds a new dimension to its global missionary efforts. So far, CBN has established ninety-seven WorldReach Centers in fifty-nine different countries.[35] These centers fulfill a dual function. On the one hand, they adjust CBN's TV and radio programs to the specific cultural needs of the audiences they are seeking to reach.[36] To fulfill this task, WorldReach Centers cooperate with the leadership of indigenous religious communities and missionaries who know the relevant cultural traditions. On the other hand, WorldReach Centers enable the network to supplement its "media blitzes" with face-to-face evangelism. While CBN's media campaigns combine radio and television programs, newspaper ads, billboard information, and other channels of communication, its WorldReach Centers offer personal counseling. People are encouraged to contact the local centers via phone and mail or even visit them. WorldReach Centers aim to invite every person to search for a born-again experience. In this respect, they fulfill exactly the same tasks on a transnational level that were assigned to CBN's local phone counseling centers in the United States. Furthermore, WorldReach Centers have an additional function. They train indigenous leaders to plant their own cell churches. A person who contacts one of these centers will be asked to join its cell groups. The cell groups' strategy enables CBN to root newly converted followers in a religious community, a strategy that aims at an enduring commitment of converts to evangelical Christianity:

> WorldReach . . . has revolutionized the international ministry of CBN. . . . In essence, the various ministries of CBN are being forged together to form "WorldReach Centers" around the globe. Broadcast and relief . . . activities, through coordinated efforts of regional centers generate thousands of individual names who are "seekers" and new believers. . . . We aim

to gather new believers together in places where they can grow in faith. These can be house churches, cell churches, or small groups where people will gather to worship the Lord, study the Word together, and encourage one another.[37]

With the combination of media campaigns and local community building, CBN wants to increase its missionary impact. This is also the reason for its cooperation with other organizations such as Campus Crusade for Christ or CBN's own humanitarian aid group Operation Blessing. As international relief and development organization, Operation Blessing is another special purpose group created by Robertson. Since 1978 Operation Blessing has offered disaster relief in the United States and has delivered free food and clothing to poor Americans. Its most important transnational program is the International Medical Division, which sends teams to various parts of the world, providing basic health care services to people in need. Although all of Operation Blessing's departments offer humanitarian aid, they also promote the goal of world mission. Within the United States, Operation Blessing cooperates only with evangelical churches or projects. During their engagements outside the United States, Operation Blessing's medical teams likewise pursue a missionary task. They offer professional health care in order to reach people with a Christian message of salvation.

For the medical projects, Operation Blessing relies heavily on volunteer support. The Medical Division mobilizes hundreds of volunteer nurses and doctors who commit their time, knowledge, and money to the success of each trip. Before 1996 each medical team consisted of three to four paid employees and approximately twenty volunteers. Trips with the Flying Hospital began in 1996 and require a much larger team. An aircraft specifically equipped for medical procedures, the Flying Hospital boards more than a hundred volunteer health care professionals and nonmedical individuals for each trip. They contribute their expert knowledge and pay for the travel expenses. Motivated by a desire to carry on the task of world mission, participants in the medical teams welcome the parallel initiatives of WorldReach Centers and Operation Blessing in recent years. Although the medical teams focus on providing medical aid and religious counseling, they can now also send converts to the local World-Reach centers. The medical staff will return to the United States, knowing that local cell groups introduce converts into basic Christian teachings and rituals. Thus the global missionary initiatives of the Christian Broadcasting Network rely on the simultaneous effect of media campaigns, local community building, and evangelistic efforts of various organizations.

Think globally. Act locally. This is what American telepreachers do. They demonstrate a growing sensitivity to the limits of religious globalization via electronic media. Consequently, local centers are being formed that adjust programs to specific cultural preferences. Religious communities develop and offer viewers direct human encounters. They surpass the shortcomings of media evangelism through local missionary efforts. As observed in the beginning, globalizing and localizing tendencies interact.

Moreover, the study of various types of organizations founded by American telepreachers shows that religious communities remain linked to territorially based interaction. Even in an age of electronic media, social solidarity in the religious realm needs physical proximity. Translocal religious communities do not develop. Clearly, it is only the combination of local community building and global media campaigns that grants credit to telepreachers' missionary emphasis.

NOTES

1. Malcom Waters, *Globalization* (New York: Routledge, 1995), 1.

2. Roland Robertson, *Globalization: Social Theory and Global Culture* (London: Sage, 1992), 173–74.

3. Alan Scott, introduction to *The Limits of Globalization*, ed. Alan Scott (London: Routledge, 1997), 7.

4. Arjun Appadurai, *Modernity at Large: Cultural Dimensions of Globalization* (Minneapolis: University of Minnesota Press, 1996), 178.

5. Ulrich Beck, *Was ist Globalisierung?* (Frankurt am Main: Suhrkamp, 1997), 87.

6. David Nord, "Systematic Benevolence: Religious Publishing and the Marketplace in Early Nineteenth Century America," in *Communication and Change in American Religious History*, ed. Leonard Sweet (Grand Rapids: William B. Eerdmans, 1993), 239–69.

7. Robert Wuthnow, *The Restructuring of American Religion: Society and Faith since World War II* (Princeton: Princeton University Press, 1988), 103.

8. Jeffrey Hadden, "Precursors to the Globalization of American Televangelism," *Social Compass* 37, no. 1 (1990): 162.

9. *CBN Homepage*, www.cbnworldreach.org (1997); *CBN Fact Sheet*, Public Relations Division (1995); *CBN Homepage*; and Dennis Smith, *The Gospel ac-*

cording to the United States of America: Evangelical Broadcasting in Central America (Grand Rapids: Zondervan, 1990), 301.

10. Gerhard Schmied, "American Televangelism on German TV," *Journal of Contemporary Religion* 11, no. 1 (1996): 97.

11. Peter Horsfield, "Evangelism by Mail: Letters from the Broadcasters," *Journal of Communication* 35 (1984): 144–45; and Steve Bruce, *Pray TV* (London: Routledge, 1990), 122–23.

12. Quentin Schultze, *Televangelism and American Culture: The Business of Popular Religion* (Grand Rapids: Baker, 1991), 187; and Richard Stark, William Sims Bainbridge, "Networks of Faith: Interpersonal Bonds and Recruitment to Cults and Sects," *American Journal of Sociology* 85 (1980): 1376–95.

13. Whereas the term "televangelism" or "electronic church" refers to the religious TV programs produced by evangelicals or fundamentalists, "telechurch" points more specifically to their production and distribution departments, including their highly professionalized staff.

14. In Ben Armstrong, *The Electric Church* (Nashville: Thomas Nelson, 1979), 152–53.

15. Robert Schuller, interview by the author, 1995.

16. Schuller's Pastor of Congregational Life Ministry estimates that the congregation recruits not more than 30 percent of its new members via TV (Berit Bretthauer, *Televangelismus: Religion zwischen Vergemeinschaftung und Individualisierung* [Frankfurt am Main: Campus, 1999]). These members were initially attracted to the Crystal Cathedral by *Hour of Power*. Their decision to join the church was determined by their personal experiences within the congregation.

17. Schuller interview.

18. Bretthauer.

19. Strictly speaking, megachurches are not neighborhood communities. Their members often live miles apart and drive by smaller churches in their neighborhood to attend a larger church. However, it is still a local ministry, since it draws people from a limited geographic area. In addition, active members of a large church tend to move closer to it (Charles Trueheart, "The Next Church," *Atlantic Monthly*, August 1996, 37–58).

20. Wolfgang Streeck, "Vielfalt und Interdependenz: Überlegungen zur Rolle von intermediären Organisationen in sich ändernden Umwelten," *Kölner Zeitschrift für Soziologie und Soyialpsychologie* 39 (1987): 452–70; and Alfred Dubach, "Bindungsfähigkeit der Kirchen," in *Jeder ein Sonderfall?* ed. Alfred Dubach and Roland J. Campiche (Zürich: NYN Buchverlag, 1993), 133–72.

21. Bretthauer.

22. Donald Horton and Richard Wohl, "Mass Communication and Parasocial Interaction: Observation on Intimacy at a Distance," in *Inter/Media: Interpersonal Communication in a Media World*, ed. Gary Gumpert and Robert Cathcat (New York: Oxford University Press, 1986), 185–206; and Donald Hor-

ton and Anselm Strauss, "Interaction in Audience Participation Shows," *American Journal of Sociology* 62 (1957): 579–87.

23. The address is www.crystalcathedral.org.

24. Bobby Alexander, *Televangelism Reconsidered: Ritual in the Search of Human Community* (Atlanta: Scholars Press, 1994), 67.

25. Stewart Hoover, *Mass Media Religion: The Social Sources of the Electronic Church* (Beverly Hills: Sage, 1988), 217.

26. Alexander, 6.

27. Henry Jenkins, *Textual Poachers: Television Fans and Participatory Culture* (New York: Routledge, 1992).

28. Bretthauer.

29. Wuthnow.

30. Hoover, 70.

31. Alec Foege, *The Empire God Built: Inside Pat Robertson's Media Machine* (New York: John Wiley and Sons, 1996), 7.

32. Foege, 15.

33. Hoover, 82.

34. Bretthauer.

35. *CBN Homepage* (1997), www.cbnworldreach.org.

36. Hadden, 164.

37. *CBN Homepage* (1997).

DAVID BATSTONE

Dancing to a Different Beat:

Emerging Spiritualities in the

Network Society

W hat the printing press did for Europe in the sixteenth
century, the convergence of telecommunications media
is doing in our own time. Individuals connect today
with little regard for space and time and interact with machines
with virtually the same degree of subtlety they expect from other
human beings. We live in complex networks, globally distributed,
which constantly transmit information back and forth across processing units, be they microelectronic chips or organic brains. This
telecosm of hyperlinked chips brings together the world's economies
and cultural movements.

Global relationships are changing radically as a result. Mixed alliances of commercial, governmental, and nonprofit ventures do business with each other in ways that break conventional molds. Their
collective systems, or nets, invest in new concepts or the means to
create them. The Internet is both a metaphor for and stimulus to that
network. Multidirectional networked media like the Internet are not
just a continuation of the mass media; they represent an important
shift because they create a new collective mental space.

As the millennium turns, "net" replaces "community" as a meaningful way to name our existence as social beings. Community implies a stability among personal relationships, identifiable roles and
obligations, and practical activities that bind its members together
in some kind of common venture. In our agrarian past, that venture
might have been as simple as the struggle for survival, or as complex

as the duties demanded by extended kinship networks. In the industrial era, community gradually came to be applied to associations who shared an ethnicity, a religion, a gender, or perhaps landed in the same labor pool. Hence, whereas communities once were known as sites that held people together despite their differences, their defining feature in mass culture became homogeneity. It was not much of a leap from there to identify communities as markets that bring customers together in one place, cheaply and easily.

In a network society, heterogeneity and difference reign. The institutions that once bound people together in small-town America—the bank on Main Street, the neighborhood church, the local union hall—are becoming artifacts of nostalgia. We meet others today in transitional sites that offer services and relationships that address ever smaller parts of our lives. Those tissues of a self are linked associatively, yet rarely in a unitary way.

Should we not expect, then, that the ways we construct transcendence in a network society would change radically as well? If connection across heterogeneity is a force of consciousness that frames both consumption and production, pluralistic meaning systems seem unavoidable.

At least that is what I discovered in an extensive study of "emerging spiritualities" in the San Francisco Bay Area.[1] My research demonstrated an exceptionally high interest in spiritual rituals, yet the forms they took were an amalgamation of various ancient traditions. For most people I interviewed, spiritual practice had little to do with rigid belief systems; experience is what counts.

It is not uncommon these days for religious practitioners to have self-made altars in their homes, adorned with personal mementos from significant life events. One popular renewal center placed at the front of its meditation room small statues of Ramakrishna, Sarada Devi (Ramakrishna's wife), Jesus, and Buddha. Above this altar was a sign: "[We] do not care for dogmas or sects, churches or temples; they count for little compared with the essence of existence in each of us." Even within more traditional centers of religious reflection, I observed a prolific manufacturing of theologies and images.

Dharma master Heng Sure, for instance, passes on to seekers who trek to his Berkeley Buddhist monastery a practical wisdom that has been been carefully tested for well over two millennia. Many of his students were raised in Christian churches or Jewish synagogues. Whereas other religious teachers might seize the opportunity for potential converts, this Buddhist monk simply hopes for greater enlightenment. "If Buddhism helps them, so be it, but it might turn out that they just need to be better Christians, or better Jews."

Or maybe all three at once. An increasing number of Americans are adopting multiple religious traditions, held simultaneously, each for what it uniquely offers. The demand to espouse a single religious faith is losing its force. Heng Sure himself grew up in a Methodist church in Ohio. After an eventful spiritual quest, he pursued the path of Ch'an Buddhism, an expression of Buddha's teaching that flowered in China. While he today ardently practices traditional Buddhist disciplines, he nonetheless values his Christian roots: "I feel no energy to remove one for the other."

These emerging spiritualities are regularly denigrated by journalists and scholars of religion alike. Typically they are thrown into the catchall category of "New Age movement." Even less flattering are characterizations such as "cafeteria spirituality," thereby implying that adherents have no formal attachment to religious institutions but pick and choose from whichever ancient wisdom or worldview that takes their fancy.

"Cruising the Spiritual Marketplace" is the title of a feature article on new religious movements published in the *San Francisco Chronicle*.[2] Written by Donald Lattin—the newspaper's senior religion editor, who has also coauthored the sociological survey "American Religion in the New Millennium"—the article contains a series of terms and assumptions that are common currency among the religious intelligentsia.[3] Citing numerous surveys showing that Americans are less loyal to historic religious traditions, but quite invested in spiritual matters, Lattin concludes that "the breakdown of organized religion" has resulted in a "free market of faith and spiritual practice." Given that no one seems to have a monopoly on spiritual truth, "new revelations roll out every season, like the latest product lines from Ford, Chrysler and GM." The best metaphor Lattin can find for this inchoate and rootless social milieu is to say that people move from one religion to another "[just] like they change Web browsers on the Internet, searching for the best connection."

Although Lattin intended to use the Net metaphor pejoratively, he has inadvertently stumbled on a useful tool for understanding what lies behind the rise in emerging spiritualities. For while emerging spiritualities are surely no less susceptible to the forces of consumerism than are more traditional American religious movements—and as such are to be no less put under scrutiny—they are a reflection of the network society wherein they are taking shape and are to be valued as a fruit of an authentic religious quest.

EARLY TREMORS: THE BEAT MOVEMENT
IN THE UNITED STATES

The American search for spiritual connection via religious plurality did not begin with the network generation.[4] Early tremors can be traced at least as far back as the Beat generation.[5] Although their writing methods and brazen lifestyle were deemed downright quirky in the 1950s, the collective aesthetic of Jack Kerouac, William Burroughs, Gary Snyder, Michael McClure, Allen Ginsberg, and friends portends streams of consciousness that emerge with remarkable clarity in the digital age.

For quite some time, the Beats have suffered a reputation as fashionable dabblers in the exotic East. Some of their own contemporary critics meted out even harsher judgment. One reviewer distinguished Kerouac's *On the Road* from true literature by its "poverty of emotional, intellectual, and aesthetic resources, an ineptitude of expression, and an inability to make anything dramatically meaningful."[6]

But what marked the writings of the Beats and defined them as a movement was not so much a common political stance or even a shared literary style but a self-directed spiritual quest for a "new consciousness." Nearly every one of the Beats claimed to be a writer with a deep religious interest. In an influential *New York Times Magazine* essay, Beat author and chronicler John Clellon Holmes claimed that the movement "exhibits on every side, and in a bewildering number of facets, a perfect craving to believe . . . the stirrings of a quest."[7]

It all starts, and ends, "on the road." Dean Moriarty and Sal Paradise, the main characters in Kerouac's groundbreaking novel, search for something they can believe in and all the ecstasy and transcendence they can stand along the way. Kerouac leads them into full contact with the unknown, where flashes of revelation appear from the most unlikely sources. Dean and Sal discover by trip's end that the mystery of the open road lies not in any particular destination but in the perennial drift toward connection.[8]

That message would fit comfortably on the dust jacket of Sherry Turkle's latest who-are-we-now treatise, *Life on Screen*. The MIT professor tracks "personal identity in the age of the Internet" and finds that we invent who we are as we move in and out of social encounters and cycle through a number of social roles. We build a sense of reality, in other words, out of the associations we make. Turkle identifies the Internet as "a significant social laboratory for experimenting with the constructions . . . of the self that characterize postmodern life."[9]

Dean and Sal never journey into cyberspace, of course, but that did not make it any less difficult for them to separate the real from the virtual. Astute social observers of the fifties depicted postwar America as a "one-dimensional society" run by "organization men" who produced mass culture for the consumption of "lonely crowds."[10] The real was defined uniformly, and any retreat from its standards was akin to treason. "What is good for GM is good for America" ran the slogan that dictated behavior ranging from the economic to the personal. The open road, then, offered Dean and Sal access to an unmediated America, free from the rigid Protestant-Catholic-Jewish faith of cool reason.

In Kerouac's personal diaries logged during the time he was writing *On the Road* can be found a lengthy quote taken from a D. H. Lawrence essay on Walt Whitman:

> Not by meditating. Not by fasting. Not by exploring heaven after heaven, inwardly. . . . Not by exaltation. Not by ecstasy. Not by any of these ways does the soul come into her own. Only by taking the open road. Exposed to full contact. On two slow feet. Meeting whatever comes down the open road. In company with those that drift in the same measure along the same way. Towards no goal. Always down the open road.[11]

Just so, a band of disaffected literati, hungering for fresh sources of information, sought connections with those most beaten-down by society. Hoboes and racial outcasts intrigued Kerouac especially, while Ginsberg gravitated toward sexual outlaws and Burroughs befriended drug addicts and criminals. Raised in middle-class malaise, these writers desired to see a world that was set free from control and conformity.[12]

Inspired by the rawness of his encounters, Kerouac changed his writing method to mirror the movement of time. Writing was dead, he argued, once it was made to bow before prescribed rules, narrow selectivity, punctuation, and revision. He wanted his writing to bop as spontaneously as the improvisational scat of Charlie Parker, the action painting of Jackson Pollack, or the trance writing of W. B. Yeats. Exhausting the forms of language would give Kerouac, he hoped, new insights into how the world might be put together. He likened his writing method to "swimming in a language sea," an unintended yet colorful description of hypertext for a digital generation.[13]

Starting with *On the Road*, Kerouac recorded whatever impressions or memories spilled out of his mind, deliberately repressing his obsession for finding the "right" word or idea. He quickly ran into an obstacle, however. His chain of thought was broken each time he had to feed a new sheet of paper into the typewriter. Hence, to preserve an uninterrupted flow, he began typing on continuous rolls made up of twelve-foot-long sheets of drawing paper. He subsequently wrote *The Subterraneans*, a barely fictionalized account of one of his love affairs, in only three days in 1953.[14]

Kerouac felt that he had stumbled on "the only possible literature of the future," and he foresaw a day when the means of communication would facilitate not only spontaneous prose but a more immediate exchange of ideas as well. Although his insights clearly point to the arrival of E-mail, at the time Kerouac only could imagine its advent in science fiction terms, calling it "Space Age Prose." "It may be they won't be reading anything else but spontaneous writing when they do get out there, the science of language to fit the science of movement," wrote the prescient Kerouac.[15]

To help Ginsberg and Burroughs appreciate his transformation as a writer, Kerouac prepared for them a laundry list of attitudes and techniques that he considered "essential for spontaneous prose." One pithy phrase captures the spirit of his list: "Something you feel will find its own form."[16]

Kerouac's "essentials" read like a survival manual for the denizens of electronically mediated virtual communities. Cyberspace author Allucquére (Sandy) Stone in fact suggests that success in online encounters requires the ability to perform "lucid dreaming in an awake state."[17] Stone, who directs the University of Texas multimedia laboratory, believes that people who participate in multiple-user dungeons (MUDs) and other simulated environments sign off having gained interactive ways of processing information that enhance perception in physical environments as well. Their imaginations do not stop firing once they leave their avatar, she contends.[18]

Four decades ago, Burroughs was already frustrated by the inherent limitations of communicating information solely through a two-dimensional sheet of paper. He astonished readers with his preface to *Naked Lunch*, brazenly claiming that the words as they appear in the book could have worked just as easily in any order. His description of the ideal presentation of the book has more the feel of a Web page than hard copy: "[It] spills off the page in all directions, kaleidoscope of vistas, medley of tunes and street noises, farts and riot yipes and the slamming steel shutters of commerce."[19]

While other Beats followed Kerouac into a spontaneous prose, Burroughs developed a montage style of writing that, he argued, mirrored the process of human perception more faithfully than representational writing. Using a crude cut-and-paste method, he constructed his tales like a Web designer mixes and matches .gifs on a page. His stated goal was to impose neither plot nor continuity, but to splice together as many images as possible simultaneously.

While the industrial world touted empirical reason as the sole path to the truths that really matter, the Beats trusted in the dawn of a new age that would value intuition and imagination as equally critical to the production of knowledge. Reason alone was incapable of keeping pace with a world of rapidly changing images.

One thought logically following another, centrally organized, fit a mass consumer, a mass media, and a mass political structure. The Beats insisted that the new consciousness be discontinuous. They reveled in chaos, where patterns emerge but last no longer than the period for which they are relevant or meaningful. If nothing is fixed or permanent, creativity can run amok. Just imagine what they could have done with today's Web!

The Beats, of course, turned to fiction and poetry as their tools for creativity. Virtual writing gave them license to make associations and blur lines that bent the rules of publicly ordered social life. Connections that made no sense (or were not allowed to exist) in the real world took on a dynamic life of their own in their fictive environments.

Even when their subject matter was autobiographical, which it often was, the Beats usually danced behind the masks of their characters and tropes. Kerouac, for example, detailed in each of his novels the names and places of his daily encounters, yet he freely fictionalized these slices of reality whenever it served the movement of the story.

Keeping up with the flow of reality, they believed, required constant reinterpretation. Philip Whalen, then Beat writer and now Buddhist monk, succinctly articulated the spirit of the Beats in his poem "Sourdough Mountain Lookout":

> What we see of the world is the mind's
> Invention and the mind
> Though stained by it, becoming
> Rivers, sun, mule-dung, flies—
> Can shift instantly
> A dirty bird in a square time[20]

These "material-symbolic-psychic" connections lie at the heart of Donna Haraway's contemporary theories of technoscientific culture. Haraway, a professor in the History of Consciousness program at the University of California Santa Cruz, shares the Beats' passion to affect the language and concepts on which a worldwide web of relationships depends. Her ultimate interest is to pursue "which connections matter, why, and for whom." Although computers alone do not really cause anything, she believes that hypertext defines paths of action that have the potential to remake entire worlds.[21]

Haraway points to Mosaic—the early precursor to today's Web browsers—as a primary medium of global information about business, academic, and cultural action. The consciousness Mosaic created was vital for the distribution of valuable goods such as freedom, justice, well-being, wealth, skill, and knowledge. Mosaic's actual configuration, however, resulted from daily negotiations over the way subjects interacted. What matters in technoscientific world building, Haraway concludes, are "enrollments" (who shows up) and the "hybrids" they produce in unrestricted intercourse.[22]

The Buddhist concept of "emptiness," which appears regularly in Beat writing, is in many respects parallel to Haraway's notion of "hypertext mystification." Many of the Beats found solace in Buddhism for the very reason that it offered channels for linking a solitary mind to a deeper consciousness of the universe, yet without losing oneself in groupthink.

"Emptiness implies a common space, yet not a common mind with archetypes and messages running back and forth," explained Ginsberg in an interview. "Just as the Internet represents a collective body of information, creativity is distributed throughout the network."[23]

Given their historical context, the Beats were ever wary of efforts to collectivize creativity, be their motivation utopian or fascist. Limits on communications in 1950s America reduced politics, reason, and ethics to a narrow technoscientific project called the Cold War. The web of secrecy ran from the bedroom to the top of the government, thus tightly regulating the kinds of intercourse that were permitted. In this claustrophobic environment, the writings of the Beats begged for candor about sexuality, politics, drugs, and money.

Burroughs exposed the dark side of this state regimentation in his drug-soaked parody of social control, *Naked Lunch*. The "Senders" are a scientific-industrial elite who gather at a National Electronic Conference in order to map out the future of the social order. They pass a legal mandate requiring every surgeon to install a miniature transmitter into the neural pathways of the citizenry, so that subjects will send messages of their internal feelings and thoughts back to the state. But the Senders decide a citizen must never receive a message, lest he "recharge himself by contact." Burroughs later reveals the Senders' rationale for one-way telepathic control: "Power groups of the world frantically cut lines of connection."[24]

The Beats were above all willing to experiment with candor, even when it meant letting worn ideas and secure structures die. Candor implies getting as close to the real as you can while accepting that this moment, too, will dissolve. It is the confidence that what is true and what is beautiful do not need a fortress of ideologies to uphold them but will manifest themselves in their own way.

Ginsberg was never one to take restrictions on his free expression lying down. In 1957 U.S. Customs agents impounded on charges of obscenity a shipment of his London-published poetry collection *Howl*. The ensuing court battle catapulted the Beats off the pages of obscure literary rags and into the national spotlight. An unrepentant Ginsberg sustained to the end of his life that state censorship degrades democracy. "It's all about mind and body control for the sake of power. And today the fight continues over the Internet."[25]

Ginsberg was legendary for not only writing with, but also living with, candor. One night during the performance tour for *Howl*, a heckler in the audience dogged the poet throughout the entire reading, accusing him of talking nonsense. His performance completed, Ginsberg turned the stage over to fellow Beat Gregory Corso, who was immediately subjected to the same abuse. Not nearly so patient, Corso challenged the heckler to a verbal duel, using weapons of "images, metaphors, magic." But the heckler wanted a fistfight and continued to taunt the poets, calling them cowards and asking what they thought they were doing onstage.

"Nakedness," Ginsberg quickly replied, then walked into the audience after the heckler. He challenged the heckler to demonstrate his bravery by taking off his clothes. Tired of waiting, Ginsberg stripped off all of his own clothing, hurling his pants and shirts after the retreating heckler. "The poet always stands naked before the people," announced Ginsberg to the now hysterical audience.[26]

Candor is still a rare commodity in our culture of endless simulation. Most of us live uncertain of the ideas, skills, and strategies that permit success in a given location. The legacy of the Beats suggests that neither a new set of facts nor reason can deliver a solution. The secret, wrote Kerouac, is to live fully "in the dignity of your experience, language, and knowledge," and the right connections will follow.[27]

THE ESSENTIALS OF EMERGING SPIRITUALITIES

Stephen Prothero, in his *Harvard Theological Review* essay treating the Beat movement as spiritual protest, prosaically depicted the Beats as wanderers who tried "not to arrive but to travel, and in the process, to transform into sacred space every back alley through which they ambled and every tenement in which they lived."[28] Just so, alternative spiritual seekers in the network society aim to make contact with the sacred in moments of connection, not only to other human beings but with nature and amid the stream of life events. They have the power to communicate with one another at will all over the world and with the ability to see and hear every imaginable point of view.

It's hard to imagine how fixed theologies like those of most organized religions will survive intact the on-line scrutiny given to ideas, opinions, and proclamations. The network is a natural leveler of established institutions. Once individuals get their hands on the machinery of communications, they make and disseminate their own personal theologies.

To speak of "emerging spiritualities," however, is not to describe a sect or a cult. There is no organization one must join, no creed one must confess. Many of their practitioners disassociate themselves from any movement altogether, though they embrace core aspects of their thinking. My field study of emerging spiritualities in the San Francisco Bay Area (admittedly a skewed sample on which to project a national prototype) revealed that more than two-thirds had attended a church or synagogue at least twice a month while they were growing up, four-fifths mixed elements of Asian and traditional Western religions, more than half believed in reincarnation, and three-quarters balked at being identified as "religious," preferring the label "spiritual."

The most salient feature of a network is that it contains no clear center and no clear outside boundaries. And we are only beginning to see the anxiety, loss, excitement, and gains that people experience as our world shifts to a web of network societies. Nonetheless I will attempt to identify some of the core values and characteristics of emerging spiritualities, using a select twelve of Kerouac's "essentials of spontaneous prose" as my categories.[29]

1. Submissive to everything, open, listening. A popular saying makes its way around cyberspace: Information wants to be free. In the network society, individuals experience unprecedented freedom of expression and access to diverse points of view. They seek and find their own truths and encounter virtual networks with fresh ideas about spirituality. Boundaries are constantly compromised. In their demand for interactivity, the practitioners of emerging spiritualities realign the relationship between dispensers and receivers of dogma. Where they find resistance, they are more likely to shape new kinds of institutions than to accept the ones they already have.

2. Accept loss forever. Ambiguity and doubt aren't considered retreats from faith, but a new way of being faithful. Doubt is the spiritual fruit of a soul living with the truth of uncertainty. The Buddhist concept of emptiness particularly resonates in a network: all things lack independent existence and as such exist only in relation to all else that exists—much like a Web site does not exist independently but is a temporary arrangement of meaning. Emptiness applies to the self as well, since we build associative tissues of a self in the many nets to which we are linked. And it is widely believed that every bit of information one absorbs, no matter where it comes from, leads to personal change. Many feared for some time that the self would disappear with the advance of technology; rather, it seems the self has become mediated.

3. *Write on, can't change or go back, involuntary, unrevised, spontaneous, subconscious, pure.* The logic of the network is not linear or causal but associative. Chance connections displace necessary relations. Throughout most of the twentieth century, ideology and dogma overwhelmed our public discourse. Now information technologies make it possible to encounter more personal connections than ever before, broadly distributed across the globe. The network generation values personal experience over ideology, testimony over dogma, compassion over moralizing. This sensibility resembles Kerouac's description of a Beat ethic: "continual conscious compassion."[30]

4. *Telling the true story of the world in interior monologue.* The network generation is individualistic and idiosyncratic. Personal experience is critical. Religious belief must be experienced, not taught or mandated. You do not join to belong. Its only commandment: "Be yourself." Spiritual qualities are separated from the outer world of actions and ethics except where that world is redefined in spiritual terms. All life—all existence—is the manifestation of Spirit. In a similar way, all religions are expressions of this same inner reality. It's expected to be different for every person who sits down to meditate. The search for a center, a teacher, a tradition, is a part of the path that everyone must walk for oneself.

5. *Work from the pithy middle eye out, from the jewel center of interest, swimming in language sea.* Perhaps most characteristic of emerging spiritualities is the variety and all-inclusiveness of their parts. By and large, the network generation shares a deep mistrust of "authorized versions" and a preference for nonhierarchical models of operation. This attitude is highly informed by a bias against rational thought or systems of belief and toward intuition and holistic paradigms. Unlike a print medium, telecommunication moves against uniformity. When a text is sent out over the Net, it is ever vulnerable to revision, or perhaps better put, it invites revision. So in practice, rituals and beliefs are chosen and tailored by virtue of what you get from it, what it does for you, and how it makes you feel.

6. No fear or shame in the dignity of your experience, language, and knowledge. Emerging spiritualities typically grant equality to women, are not sexually repressive, and take a holistic, ecologically aware approach to the divine. Their practitioners feel free to arrange their lives in ways that work for them, sometimes choosing marriage, sometimes not, having children when they want them, if at all. They are not self-conscious about their sexual choices—straight, gay, or otherwise.

7. In tranced fixation dreaming upon the object before you. In the modern age, science dealt with materiality, while spirituality was circumscribed to nonmaterial spaces. Emerging spiritualities seek to reconcile immaterial space with the scientific mind; cyberspace itself is precisely such an immaterial space and represents a conceptual bridge. One of the fundamental aims of emerging spiritualities is to extend our sense of self and thereby overcome feelings of separateness with other human beings, nature, and the cosmos. The same approach is applied to arrive at a more holistic view of technology. The merging of human with machine and technology is seen as part of the mystical task of union with the universe.

8. Something that you feel will find its own form. A mantra of the network society: Don't let ritual become routine. When life is happening, our symbolic acts have meaning; to the contrary, symbolic acts alone cannot make life happen. The goal is to find a resonance between the form in virtual reality and the form in physical life. Homemade altars and ceremonies decorated with mementos and artifacts that personalize an experience with the sacred are commonplace among practitioners of emerging spiritualities. Group ceremonies often include sharing of food, fire and burning candles, purification with water, fragrances, and intimate offerings. All are intended to create a sacred environment in which practitioners hope to be touched by the transcendent.

9. In praise of character in the bleak inhuman loneliness. Emerging spiritualities treat suffering as a spiritual challenge. Suffering inspires a bond through which we all touch each other. The only real disaster, ultimately, is a lack of connection to the Spirit. The materialistic bent of European culture has led us to the delusion that we are alone on this earth, unrelated to those who lived before us, those who will come after us, and those cultures and species who currently share the planet with us. Healing oneself spiritually contributes to healing the greater network, from the inner consciousness to the collective consciousness. If a practitioner of an emerging spirituality speaks of the divine, the Spirit is immanent, immersed in the struggle of the world.

10. Be crazy dumbsaint of the mind. Meditation, not prayer, is the vehicle to transcendence. Meditation is directed to the inward Spirit, in order to center and focus the self, to strengthen awareness, to relax the body-mind, and to train right response. It is not identified with any particular religion but rather is assumed to be the practice of a universal spiritual culture. Allen Ginsberg was fond of quoting his teacher Chögyam Trungpa: "First thought, best thought."[31] So meditation should lead to a state of mind that is fresh and responsive, never hampered by concepts but using their energy for whatever purpose is beneficial.

11. Blow as deep as you want to blow. In the network society, the local becomes global without being universalized. There is no end to the network. Every destination is a point of departure, and every point of departure is a destination. So emerging spiritualities see the universe as an endless dynamic of wholes and processes that serve as a doorway into the deeper structure of reality. A popular myth is the story of the god Indra in the Hindu tradition. Indra is said to have cast a fishing net to encircle the entire universe. A brilliant jewel rested at each link in the net where two ropes crossed. Each jewel reflected every other jewel simultaneously; to look into any one jewel, one would find within it the entire universe. The lesson: once one becomes aware of the smallest spark of divinity, one touches the whole.

12. No time for poetry but exactly what it is. Popular culture is not merely entertainment in a network society but a common language and a shared point of reference. Creations of popular culture move beyond the individual imagination and tap roots that feed a collective social mind. Their images fit, represent, speak, titillate. With unique intensity, pop culture absorbs images and events and sends them back into the network, altogether altered and disguised. They both mirror the society and modify it. In his book *Virtual Faith: The Irreverent Spiritual Quest of Generation X*, Tom Beaudoin decries traditionalists who see pop culture as "a cultural wasteland devoid of spiritual symbols." Most practitioners of emerging spiritualities agree with Beaudoin: popular culture contains the elements "sufficient to begin funding a new theology by, for, and about a generation."[32]

TO REENCHANT THE WORLD

In his book delineating "new rules" for the network economy, Kevin Kelly warns: "Because the nature of the network economy seeds disequilibrium, fragmentation, uncertainty, churn, and relativism, the anchors of meaning are in short supply. We are simply unable to deal with questions that cannot be answered by means of technology."[33]

In this uncertain environment, many Americans desire to encounter a sense of awe and wonder that gives meaning to their place in a bewildering network. But to do so, they deem it necessary to engage in a total redefinition of sacred time and space. In their emerging spiritualities, the divine cannot serve as a transcendent authority figure, nor is humanity an isolated fact of nature. The Spirit—which is to be found wherever and whenever the seeker recognizes the mystery of each moment—is a force that makes physical communion possible. The dream: to reenchant the world.

NOTES

1. The study was commissioned by *Soma* magazine. An anecdotal account was published in *Soma* (May and June 1996).

2. Don Lattin, "Cruising the Spiritual Marketplace," *San Francisco Chronicle*, 29 November 1998.

3. Don Lattin, *Shopping for Faith: American Religion in the New Millennium* (San Francisco: Jossey-Bass Publishers, 1998).

4. An earlier rendition of this section on the Beat generation and the network society was published in *Wired:* "Cyberbeats," *Wired* 6 (March 1998): 116–22.

5. These spiritual roots could also legitimately be traced much further back to the transcendentalists, a school of thought influential among New England writers in the mid-1800s, including such luminaries as Ralph Waldo Emerson and Henry David Thoreau. For example, see Catherine L. Albanese, ed., *The Spirituality of the American Transcendentalists* (Macon: Mercer University Press, 1988).

6. Norman Podhoretz, "Letter to the Editor," *Partisan Review* 25 (summer 1958): 476. In the preceding issue of the *Partisan Review* (spring 1958), Podhoretz wrote a more lengthy critique, equally scathing, of the Beat movement: "This is a revolt of the spiritually underprivileged and the crippled of soul" (316).

7. John Clellon Holmes, "This Is the Beat Generation," *New York Times Magazine*, 16 November 1952.

8. Jack Kerouac, *On the Road* (New York: Penguin Books, 1991).

9. Sherry Turkle, *Life on Screen: Identity in the Age of the Internet* (New York: Touchstone Books, 1997), 268.

10. Herbert Marcuse, *One-Dimensional Man* (Boston: Beacon Press, 1964); David Riesman, *The Lonely Crowd: A Study of the Changing American Character* (New Haven: Yale University Press, 1950); and William H. Whyte, *The Organization Man* (New York: Simon and Schuster, 1956).

11. As cited in Steve Turner, *Angelheaded Hipster: A Life of Jack Kerouac* (New York: Viking Penguin, 1996), 25.

12. Stephen Prothero, "On the Holy Road: The Beat Movement as Spiritual Protest," *Harvard Theological Review* 84, no. 2 (1991): 210.

13. Turner, 145.

14. Turner, 143; and Jack Kerouac, "Essentials of Spontaneous Prose," in *Big Sky Mind: Buddhism and the Beat Generation*, ed. Carole Tonkinson (New York: Riverhead Books, 1995), 28.

15. Jack Kerouac, "First World," *Escapade* (June 1959).

16. Kerouac, "Essentials of Spontaneous Prose," 28.

17. As cited in Susan Stryker, "Sex and Death among the Cyborgs," *Wired* 4 (May 1996): 135.

18. Stryker, 135–36.

19. William S. Burroughs, *Naked Lunch* (New York: Grove Press, 1987), 207.

20. Philip Whalen, "Sourdough Mountain Lookout," *Blue Sky Mind: Buddhism and the Beat Generation*, ed. Carole Tonkinson (New York: Riverhead Books, 1995), 203.

21. Donna Haraway, "What Does It Mean to Be an American?" radio interview by David Batstone, host and executive producer, BusStop RadioNet Productions, 1997.

22. Donna Haraway, *Modest Witness@Second Millennium* (New York: Routledge, 1996), 94.

23. Allen Ginsberg, interview by David Batstone, San Francisco, 19 December 1996; a portion of the interview was published as David Batstone, "Allen Ginsberg's Last Words," *Black Book* (summer 1998): 42–44.

24. Burroughs, 147–49.

25. Ginsberg interview by Batstone.

26. Ginsberg interview by Batstone.

27. Kerouac, "Essentials of Spontaneous Prose," 29.

28. Prothero, 211.

29. Kerouac, "Essentials of Spontaneous Prose," 28–29.

30. Jack Kerouac, "The Art of Fiction LXI," *Paris Review* 43 (summer 1968): 85.

31. Ginsberg interview by Batstone.

32. Tom Beaudoin, *Virtual Faith: The Irreverent Spiritual Quest of Generation X* (San Francisco: Jossey-Bass, 1998), 144.

33. Kevin Kelly, *New Rules for the New Economy: Ten Radical Strategies for a Connected World* (New York: Viking, 1998), 159. Kelly, however, reaches a different resolution: "Because values and meaning are scarce today, technology will make our decisions for us" (160).

INDEX

Islam in, 43n. 13; religious nation-
alism in, 70–71; slaves' liberation
from, 40
Eiselen, W. M. M., 141
Ejidos (communal lands), 89
Emerging spiritualities/religious
plurality, 227–29, 235–40, 240n. 5
Emerson, Ralph Waldo, 240n. 5
Empiricism, 57
Emptiness, 233–34, 236–37
Engels, Friedrich: *The Communist
Manifesto,* 60–61
England, 35, 59
Enlightenment, 38, 55–56, 58
Epistles, 111
Eschatology, 12
ESPN (network), 26, 27
Esso, 138
Ethiopia, 44n. 36
Ethnic cleansing, 72
Ethnicity. *See* Race/ethnicity
Ethnocentrism, 49
Eugenics, 110
Euro-Asiatic system, 34, 42n. 8
Eurocentrism, 49
Europe, 33–34, 42n. 4
European colonies, liberation of, 36,
43n. 21
Evangelical movement, 110–11. *See
also* Missionaries
Evangelical pietism, 125, 126–27
Exxon, 139

Faith Partners, 211
Falwell, Jerry, 208, 211
Family Channel, 218
Far East Broadcasting Company,
204–5
Fast-food corporations, 27
First Commandment, 115
First National City Bank of New
York, 138
First World system, 34

Flying Hospital, 222
Ford Motor Company, 139
France, 75
Franciscans, 93–94
Fraser, Alexander, 122
Freedom of expression, 236
Freeman, Thomas Birch, 124
Free markets, 16, 17, 20, 29
Freemasons, 68, 71
Freetown, 124
Freitag, Sandra, 181–82
French Revolution, 58
Froude, J. A., 107
FUNCINPEC, 189, 200n. 2

Gamaa i-Islamiya (Islamic Group),
70–71
Gandhi, Indira, 66, 72
Gandhi Museum kolam competition,
174–78, 183–84
Garrard-Burnett, Virginia, 92, 96–97,
98
Gay, Peter, 55–56
General Electric, 139
General Motors (GM), 139
Gérard, Albert, 117
Germany, 59, 75
Ginsberg, Allen, 229, 230, 231, 234–
35, 239
Glassie, Henry, 184–85
Globalization: definition of, 203;
faddishness of, 2; meanings of,
2–3; negative vs. positive effects
of, 3; theories of, 47–51, 61–62,
88, 100n. 1. *See also* Religion of
globalization
God: capitalist wealth as, 9–10, 12,
28; potency of, 19; revelation of,
115; revelation of, in religion of
globalization, 19–28, 29; as ultimate concern of believers, 9. *See
also* Theology
Goldstein, Baruch, 67, 75

CONTRIBUTORS

Dwight N. Hopkins is Associate Professor of Theology, University of Chicago. He is the author of *Down, Up, and Over: Slave Religion and Black Theology* (Fortress, 2000); *Introducing Black Theology of Liberation* (Orbis, 1999); *Shoes That Fit Our Feet: Sources for a Constructive Black Theology* (Orbis, 1993); *Black Theology in the U.S.A., South Africa: Politics, Culture, and Liberation* (Orbis, 1989); and the forthcoming *Heart and Head: Critical Reflections on African American Religious Discourse* (Palgrave-St. Martin's Press, 2002). He is the editor of *Black Faith and Public Talk: Critical Essays on James H. Cone's Black Theology and Black Power* (Orbis, 1999); with Sheila Greeve Davaney, *Changing Conversations: Religious Reflection and Cultural Analysis* (Routledge, 1996); with George C. L. Cummings, *Cut Loose Your Stammering Tongue: Black Theology in the Slave Narratives* (Orbis, 1991); with Simon S. Maimela, *We Are One Voice: Essays on Black Theology in South Africa and the U.S.A.* (Skotaville, 1989).

Lois Ann Lorentzen is Professor of Social Ethics, University of San Francisco. She has edited (with Jennifer Turpin) *The Women and War Reader* (NYU, 1998); (with Jennifer Turpin) *The Gendered New World Order: Militarism, the Environment, and Development* (Routledge, 1996).

Eduardo Mendieta, Associate Professor of Philosophy, State University of New York at Stony Brook. He is the editor of the following: with Linda Martín Alcoff, *Thinking from the Underside of History: Enrique Dussel's Philosophy of Liberation* (Rowman and Littlefield, 2000); with David Batstone, *The Good Citizen* (Routledge, 1999); *Ethics and the Theory of Rationality: Selected Essays of Karl-Otto Apel,* vol. 2 (Humanities, 1995); *Towards a Transcendental Semiotics: Selected Essays of Karl-Otto Apel, Rorty, Taylor, and the Phi-*

losophy of Liberation, by Enrique Dussel (Humanities, 1996; Humanity Book, 1999).

David Batstone is Associate Professor of Social Ethics, University of San Francisco. He is the author of *From Conquest to Struggle: Jesus of Nazareth in Latin America* (SUNY, 1991). He is editor of *New Visions for the Americas: Religion and Social Transformation* (Fortress, 1993) (and with Eduardo Mendieta) *The Good Citizen* (Routledge, 1999); *Liberation Theologies, Postmodernity, and the Americas* (Routledge, 1997).

Berit Bretthauer studied at the New School for Social Research in New York between 1991–1994. She finished her Ph.D. as an assistant professor at the John F. Kennedy Institute in Berlin. During her academic career, Berit Bretthauer has been focusing on American fundamentalism, the sociology of religion, and religious television. She has published several articles and a book, *Televangelism—Religion Between Individualism and Community*, on the subject.

Enrique Dussel is professor of philosophy at Universidad Autonoma Metropolitana-Iztapalapa, and the Universidad Nacional Autonoma de Mexico. He has authored more than twenty books on religion, sociology, history, and law, many of which have been translated into English, including *The Invention of the Americas* (1995), *The Underside of Modernity* (1996), *Ethics and Community* (1988), *Philosophy of Liberation* (1985), and *Ethics and the Theology of Liberation* (1978). A translation of his *Etica de la Liberacion: en la edad de globalizacion y de la exclusion* (1998) is forthcoming from Duke University Press.

Mark Juergensmeyer is Professor of Sociology and Director of Global and International Studies at the University of California, Santa Barbara. His books include *Terror in the Mind of God: The Global Rise of Religious Violence* (California, 2000), *The New Cold War? Religious Nationalism Confronts the Secular State* (1993), and the forthcoming *Global Religions* (Oxford, 2002).

Vijaya Nagarajan received her Ph.D. in South Asian Studies at the University of California, Berkeley, in 1998, with an emphasis in religion, art history, and anthropology. She is Assistant Professor in the Department of Theology and Religious Studies at the University of San Francisco. She has been teaching courses on religion and environment, religion and nonviolence, and comparative religious traditions. She is working on a book on the kolam, and is a research associate in the Women's Studies in Religion Program at Harvard University during the 2001–2002 academic year. She is also co-director of the Institute for the Study of Natural and Cultural Resources.

Kathryn Poethig is Assistant Professor of Global Studies at St. Lawrence University, New York. She has an M.Div. from Union Theological Seminary, New York, and a Ph.D. in Religion and Society from the Graduate Theological Union. Her research applies transnational theory to religion, citizenship, and hybrid identities in Southeast Asia. Her current research is concerned with the globalization of moral discourses (transnational feminisms, human rights, liberation ethics).

Lamin Sanneh is D. Willis James Professor of Missions and World Christianity and Professor of History at Yale University Divinity School. His books include *West African Christianity: The Religious Impact* (Orbis Books); *Translating the Message: The Missionary Impact on Culture* (Orbis Books); *The Jakhanke Muslim Clerics: A Religious and Historical Study of Islam in Senegambia* (University Press of America); *Encountering the West: Christianity and the Global Cultural Process: The African Documents*; and *Piety and Power: Muslims and Christians in West Africa* (Orbis Books).

Linda E. Thomas teaches theology and anthropology at the Lutheran School of Theology at Chicago. Her latest book is *Under the Canopy: Ritual Process and Spiritual Resilience in South Africa.* She is currently conducting ethnographic research among black Christians living in poverty on the South Side of Chicago. Her intellectual interests include race, gender, and class analysis.

Library of Congress Cataloging-in-Publication Data

Religions/globalizations : theories and cases /

edited by Dwight N. Hopkins . . . [et al.].

p. cm.   Includes index.

ISBN 0-8223-2785-6 (cloth : alk. paper)

ISBN 0-8223-2795-3 (pbk. : alk. paper)

1. Religion and culture.   2. Globalization—

Religious aspects.   I. Hopkins, Dwight N.

BL65.C8 R457   2001   291.1′7—dc21   2001033111